To Hell in a Handcart

To Sandra,

In memory of William May

With best wishes,

[signature]

(March 2020)

To Hell in a Handcart

Diaries of a PoW

John B Shanks

Transcribed by
Jeni Kingston

Matador
9 Priory Business Park,
Wistow Road, Kibworth Beauchamp,
Leicestershire. LE8 0RX
Tel: 0116 279 2299
Email: books@troubador.co.uk
Web: www.troubador.co.uk/matador
Twitter: @matadorbooks

ISBN 978 183859 228 8

British Library Cataloguing in Publication Data.
A catalogue record for this book is available from the British Library.

Printed and bound by CPI Group (UK) Ltd, Croydon, CR0 4YY
Typeset in 11pt Sabon by Troubador Publishing Ltd, Leicester, UK

Matador is an imprint of Troubador Publishing Ltd

This book is dedicated to the future;
to John's beloved grandchildren and the freedom they enjoy,
bravely and unselfishly fought for by so many.

Contents

Dad aged about 18.

Foreword

Much to his parents dismay, my father, John Burton Shanks, lied about his age and signed up to help the war effort when he was 17 years old. At school he had been a member of the OTC (Ordnance Training Corps) but, as a farmer's son, he wasn't required to join up, however his desire to get into a cockpit and 'do his bit for King and country' was too great.

As a result, his schoolboy intention to study engineering at university was consequently scuppered. Nevertheless, his familiarity and knowledge of farm machinery probably helped him achieve his desire to become a Spitfire and Hurricane pilot for the Royal Air Force at the tender age of 20.

After just 17 hours instruction in a Tiger Moth, spanned over 12 days, Dad flew his first solo and, within months, was himself an instructor.

According to his Log Book, he was considered an 'Above Average' pilot but it seems he was unhappy to be away from the action as shown in the following letter (pages 1 and 2 are lost…):

"page 3
Don't think I've become resigned to it in the slightest bit,
no – fear. If I do have to go instructing, the first thing I shall
do is put in an application for transfer to ops, and I'll keep
at them, by Jove!

Dad aged about 20.

While on the subject of this instructor business here is a little poem, I don't know who it was written by, which I think is extraordinarily apt and good.

THE FLYING INSTRUCTOR'S LAMENT

"What did you do in the war, Daddie,
And how did you help us to win?"
"Circuits and bumps and turns, laddie,
And how to get out of a spin."

Woe & alack and misery me! I trundle around the sky,
And instead of machine gunning Nazis, I'm teaching young hopefuls to fly,
Thus is my service rewarded, my years of experience paid,
Never a Hun have I followed right down, nor ever gone out on a raid.
They don't even let us go crazy, we have to be safe and sedate,
So its nix on inverted approaches, they stir up the CFI's hate.
For it's oh such a naughty example, & what will the AOC think!
But we never get posted to fighters – we just get a spell on the Link.

So its circuits & bumps from morning till noon, and instrument flying till tea;
"Hold her off: give her bank: put your under-cart down:
You're skidding: you're slipping" – that's me;
And as soon as you're finished with one course,
Like a flash up another one bobs;
And there's four more to show round the cockpit,
And four more to try out the knobs.

But sometimes we read in the papers of the deeds that old
pupils have done,
And we're proud to have seen their beginnings,
And shown them the way to the sun.
So if you find the money & turn out the 'planes,
We'll give all we know to the men,
Till they cluster the sky with their triumphs
And burn out the Beast from his den!

Anon

Not bad, eh! & it's just like that.

Today is the first day we've had really decent weather.
It's absolutely glorious. I only hope it's the same up your
way & keeps like this till next weekend at any rate, for
with any luck I shall be home next weekend for 48hrs leave
before going to my next station, so please don't make any
arrangements or having crowds of visitors next weekend,
& please keep some mushrooms back if you have any.

Well, I think that's all for the moment so cheerio for
now and here's lots of love to you all,

Love John xxxxxx"

Dad's desire to see action was finally met when he was relocated to Biggin Hill and Gravesend to be part of 124 Squadron in May 1942. He went on several sorties, but it was on 19th August, during the Battle of Dieppe or Operation Jubilee, known as the greatest air battle, that dad's war-time flying career came to an abrupt end.

Like many others, Dad spoke rarely about the war, and never told us that he had documented his experiences as a PoW.

Dad in his beloved Spitfire.

Throughout this editing process, I have wondered what he would think if he knew that his diaries were being made publicly available. Yet I feel the diaries represent an invaluable historical document that stands to play its part in preserving the memory of the Second World War, the experiences of the young servicemen that fought so bravely, and the huge impact that the conflict had on families across Britain and indeed across the world.

Almost 75 years after peace was declared on 8th May 1945 the memory of World War II is rapidly fading from public consciousness. As this document so clearly demonstrates, Dad believed in the value of making personal sacrifices in the name of building a more peaceful and prosperous world.

Ultimately, I have therefore concluded that he would be supportive of any attempt to ensure that we learn the lessons of the past and pass on stories and materials that can promote intergenerational learning and understanding.

Dad was a wonderful storyteller, and I believe that he would be proud to know that this story – which so vividly brings alive the despair and struggle, but also the hope and camaraderie, that comprised his wartime experience – might help to promote reflection on how far we have come since 1945 – and how far we have yet to travel.

PLEASE NOTE – I have tried to keep as faithful to the text of Dad's diaries as possible, therefore any words emboldened, or spaces marked with an underscore, are words I have been unable to read; either due to the degradation of the paper or illegibility of the script. It is possible that some of the words are unfamiliar to me as they are either 'of the time', PoW slang or even translations of German or Polish words. For ease of reading however, I have added spacing, paragraphs and the occasional comma and question mark. To explain some abbreviations, ranks, people or place names, I have made my own additions in bracketed italics.

From bottom left; Basil, Tommy, Gordon, Warwick and Dad

1942

August 19th saw the Commando raid on Dieppe. My first trip was at dawn when we had a wizard view of the landing operations but the only opposition we got was some flak from our own warships. On my second trip I attacked first a FW 190 with no observed results – he was again too fast – and then Pete and I attacked a Do217E. After Pete had finished his attacks I went in and gave him everything I had. After jettisoning his bombs he crashed. Unfortunately for me, shortly afterwards I had engine failure and had to crash in small field.

After an unsuccessful attempt to destroy the aircraft, I tried to get back to the beach. After 6 hours of this when I was twice almost picked up by the Huns, I realised the boys had all left so I hid in a ditch in a wood until night-time when I hoped to make my way south towards Spain. Unfortunately, a Hun army officer must have spotted me for he came up and, of course, then the game was up.

I was treated quite well and later that night taken by car – a mad ride – handcuffed to another chap, a F/O *(Field or Flying Officer)*, to a prison at Beauvais, north of Paris. I was there kept in solitary confinement for two days with guards of the Todt organisation.

Six of us were then taken on the Friday to Dulag Luft *(Oberusel or Wetzlar)* at Frankfurt, via Paris. We travelled by first-class express. A Norwegian P/O *(Pilot Officer)* in my carriage told us he was going to try and escape although he was already handcuffed. At midnight he made a most foolish attempt, as the train was full of troops and going quite fast. He failed in his attempt and was shot when coming back into the carriage. He was shot through the chest.

Never will I forget his delirious screams and moans as we continued on our way. A ghastly nightmare. He was taken off at Metz but later died. I was kept in solitary confinement for 4½ days with no cigs or books during which time I had Hun interrogations. I would give them no information so they eventually gave it up as a bad job.

Food was 2 slices of brown bread and marg *(margarine)* for breakfast, soup for dinner, 2 slices of brown bread and marg for tea. I was terribly hungry and disappointed at my misfortune.

Conditions were much better out of the 'coda'. Here I met only one fellow I knew – Leo Armstrong of 401 squadron. Everyone else I mistrusted, imagining them all to be stool pigeons. I don't think my fears were entirely ungrounded.

On Sept 7th 99 Sergeants and 40 Officers left Dulag for Stalag VIIIB at Lamsdorf. On the train I met that singular character F/Sgt James (Phooey on 124) who managed to scrounge his way to Sagan. His anecdotes were most amusing.

On the journey up I noticed wide expanses of land under what seemed intense but messy cultivation. The towns and villages impressed me as being very neat and clean. There was a noticeable lack of man-power especially in the fields where most of the work was done by women or children. The children were up and going to school at 6.45am and still in the fields at dusk.

We were in the train for 2½ days on very meagre rations. We also saw ploughs drawn by bullocks and sometimes a bullock and horse shackled together. The horses visible were of very poor quality for farm purposes, mostly half-draughts.

On the journey, our boots were taken off us to prevent escape. Potsdam looked a very beautiful city. We found it extremely cold in Eastern Germany especially in early mornings but it was warm during the day. I only had battle dress, shirt and flying boots. These were taken off me before entering the camp when I was given most uncomfortable wooden clogs, causing my insteps to swell very badly.

At the camp the RAF (it was an army camp really) were treated as dirt and got the blame for every little misdemeanour. We were considered as intruders until the main camp at Sagan should be completed. The hut which was our home was 20 yards long by 10 yards wide and 10ft high, accommodating 185 men. Our whole existence seemed to centre around tins. We ate out of them, drank out of them, kept our food in them and our home-made stoves, for which we had hardly any fuel, were made out of them.

Our food was mainly Red X but managed to get along reasonably well with ½ parcel and 35 cigs per man per week. We were in an enclosed compound and got hardly any exercise. At the school there were not many books but a few crude classes in progress. I took Seaman, Advertising, Salesmanship and Electricity. The canteen was very poor with hardly any stock but since we had no money we didn't really worry very much.

We had roll call at 7:00 am and 5:00 pm.

Telephone No. : SPRINGWELL (GLOUCESTER) 2042
Telegraphic Address :
  RECORDS TELEX, GLOUCESTER.
Any communications on the
subject of this letter should
be addressed to :
AIR OFFICER i/c RECORDS,
  Address as opposite,
and the following number
quoted :—
  07/1192260
  Your Ref. :

RECORD OFFICE,

ROYAL AIR FORCE,

GLOUCESTER.

Date 21st August 1942

Dear Sir,

     I regret to confirm that your son, No.1192260
Sergeant John Burton SHANKS of No.124 Squadron, Royal
Air Force, is missing, the aircraft of which he was the
pilot and sole occupant having failed to return to its
base on the 19th August 1942 from an operational flight.

     This does not necessarily mean that he is killed
or wounded. I will communicate with you again immediately
I have any further news and would be obliged if you on your
part, would write to me should you hear anything of your
son from unofficial sources.

     May I assure you of the sympathy of the Royal
Air Force with you in your anxiety.

     I am,
        Dear Sir,
        Your obedient Servant,

        Air Commodore
        Air Officer i/c Records,
        ROYAL   AIR   FORCE.

W.I.Shanks, Esq.,
The Hollies,
Burton Pattingham,
Nr. Wolverhampton,
Staffordshire.

Missing in action.

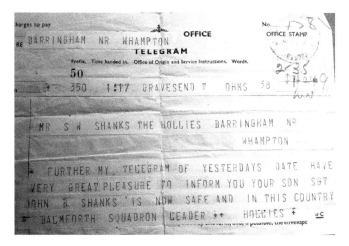

Charges to pay

RE BARRINGHAM NR WHAMPTON   OFFICE

TELEGRAM

No.

OFFICE STAMP

Prefix. Time handed in. Office of Origin and Service Instructions. Words.

50

350   1117   GRAVESEND T   OHMS   38

MR S W SHANKS THE HOLLIES BARRINGHAM NR
WHAMPTON

= FURTHER MY TELEGRAM OF YESTERDAYS DATE HAVE
VERY GREAT PLEASURE TO INFORM YOU YOUR SON SGT
JOHN B SHANKS IS NOW SAFE AND IN THIS COUNTRY
BALMFORTH SQUADRON LEADER ** HOLLIES +

Wrong Information.

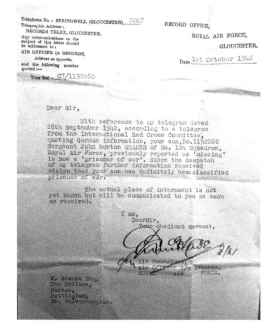

Telephone No. : SPRINGWELL (GLOUCESTER) 2047
Telegraphic Address :
RECORDS TELEX, GLOUCESTER.
Any communications on the
subject of this letter should
be addressed to :
AIR OFFICER i/c RECORDS,
     Address as opposite,
and the following number
quoted :—
     Your Ref. : C7/1192260

RECORD OFFICE,
ROYAL AIR FORCE,
GLOUCESTER.
Date 1st October 1942

Dear Sir,

     With reference to my telegram dated
26th September 1942, according to a telegram
from the International Red Cross Committee,
quoting German information, your son, No.1192260
Sergeant John Burton SHANKS of No. 124 Squadron,
Royal Air Force, previously reported as 'missing'
is now a 'prisoner of war'. Since the despatch
of my telegram further information received
states that your son has definitely been classified
prisoner of war.

     The actual place of internment is not
yet known but will be communicated to you as soon
as received.

         I am,
           Dear Sir,
           Your obedient Servant,

             Air Commodore,
             Air Officer i/c Records,
             ROYAL AIR FORCE.

W. Shanks Esq.,
The Hollies,
Burton,
Pattingham,
Nr. Wolverhampton.

Correction.

OFFICERS' MESS,
ROYAL AIR FORCE,
DEBDEN,
SAFFRON WALDEN.
TEL. SAFFRON WALDEN 280 & 281.

24.8.42.

Dear Mr Shanks

I am sure that yourself and Mrs Shanks must have been heart-broken to finally hear that your son John is missing.

I sincerely apologise for the double agony you have suffered by being wrongly informed that he was safe. Although I was passing information received from higher authority,

I personally feel in some way guilty for this appalling mistake. Please try and forgive myself and the originators of the mistake if you possibly can.

The circumstances of the accident all point in favour of John making a safe forced landing on enemy territory. He was attacking an enemy bomber at low altitude and was seen to shoot

it down. However, it jettisoned its bomb just before crashing and we believe that John's aircraft was damaged by the shrapnel from the exploding bomber. We definitely heard John say that his engine had stopped and he was making a forced landing. He was a first-class pilot and there is no reason why he should not have done this successfully.

So myself and the rest of the squadron think, not with undue

optimism that John will be O.K. but a prisoner of war.

Please try not to be too down-hearted if you do not receive any definite information for some time. Myself and the rest of the boys will be eagerly awaiting the same news.

Hank, as we call him, is a great friend of us all. He is really first class, both as a pilot and as a fellow.

Yours sincerely
Tom Bakersfield
S/Ldr

Letter from Squadron Leader.

Dear Mr Shanks,

I am sure that yourself and Mrs Shanks must have been heartbroken to finally hear that your son John is missing.

I sincerely apologise for the double agony you have suffered by being wrongly informed that he was safe.

Although I was passing information received from higher authority, I personally feel in some way guilty for this appalling mistake.

Please try and forgive myself and the originator of the mistake if you possibly can.

The circumstances of the accident all point in favour of John making a safe forced landing on enemy territory. He was attacking an enemy bomber at low altitude and was seen to shoot it down. However, it jettisoned its bombs just before crashing and we believe that John's aircraft was damaged by the shrapnel from the exploding bombs. We definitely heard John say that his engine had stopped and he was making a forced landing. He was a first class pilot and there is no reason why he should not have done this successfully.

So myself and the rest of the squadron think, not with undue optimism, that John will be O.K. but a prisoner of war.

Please try not to be too down-hearted if you do not receive any definite information for some time. Myself and the rest of the boys will be eagerly awaiting the same news.

Hank, as we call him, is a great friend of us all. He is really first class, both as a pilot and as a fellow.

Yours sincerely,
Tom Balmforth
Squadron Leader

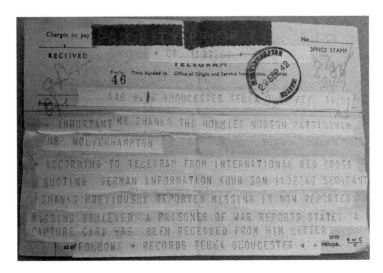

Finally, accurate information.

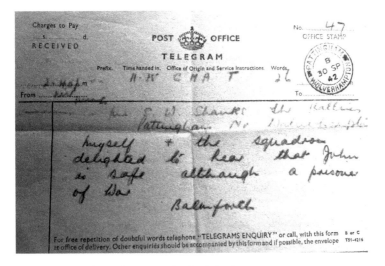

Squadron Leader's delight at news.

Sept 15th

This morning I heard Lord Haw-Haw announce my name as a PoW.

The sanitary arrangements here are disgusting. No toilet paper at all. For sleeping we only have one blanket which makes it very cold at night.

Last night, 10 people attempted to escape but all were caught. The enraged guards ran amok in our billet, screaming hysterically and bashing everyone they could with rifle butts and bayonets. I was not a little scared and broke all high jump records in getting on top of my bed.

Sept 16th

A few more of the sordid details. Our rations issued by the Huns are 1 small bowl of soup and a fifth of a loaf a day on 5 days a week with 2 small bowls and a seventh of a loaf on the other two days. Spread over a week, they usually give us some marg and honey from the Argentine. Biscuits (about 8 cream crackers from England and Canada), a small piece of German sausage (horrible), a little cooking fat, a little tea and sugar, a tin of corned beef and a tin of M & V *(meat & veg stew)*. According to the medical authorities, this is just <u>below</u> starvation diet so thank God for the Red X.

Our day is mostly spent with deciding what we shall eat and attempting to cook it. We make porridge with grated biscuit, raisins and milk powder, rissoles with corned beef, breadcrumbs and spuds (issued by the Huns each day). Fry spuds and tinned meat with a little grated cheese and have bread and butter with either jam, honey or cheese. The

Ablution block.

Huns give us a little cheese during the week but it is inedible in the raw with an abominable smell. Our drink is either tea, coffee or cocoa. It is inadvisable to drink cold water as this gives everyone who has it a violent attack of diarrhoea, lasting a number of days.

The Huns, incidentally, only turn on the water when they feel like it which isn't very often, so we have a little difficulty in keeping clean.

Also during the day we play a lot of cards and go to appropriate classes. These are given by ex-school teachers, advertising agents etc. There is a possibility of a game of football but I think it is rather remote. We, the RAF, are not, like the Army, allowed to walk out of the compound around the camp, but last Sunday we were allowed to witness an entertaining boxing competition.

Each week there is the usual issue of 'The Camp', the PoW

newspaper given by the Huns and full, of course, of the most ridiculous propaganda. Also we are allowed to listen to Lord Haw-Haw each morning at 7.30.

The usual flock of rumours keep pouring in, the latest being that the Hun won a Commando raid in Boulogne three nights ago and that there was a 1000 bomber raid on Bremen 6 nights ago. We shall not get the real news until the next crowd comes in, in about one weeks' time.

As for cigs, we have to economise by taking the tobacco from cig ends and keeping it in a tin. Cig papers are obtainable at the canteen.

I have taken on a bet with one fellow that the war will be over by Sept 14th 1943. A £1 bet.

Sept 17th

Last night there were four short but very interesting talks given; on hospitals by the head surgeon of Sydney hospital; pre-war Poland by a Pole; slaughtering by a butcher and some experiences by an insurance agent. Passed the evening very well.

Today it is beautifully sunny, but there is a strong wind and it is definitely getting colder. Apparently, we lost two destroyers *HMS Sikh* and *HMS Zulu* at the commando raid on Tobruk. Stalingrad is still nobly holding out and, from reading between the lines of Lord Haw-Haw's broadcasts, it is apparent that the Germans are doing badly in Russia.

I have not yet described the camps that I've been to. That at Frankfurt was situated in a small valley surrounded by hills covered in sweet-smelling pine trees. It was very beautiful and the weather, while we were there, was extremely good.

Nearby were some of the very neat-looking black and white striped farm cottages. I think we could learn something from the Huns there. Working on the camp were Russian PoWs who ate anything they could lay their hands on, even old crusts of bread thrown outside. Also working in the fields nearby were old Polish women (peasants) imported by the Huns.

The camp had a playing field opened each afternoon where the boys played soccer and tenniquoits. It had an extremely good dance band which entertained certain nights each week and there was an excellent impromptu concert on the Sat night, better than any ENSA concert I had seen. We also saw, on the Wed night, a German submarine film of the last war. The cooking there is done communally which is a much better idea than the way we do it here. 4 meals each day. The beds etc were quite good and there was a decent library.

Here the camp is situated in a wide, desolate, flat, sandy plain, with some pine forests around. There is nothing distinctive about it at all except that it smells.

Sept 18ᵗʰ

And very cold too. God knows what it is going to be like in the winter.

Our barrack commander is getting particularly officious. Last night the RAF were allowed to go to an RAF concert. The music and singing were very good indeed but the sketches were rather weak. The Army provided an excellent band. There are reports this morning that there was another big bomber raid last night and that the Huns are retreating from Stalingrad.

Drying laundry.

Sept 19th

A very bright day but still cold.

Cards last night.

There is still fierce fighting around Stalingrad but the Huns seem loathe to mention the fighting further north at Voronezh, Orel etc.

It's a pity I smoke for the main method of buying food etc is by cigarettes. The present rate of exchange is 30 cigs for a packet of raisins or prunes and 30 cigs for a packet of tea.

Sept 20th

Again, very sunny and much warmer.

Stan's birthday today so we are going to try and eat a little more. He has made a cake which is cooking right now. We have to be very careful because the guards come round and smash up our stoves if they see us burning wood since they think we are burning bed-boards.

There was quite an amazing spelling bee and quiz competition last night. We saw a soccer match yesterday afternoon between the RAF and Army. The RAF won 3-2. Terrible pitch.

Apparently, there was a combined raid by Russians and RAF on Berlin about a fortnight ago. From the wireless this morning, it is evident there has been a decrease in shipping losses and that the Huns are very worried about a threatened 2nd Front and that there was a big raid some place night before last.

I wrote another letter home (my third) yesterday. Oh! For more food.

Sept 21st

Again a very warm and sunny day.

Yesterday afternoon we went to a Church of England service which was quite enjoyable although the padre did not give a very good sermon. He said he was very tired.

We had a very good meal at tea-time when we ate Stan's birthday cake. It was a little doughy so we will benefit by the experience next time we try one.

The Huns are claiming successes with a big convoy bound for Russia. The fighting for Stalingrad still goes on and the fighting in the Middle East seems to be flaring up.

Today we have been issued with more clothing including a good pair of boots which are a treat to wear after the clogs, a pair of pants, shirt, two hankies, a collar and tie and two pairs of socks.

Sept 22nd

And still very sunny.

Nothing happened last night except that during the night one of the boys paying a visit to the night latrine when one of the dogs tried to attack him through the window. He closed the window when the dog broke the glass but it kept him off.

Stan is today down with diarrhoea.

Fighting still goes on for Stalingrad.

This am *(morning)* I met Penny. How I've missed him before I don't know. We had a very interesting chat about old times and the squadron.

Sept 23rd

80 new boys came in yesterday. They have no information at all and are practically all bomber crews. I don't know any of them. There have been a lot of big raids especially on Bremen.

We now have 125 men in our room which is like the black hole of Calcutta. I felt very miserable yesterday mainly on account of the disorganisation and the fact that I have a very bad cold in the head.

Lord Haw-Haw did not mention Russia this morning.

Cloudy today but still warm.

There are rumours that Russia has declared war on Japan; that there was a parachutist raid on Bremen and that the Russians have thrown 1,000,000 men onto the Stalingrad front.

Life in the barracks.

We now have Indians in the compound who use the same latrines and same ablutions which is yet another flagrant violation of the prisoners of war convention.

Sept 24th

Trouble in the camp. Last night our barrack had a mass meeting with the compound C.O. presiding to decide the fate of our barrack commander. It was decided to chuck him out and have a new man elected which was duly done. He has been much too officious and uncivil. Good show.

Today my cold is much better and my browned-off feeling has worn off. Things are getting a bit more settled down. It is very interesting listening to the Indians of whom can speak no English. They are very ignorant and childish and very unintelligent – one of them is under the impression that there were only 100 British planes at Dieppe and 1 USA bomber!!

This morning it appears that the Russians are attacking strongly at Stalingrad. The Huns seem to be putting out peace feelers. I have a feeling that something very big is happening. Rumour has it that the Russians have Port Arthur in Manchukuo.

This afternoon some startling news. Reports purporting to come from official German news are that we have recaptured Tobruk and that there is fighting in Benghazi; that there was a 1500 bomber raid on Berlin not long ago and that there is discontent in the Rhur.

Sept 25th

Again it is very warm today.

Yesterday afternoon we were allowed to go and see a soccer match between the RAF and the Army. RAF won 6-2. It was an exceedingly good game with a very high standard of football.

Lord Haw-Haw said there was still fighting round Leningrad but I don't think the Huns are doing so well.

Sept 26th

Still very warm and sunny.

Last night the barrack had a most farcical moan session. I didn't realise we had so many old women in the block. The highlight of the evening was a false alarm *"Achtung, Achtung"*. I have never seen such a scramble or so many white faces.

We also heard an alleged Churchill speech on August 26th. He said there were 2½ million Yanks in England; we had

80,000 air crew; that there were 12,000,000 allied troops; that we had 80,000 tanks. He promised a 2nd Front before Xmas; victory in Egypt this year.

This morning Lord Haw-Haw was very busy making excuses for the non-capture of Stalingrad.

Sept 27th

Very cloudy and colder today.

For the first time the gates were opened and we are now allowed to walk around the camp. Had an interesting chat with some army fellows. Did not have the news today.

Cards yesterday, when I won 5 cigs. We play 500 a cig a game. What a bind this awful life is.

Sept 28th

Warm and sunny again.

The Huns did not let us hear Lord Haw-Haw this morning. We are hoping no news is good news.

Last night we went to an impromptu concert given by some of the boys. Very good. An excellent comedian compere.

Went to a soccer match in the afternoon. Spits v Harris. Spits won 2-1. Not a very good game. Played soccer myself this morning. Am terribly unfit and find it very difficult to stand the pace. We won 5-2.

Sept 29th

Yet another sunny day gone by.

I wrote my 4th letter home last Sunday.

Again no news from Lord Haw-Haw. Wild rumours of an invasion and a Russian break-through on a 100 mile front.

Enrolled in the school yesterday; taking Agriculture, Veterinary and Building Construction. Had my first three lessons today. Feeling pretty browned off again.

Sept 30th

The most beautifully warm and sunny day we've had.

There are many rumours that the 2nd Front has already started. Stalingrad still holds out.

Went to another class today. The main trouble is that the lecturers on Agriculture and Veterinary are Australian and New Zealanders and they deal mainly with conditions in those countries.

Went to a very interesting and amusing lecture on New York by a New Yorker, a chap called Armstrong.

Oct 1st

And still sunbathing weather.

Went to four lectures today.

No fresh rumours today. We had a most enjoyable game of whist (a whist drive) in the barrack in the evening. Some useful prizes of clothes were given.

Oct 2nd

The weather seems to be breaking at last, thank God! The worse the weather is the better – for it will be worse for the Huns in Russia.

The news this morning was quite good. Apparently there has been a big British attack in the desert and the Aussies have been attacking in New Guinea. Apparently the Germans were displeased by Hitler's recent speech.

Have decided to study for London Matric in December.

Oct 3rd

Stalingrad still holds out.

I am still undecided about the London Matric for I think the conditions for study – and it would entail quite a lot – are most unsatisfactory. I think I shall just content myself with individual study.

In a very interesting discussion last night we decided that the 2nd Front would quite obviously not materialise before the middle to the end of October and then it could coincide with an offensive in the Middle East in cooler weather and with an offensive in Russia in the winter when the Russians are much better in attack.

Oct 4th

Went to a lecture on Rumour last night. Extremely good but soon after the entry of a Hun it ended abruptly.

About 9pm, 90 new arrivals came. Terrific panic. Some of the boys went for bed-boards etc for them and brought back some extra. The guards in the compound realised what was happening and ran riot. Scrambles into barracks; some chaps taken and put up against the wire, being threatened with shooting. One fellow, in nightshirt only, beaten up because he had no disc! Riot and stabbings in the Indian compound.

The new chaps have no important news except that the desert campaign seems to be going very well, confirmed by Lord Haw-Haw this morning. The latest rumour is that British and Yank troops are in Finland.

Oct 5th

Today has been an absolutely beautiful day. Sunbathing most of the day although it was extremely cold in early morning.

Lord Haw-Haw making more excuses for the non-capture of Stalingrad.

Carried on with my study of chemistry.

Oct 6th

I forgot to mention that I sent off a letter to Mary on Saturday.

Today was calamity. The Hun authorities have stopped all our privileges and Red Cross food. We are confined to the compound, no school or concerts etc. The reason they give is an account of treatment of PoWs in England.

The RAF immediately comes into its own by giving this morning an open air concert with band etc for the benefit of the compound and the repats. Wizard.

This evening we had a very entertaining whist drive in the barrack, the entrance fee being one cigarette, which were redistributed as prizes.

Oct 7th

The winter seems to be coming on. It is much more cloudy and colder.

Mary.

Still fighting in Stalingrad. Our privileges were returned today including Red X parcels etc. which rather confirms that their excuse was somewhat suspicious. There are rumours that Dunkirk was occupied for two days recently.

Cards in the morning and afternoon. In the evening we went to a most interesting and amusing lecture on Rumours by Dan Edgar. It was complete this time.

Oct 8th

Again the gates have been closed. We don't know what for this time.

It was a beautiful warm morning but it clouded over in the afternoon.

All the troops from Dieppe were today herded into another compound and are still locked in the barracks with their hands tied in front of them and 100 or so Huns yelling round them. Shameful treatment! The rumours are that;

1. They refused to work
2. It is a reprisal for treatment of PoWs at Dieppe by us, of course.

We have rumours that the Huns are retreating from Stalingrad.

I today heard that Szumski, Domiter, Galazka, Olsewski, Sodlewski are all killed.

Oct 9th

Again the loss of privileges went on and the troops still have their hands tied. We have no Red X food so are living entirely on Germans rations and are to be treated like the Russians. This is a reprisal for the treatment of Huns at Dieppe and in the Channel Islands during a raid on Oct 4th.

The weather is bad. Rain most of the day and a very cold wind.

I have been suffering from a gum boil which for the last three days has been extremely painful so that I could hardly bear to eat or talk. Luckily it burst at 1.45 this afternoon, but not before it gave me a splitting headache and stomach ache with pain in my neck, ear and jaw. Blast this place!!

Oct 10th

What a day! It is very cold now.

At about 10.30am Laurie came in and said "Prepare for the worst boys, It's our turn now". With that we were put in another barrack which brought the complement up to 190 in one room!

At 11.00am we were all paraded and with about 200 Huns (steel-helmeted and armed to the teeth) in attendance with the Camp Commandant. An interpreter read out that they had not received a satisfactory reply from England so we were going to be tied up. This was done at about 12 noon. At about 4.30pm we were lined up in the barrack and an interpreter read out that "By order of the German Fuhrer and German people the bonds will be released for the time being."

Contrary to German expectations the announcement was heralded with a stony silence. Accordingly they were taken off.

Oct 11th

Panic again! This morning, since the German Government had received no favourable reply from the British, our hands were again bound at 08.00hrs. They were taken off for 1hr at 11.00hrs and put on again at 12.00hrs. They were then taken off at 21.00hrs.

There was no moaning from the boys and the guard seemed surprised to see us laughing and joking and singing loudly. Some of the guards were quite good and chatted with the boys who could speak German. One refused to believe that there had been any 1000 bomber raids!! They all said the fighting in Russia was very hard, and one went so far as to say that if the 2nd Front was opened the war would be over in 6 weeks. If it wasn't opened it would be over in 6 months. There is a rumour that 33 divisions have landed at Le Havre.

We are now living on purely German rations with just a little Red X. It is also very cold.

Wrote home today.

Oct 12th

Again we were bound rigid at 08.00hrs released at 11, bound at 12, released at 9pm. No one really minds the binding which is a bit inconvenient, but we dislike the overcrowding and smelly atmosphere.

Cold again.

Oct 13th

Same old routine. Cold early morning, warm during the day.

The guards are frontline troops and very young. They seem to consider this as much of a nuisance as we do.

Oct 14th

Again this tommy-rot. And again extremely cold early morning but warmer during the afternoon.

Kept us out on parade this morning because Joe *(a particularly brutal and infamous guard)* miscounted although it was pouring with rain.

A rumour today that 3 Hun armoured divisions have been annihilated at Stalingrad. According to a Hun newspaper the British have admitted tying up Germans at Dieppe and Sark.

The guards are mostly frontline troops on rest and are mostly very young. They are, of course, bedecked with iron crosses and seem to be getting very browned off. They will not commit themselves regarding the Italians and say the war in Russia is very hard. When asked how long the war will last one said with commendable tact "That rests with God".

None of them seems to have any concrete opinion of how long it will last.

Oct 15th

Yet again...... The guards get more and more lax. This morning three *'unter-offiziers' (sergent or staff sergeant)* were talking to us, one of whom could speak a little English. He thought this tying up to be very stupid. They asked if anyone could play an instrument and after posting guards at each end of the block to "look out for the enemy" as one said, undid one of the boy's hands. He then played his guitar to the accompaniment of the boys' voices. They were amused at "We'll hang out our washing…." which was apparently a popular song in Germany.

There are persistent rumours of a 2nd Front, Turkey is supposed to be in the war, and we are supposed to have had 75,000 casualties in the 2nd Front.

Oct 16th

I am getting tired of repeating the childish whims of the two governments and so are the guards. One of them told us today that his father was a PoW in Japan for 6 years during the last war and then in 1920 went to England. Terrible treatment in Japan, but ok in Blighty. Another one said the figures of Allied and Russian losses issued by the Huns were untrue. Another said he was shortly going to France.

Rumours today are again of the 2nd Front where we are supposed to be landing 3 divisions a day; and that our bonds will be taken off by 2pm tomorrow.

We had a much needed shower today.

Oct 17th

What a day for rumours. That the 2nd Front is really in progress; that we are fighting at Rouen; that we are fighting in Paris; that there has been a 75km advance; that there have been gigantic 2000 aircraft battles; that we lost 300 aircraft yesterday; that the Yanks made a 500 fortress raid at night and lost 38; that we are from 7pm tonight to be treated like Russian prisoners and have our feet bound etc; that the Hun PoWs in Canada have had their hands and feet bound and a rope around their necks; that the Camp Commandant has been posted on account of his leniency; that there is martial law in England; that 3 parsons have already been shot for preaching against the Government.

On top of all this it has been bitterly cold and wet with a howling gale.

I am getting increasingly hungry and have alternating spasms of despair and hope.

Oct 18th

What a terribly cold wet day.

We have to parade in pools of water, pouring with rain and no coats! There is a layer of snow on the Czech mountains today.

Our food is just barely sufficient to live on. We have two thin slices of brown bread for breakfast with either fat and salt or marg; a small bowl of soup and one potato for lunch; and another two slices of bread etc and about 3 or 4 more spuds for tea. We have a brew of tea at 4pm and mint tea at 6pm. This is a day's food. This is now telling on the boys, evident by the boys' pale faces and black eyes.

There are no rumours today except that the Russians are pushing the Huns back on an 800 mile Front.

Today one of the Army boys, with his hands tied, was stabbed in the back with a bayonette. He is in a bad way in hospital and has lost a lot of blood.

Oct 19th

An extremely cold bitter day. It is impossible to sleep well at night owing to the cold.

Fellows are going to hospital from this barrack on an average of three or four a day. This I think is due to the cold and lack of food.

We've just had terrific news. Apparently British troops have been in France for two days. The German people will be told tonight or tomorrow. It is a tonic to everyone who is wild with excitement. Tonight everyone is even wilder.

What a red letter day. We've had biscuits, cheese, chocolate, cigs, prunes and sugar. On top of that the new boys came in and said the Huns were getting a bashing everywhere. Stalingrad is a graveyard for them, shipping losses are slight, the Yanks have been heavily bombing Germany and that the war will soon be over. The latest rumour is that the 2nd Front has been in progress for 8 days and that we are now fighting at the Albert Canal.

As a damper the Huns have taken our stoves out. We can't have any brew, we can't lie on our beds during the day and our billets and dixies *(cooking pots)* must be spotlessly clean.

Oct 20th

Things certainly do happen. They're dropping down heavily on the old 'bull'. We cannot lie on our beds during the day. The stoves were taken out this morning. No brews. We have to stand away from the wire to talk. We must shave every day, keep our hair cut, be properly dressed, with caps etc on parade, complete with polished boots although we have no brushes or polish!

We had an inspection tonight. Lots of rows. We were issued with greatcoats today.

No rumours except that there has been a 200 Fortress raid escorted by fighters on Hamburg. No Luft lost. Everyone is subdued today with no news of the 2nd Front.

I wrote home and to Mary on Sunday. Both PCs *(post cards)*.

Oct 21st

Just another day. Very cold and cloudy.

Did a brew outside today. I think the rumours about the 2nd Front are untrue.

Stan was chased around by a lunatic with a bayonet today.

I heard some real news about the battles in the Far East – Coral Sea etc.

Oct 22nd

Again cold and wet.

Rumour today has it that we've captured Amsterdam.

The new fellows have come into the compound. Not much new gen. There is one Spit pilot who tells me that the old squadron has gone back to the old kites. Otherwise the 2nd Front seems to have died its natural death.

We spend most of our time reading, talking and sleeping.

Oct 23rd

No rumours today except that tomorrow we may have our bonds off to do some washing and cleaning up. The days drag very slowly but the months seem to go by fairly quickly.

In my moods of despondency Stan's presence and conversation are for some unknown reason a tonic to me. If only we could get some real news.

Oct 24th

Today, for a wonder, a rumour came true. Our bonds came off at 11:00 am for the afternoon so that we could do some washing and generally clean the place up. The wash place was like a laundry. Quite amusing but it certainly passed the day – a beautiful day – the Fates were kind.

A rumour today that the German government have received a favourable reply from England. It was a great treat to be free again.

Sandy and I stewed up the prunes and made some jam.

Oct 25th

We've been tied up again today. Again a nice day.

Rumours have been round today that the bonds will be off tomorrow. Who knows!

Also rumours that the Russians have pushed the Huns back 150 miles at Leningrad; that the battles in the Solomons are going ok; that there are Yanks in Russia.

If only I could get something to occupy my mind. If we're not careful we shall drift into a state of mental stagnation. Stan gives me great encouragement. We went to a church service this morning. The service is very welcome but I wish that man could preach.

Wrote to Mum and Dad and Tilly yesterday. Both PCs.

Oct 26th

Rumour has it that there is a big British offensive in the desert. We have supposedly captured 40,000 Huns etc, etc.

Rumour also says that we are going to move from here. The sooner the better. Today the front line guard left us and we were left with more tormenters – old stooges from Berlin.

Big bulk issue today.

Oct 27th

Quite a nice day.

Had a farcical dixie parade in the afternoon.

One of the guards say he does not believe a word of the Hun propaganda and says that unless they beat the Russians this winter, they've lost the war and that their losses in Russia are tremendous, having lost all their crack troops.

Oct 28th

Today a beautiful sunny day with a strong wind.

About 10 officers (Huns) came round inspecting the camp today. There are strong rumours that we shall be moving very shortly either to Sagan or Lubeck.

We have no news about the progress of the British offensive in the desert which is admitted by the Huns.

Oct 29th

A beautiful very warm sunny day, like an English good summers' day.

A horrible rumour that the Russians are seeking peace terms from the Huns. So help us if it's true. It appears that the rumour developed from the fact that someone misread the Hun papers.

The General looked as hard as nails and reeked of scent!!

No news of the war in the desert.

Oct 30th

A bit cooler today. We now have more discipline and a threat of being punished by having Russian police on camp and Russian prisoners sleeping next to each Englishman. The guards are…

I though one was going to beat me up today – for treading on my foot!!!

No rumours and no news today.

Oct 31st

And still amazing weather. I can't understand it. It is sunny all day and warm.

A new game was introduced into the billet tonight. Racing, complete with bookies, horses, owners etc, etc for cigarettes. Very good for passing the time away. The horses were moved on by the roll of a dice, the dice being rolled by the owner of each horse. I paid 2 cigs for a horse.

Nov 1st

Amazing! Sunbathing in November.

There are no rumours and no news. There are even no rumours of any Red X issue tomorrow. Went to a church service this morning. A much better preacher.

Nov 2nd

Got some old BBC news today. Apparently Churchill said on Oct 19th that our offensive may go on, when it starts, 'till 1944. God forbid! On the same day Lancasters made the biggest daylight of the war on an arms factory in France. 94 bombers.

A bit cooler today but still sunny.

We had a little more bulk issue but none of the usual accompanying rumours.

Nov 3rd

Had a terrible night last night. No sleep at all due to excruciating pain in my stomach. Think I've got a cold in my inside. Lots of diarrhoea. Haven't eaten at all today.

What a day for rumours – that we've captured 16,000, 30,000, 100,000 troops in Libya and even that the Huns have packed up there; that Italy has asked for a separate peace; that the first RAF crowd are leaving here by Monday.

Still very sunny.

Nov 4th

Stomach ok today. Still very sunny but cooler.

One of these guards who are all about 40-50 said they may be going to Russia. Very significant. A fellow was told by a German from Russia that it is carnage at Stalingrad, not a battle. A guard said he doesn't believe any propaganda and that he hasn't seen butter for two years. They stare goggle-eyed at our food.

Very good news in camp newspaper. They admit large Russian attacks on all fronts, make excuses for their losses, weather etc and admit that their U-boat crews, many of whom are young, have seen no action before.

Their communique from the desert admit a British breakthrough at the place and that they are having heavy losses.

Had pants, vest, socks, shirt and 50 cigs given me by an Army fellow. On the camp they are trying to mess us about as much as possible by blanket parades, dixie parades, tying up inspections etc to try and get the boys out on working parties.

Nov 5th

Very wet today.

There was a mouse in my paillasse under my head last night. Horrors!

Not much news. I became acquainted with Chapter 13 of Revelations where it is supposed to predict that the war will end in March next year.

Nov 6th

Very, very cold and wet.

The General was on the camp again today. The ban is supposed to be lifted on Tuesday.

Won more cigs at racing. Drew a house in the Grand National which came in 2nd. 30 cigs!

Very good news from the desert. The Huns admit they are retreating and the Wops say they have had heavy losses.

2oz tea now cost 50 marks i.e. £3.6s.8d

Nov 7th

A terrible wet, cold, damp, raw day.

Did some washing in the afternoon, our hands being untied. We are supposed to be fighting at Matruh and to have taken 9000 prisoners. All the boys very cheerful about the Middle East.

Nov 8th

A bit warmer today but still foggy and wet.

Went to church in the morning and wrote home in the afternoon.

In the Middle East we are claiming 9,000 PoWs, 226 tanks, 60 aircraft and 100,000 tons of shipping. There are rumours that the Huns have deserted Libya.

In the afternoon, developed a terrible headache and stomach-ache.

Nov 9th

A nasty day again.

More bulk issue and got a pullover and gloves. Didn't sleep a wink last night for headache and stomach-ache and the head went on all day. Terrible pain just behind the eyes probably due to eye strain from too much reading in bad light.

Bags of news; that we have landed at Morocco; that we are fighting at Tobruk, that the Russians have advanced 125kms south of Stalingrad; that Hitler made a defeatist speech; that we have landed at Chad and Dakar.

Nov 10th

Our first bit of snow today.

We are not to have any newspapers.

More rumours of the Morocco landing and that the French fleet has sailed from the South of France.

Feeling much better today. A bit more bulk.

Nov 11th

Bags and bags of rumours. That the Huns have reoccupied the rest of France; that we have captured 45,000 troops at M.M.; that the Russians have opened the winter offensive; that we've been heavily bombing Italy; that the French fleet has sailed.

A very cold day.

Nov 12th

Rumours that England and USA have declared war on France; that the French fleet has capitulated; that we have landed at Marseille and are fighting in France; that we've captured Darlan; that we landed in Derna and Benghazi; that we've taken 40,000 PoWs; 600 tanks, 500 a/c *(aircraft)* in the desert. Surrounded and shelling Tobruk. Morocco capitulated after ½ hrs fighting; that the battleship *Jean Bart* was sunk; that there have been 24 commando raids on Sicily in the last 7 days and that Churchill has promised England a Xmas box and it won't be North Africa.

What a red letter day for me. In the evening I played pontoon and won 50 cigs and about half an hour later received my first mail. 9 letters. One from Aunt Maggie, 1 from Aunt Kath, 3 from home, 3 letters from Mary and a Xmas card. They didn't know I was a prisoner until Sept 29th when they had my letter from Dulag.

An extremely cold day.

Someone broke into the Red X stores tonight.

Nov 13th

Again very cold. Couldn't sleep last night for excitement and intense cold.

Paid 10 cig yesterday for 3 biscuits. A loaf costs about £6.10s.0d!!!

The only rumour today is that we have taken Corsica and that the Huns are bombing Morocco.

There has been quite a lot of snow today and it's been freezing all day.

Won 20 cigs at housey-housey. Lost 9 at pontoon.

Nov 14th

Still cold and about ¼ inch of snow this morning. Snowing practically all morning. Very cold with tied hands.

Read through my mail for about the 20th time. It's great. I can almost repeat Mum's first one by heart.

Thursday's Hun newspaper has been smuggled into the compound at the cost of 50 cigs. There is supposed to be an extremely large and heavily defended convoy sailing in the Med which the Huns admit they have been unable to attack. Hitler has said the war situation is serious and Churchill says it's in the bag.

Nov 15th

Again very cold.

Went to church in the morning.

There are rumours that we've taken Tobruk and that the Huns marched into Spain from the north and we from the south. There are rumours that we have taken Corsica.

Wrote a card home and a card to Les. German guards are very lax.

Nov 16th

Very cold and wet today.

The latest moving rumour is to Stettin at the end of November.

Rumour today that the Russians have retaken Rostov; that there is revolt in Spain; that there is fighting in France between Huns and Yanks and that the Huns in Russia have withdrawn 200kms to their winter line.

The day passed quite quickly for a change, mainly because we didn't get tied up till about 1.10pm

Nov 17th

Rain, sleet and cold all day.

Biscuits and honey bulk issue.

Rumours today that we shall be tied up with chains tomorrow, the chains being 18inches apart. Should be much better. I have a slight attack of chilblain on my right hand.

Rumour has it that the Russians are attacking all along the line; that British, Yank and Hun troops are fighting in Spain; that the *Queen Elizabeth* is damaged; that the convoy got through to Gib *(Gibralter)*; that we've taken Corsica and Sardinia; that all Hun PoWs are being marched from Tobruk to Alex as a reprisal for Dunkirk; that the evacuation of Tobruk was worse than Dunkirk.

Nov 18th

Much finer and sunny today but still cold.

Had my best night's sleep last night. Wizard!

Rumours that we've taken 9,000 PoWs at Benghazi and that the Huns have landed in Tunisia.

We have fresh guards who are bastards.

Rumours that Benes made a speech when he said the war will be over by May; that Churchill has made a very aggressive one; that we've taken 192,000 PoWs including 75,000 Huns in the desert; that we've asked permission to send troops through Spain; that the Japs are making fantastic claim about a battle off the Solomons.

Turned cold and wet in the afternoon.

Nov 19th

Cold and damp.

We are still tied up with strings.

The Huns admit the loss of Derna. Churchill is supposed to have said that the bombing of Germany is about to begin... to avenge the bombing of 1940!!!

Nov 20th

Cold again, but dry.

No rumours or news at all.

Some of the boys were chained up today.

Nov 21st

Washing day in bitterly cold water. Very cold and a bit of snow.

Rumours that Benghazi is surrounded and we are fighting 150kms to the west. Turkey and Spain are supposed to have mobilised.

Spend a lot of time in the wigwam playing chess, reading and talking. Very pleasant atmosphere.

Wrote a letter to Mary.

Nov 22nd

Sharp frost during the night.

We had chains today. They are about 18inches apart and are much better.

A wild rumour that Rommel escaped from the desert in a sub which was sunk! Joke!! Also that the war in the desert is over and that we are retreating in the desert. Also that Turkey is in the war.

Lost 100 cigs at pontoon.

Nov 23rd

Lots of rumours today. That we have captured Tunis; that the war in the desert is over; that we are retreating in the desert; that we've captured Sicily; that we've landed at Genoa.

Apart from this it's been snowing all day.

We had another bulk issue.

Won 70 fags at solo.

Again no mail. Am beginning to wonder if my first mail from here got through.

I find sleeping very difficult owing to the cold and to the cold I've got again.

Nov 24th

Freezing and snowing all day.

The only rumour was that we've landed in Sicily.

Won another 50 cigs at pontoon.

The boys are preparing for Xmas.

Nov 25th

Lovely morning but very sharp frost.

Had a bath today.

The only rumour that an American Marshall said that the war would be over by Jan 1st '43 or within 3 months of that date. Really good news in the Hun paper was the admission that the Russians have broken through south of Stalingrad and at Voronezh. Also that we have captured Agadabia 100 miles south of Benghazi.

Won 170 cigs at Crown-Anchor. I now have a stock of 290. Had a little chess match with the Polish Jews. I lost – as did most people.

I have another vicious cold. Freezing hard all day.

Nov 26th

Dull morning. I have a terrible cold.

Lots of rumours today; that there was trouble between Hun and Iti troops in the desert; that Germany has withdrawn her troops from Italy; that Italy is out of the war; that Turkish troops marched into Bulgaria; that Spain has been in the war on our side for 4 days.

Thawed today. Still no mail.

Nov 27th

Milder this morning.

I had a terrible bout of coughing during the night. Slept better when it had finished.

The only rumour is that Hun troops are being withdrawn from Greece. In the newspaper the Huns admit Russian breakthroughs on 3 Fronts especially SW of Stalingrad.

Nov 28th

Snow and cold again.

No news today.

Learnt to play bridge today.

Nov 29th

Blizzard on parade.

Terrible bout of coughing during the night. Wrote a card home and to Stan.

Apparently the Huns occupied Toulon and some of the fleet scuttled itself.

Someone broke into the cookhouse last night and pinched the tea so we had mint tea this morning.

Rumours that Crete has been retaken; that there is a big convoy in the Med.

Got seconds and feel rather well today.

Nov 30th

A beautiful fine and crisp morning. The howling gale of yesterday has dropped.

A rumour today that Tripoli has been taken, also that Laval has displaced Petain.

I feel rotten with my cold. Some bulk up.

Dec 1st

Milder today. The Russians seem to be advancing pretty well.

A most distasteful incident happened today. My own and Stan's suspicions were confirmed when we caught Sandy hiding a chunk of bread cut from our day's ration. I think this has been going on for a week or two. When accused he was obviously guilty. The Rat.

Received another letter from Mum. I think I've got all my mail now. My Flt/Sgt is backdated to Aug 1st.

Dec 2nd

Very mild but snowing this morning. Heavy snow until about 3pm – about 3 or 4 inches, but warm.

The only rumours are that the Itis are withdrawing their workers from Germany and that Churchill is supposed to have made another speech when he invited the Itis out of the war or else....bombing. Also to treat prisoners well or he would allow them to be in the army of occupation.

My cold is still pretty bad and I have a pain in the chest.

The Russians seem to be attacking pretty strangely.

Dec 3rd

Dad's birthday. How I think of them on days like this.

I will now give an account of my daily routine:

Rise 06:00. Make bed etc and wash in cold water
07:00 roll call
07:20 breakfast. Tea, one slice bread, marg and potato, 1 slice toast, marg and honey, cigarette
08:00 chaining up parade
08:30 walk around compound
09:00 reading
11:15 collect and peel spuds
11:30 collect and eat soup. Today was mashed spuds and salmon followed by porridge, this being a special 2 soup day. Wash dixie and then;
12:00 reading
1:45 writing including yesterday's entry
2:00 talking

3:00 prepare tonight's supper and more talking

4:00 cup of tea

5:00 roll call

5:15 tea. 2 slices of bread and marg and spud, jam, cheese, honey, sausage or fish paste depending on the day

6:00 talking and reading

6:30 supper mashed or fried spuds

6:45 studying or games

8:00 parade for unchaining

8:30 bed

This is an average day.

Today we've had more snow and tonight it is freezing hard.

Rumours today that Crete has been evacuated by the Huns; there is fighting in Greece; and the Russians have retaken Rostov.

Dec 4th

A cold morning.

Went on the coal party and managed to pinch 2 greatcoat pockets full and stuff some more inside my blouse. Quite an appreciable amount. The civvy in charge nearly caught me once. Good fun tho' doing the Hun out of something.

There are reports that mail is to be stopped from the 9th of this month and that they are stopping the newspapers. If that's true, something big must be on.

Dec 5th

Freezing all day.

Spent all afternoon printing Xmas cards.

More rumours of fighting in Greece; of Italian unrest and that the Russians have advanced 600kms to Smolensk. Also that Churchill said he would have all allied troops in England by Jan 1st. Some hopes!

Received a letter from Aunt Maggie.

Dec 6th

Much warmer and thawed today.

Wrote a letter home and finished off my Xmas card. There seems to be very heavy fighting in Russia. No rumours at all. Let's hope it's the calm before the storm.

A howling gale at night.

Dec 7th

Cool but no snow.

2 of the Dieppe boys escaped last night. They had the dogs out this morning looking for them.

Terrible night's sleep last night.

We heard another fantastic alleged Churchill rumour. I, although an ace optimist, disbelieve it.

All the snow has thawed.

Dec 8th

Very mild this morning. Amazing this winter. Last winter was much more severe and longer. We'll see what Jan and Feb bring forth.

Had a letter today from Aunt Kate who tells me that my parcel was sent off on Oct 29th.

Rumours that the Huns are massing on the border of Greece and Turkey and that Turkey mobilised on the 28th Nov.

Dec 9th

Mild again.

A good night's sleep last night. My blasted finger won't heal.

We had a shower in the afternoon. Oh for a good Turkish bath – one of my resolution for when I get home.

Dec 10th

Slight frost last night but a beautiful morning. Very sunny but a bit cold.

Threatened this morning. There are 14 chains and 3 handcuffs missing. If they are not returned by 12 noon today we shall have to stand out on the parade ground from 9 – 12 and 1:30 – 4:30 each day; rain, hail, sleet or snow.

There were rumours yesterday that there were riots in Greece and that we are moving shortly to Sagan.

In the afternoon, very strong rumour came up that the army are moving out of the compound; that we are moving back to our old barrack; and that the chains are coming off on Monday.

Joe saw us using the *verboten (forbidden)* stove today and swore blind we were burning bed boards which we were not. Consequently the stove is now out. As a result of the threatened moves I am eating up my Xmas store of food.

Dec 11th

A beautiful morning. As usual the Huns threats did not materialise. Very sunny and warm all day.

More bulk issue. The new Lager officer says no tins are to be issued to the Lager. He even suggested that the cheese could have been made into a good soup!!! Ridiculous.

Dec 12th

Another beautiful morning.

Had a wizard night's sleep last night and feel much better for it this am.

Lots of mail this afternoon but I did not get any. Fed well all day – almost finished my stocks. We may be going down to the school next week.

Learned that the two escapists managed to get to the Bulgarian border.

Dec 13th

Lovely morning again but a bit colder.

Wrote a card to Auntie Kate and Aunt Maggie. Everyone's letters from home are very optimistic and suggest we should be home by next summer. No suggestion of Red X but bags of moving rumours.

Dec 14th

Nice day again but a bit colder.

The school did not open as I expected.

Lots of gen *(information)* that Churchill said the biggest battle in the desert has yet to be fought; that the Russians are breaking through all along the line; that Smolensk and Rostov had been retaken.

In the evening we heard that we shall be moving back to 17a tomorrow.

Got a good book on agriculture.

Dec 15th

Moved into 17a today. Blast it. We have no fires, no coal for Xmas, no decorations etc, etc. Quite a panic.

Much colder and dull today. Looks like snow.

We were chained up at 12:00 after moving and we have no books and no games. Everyone quite cheerful tonight. Bill had a very encouraging letter from his girl. I had a beautiful Xmas card from Mum and Dad.

We had a ration of Red X parcels today. Stan and I in a combine.

Dec 16th

Very cold again.

Bed in the barrack with no fires.

Lots of rumours about next week's food issue. The gen is no Red X but bulk; that the recent raid on Turin was 1000 bombers; and that the Huns are retiring to their winter line.

Wild reports that Singapore and Hong Kong are retaken.

Dec 17th

Cold sharp frost this am. Couldn't sleep for cold last night.

Rumours today that we have recaptured New Guinea and taken 75,000 prisoners! Apparently the church bells at home have been ringing for something. There seems to be intense fighting in Russia with the Ruskies attacking and the fighting in the desert seems to have flared up again.

Dec 18th

Very cold and foggy this am.

I have a shocking boil on the back of my neck which kept me awake all night. In the afternoon I kept shivering. I hope I haven't caught another cold.

The Huns say they are again returning in the desert.

Dec 19th

Warmer this am.

After a couple of aspirins and a hot drink last night I had a wizard night's sleep and feel much better this am.

Rumours that Churchill promised the continual heavy bombing of Italy; Roosevelt promised troops on Continent by early New Year; Turkey is supposed to have allowed British ships to pass through the Dardanelles; and the Pope is supposed to have gone to Ireland.

Apparently the Hun are having a lot of trouble with Sweden and France.

Played bridge in the evening.

Dec 20th

Rained very hard all night, but I had another wonderful night's sleep. This morning it was beautifully fresh, mild and the sun shining brightly.

Last night had wizard chat with Bill about food. I have decided to become a connoisseur of same when I get home.

Boil and hand now better.

Dec 21st

A bit cooler today but still fine.

We have today got our barrack locked from 7 o'clock at night.

The rumour of Singapore being in British hands seems to have died down.

Very cold in the barrack tonight. In the evening had an excellent concert which put everyone in fine spirits.

Dec 22nd

Frost last night and very nippy this am.

There seems to have been a decided stall in rumours and red hot news lately.

Rumours during the day that British troops have gone through the Dardanelles and landed at Odessa and that Oliver Lyttelton said the war would not be over by the end of 1943.

Dec 23rd

Much colder and raw today.

Getting the Xmas spirit OK. Last Sunday wrote a letter to

Mary and a card to Betty and a card to Rene *(sister)*.

Lots of duff rumours today about a second front and the troops through Dardanelles etc, etc. The Russians seem to be doing very well and pushing the Huns back.

Went to an excellent band concert, military and dance. Very, very good. I sat by a roaring fire which put me very much at home. Happy memories.

Received Xmas parcels today.

Dec 24th

What a day. Went on coal party in morning and nearly got pounced on by the civvy.

Very damp and raw today.

Had a good feed in the evening including biscuits, chocolates and sweets. Wizard. But still no mail. The gates were opened in the evening and cooking commenced. I cooked bacon and chips. Glorious.

Made an agreement with Bill to send him a farm produce Xmas parcel next year and he will send me one.

Dec 25th

Xmas day and not in the workhouse but almost as bad.

Started feeding well last night and went to bed at 12pm. It was very amusing seeing the boys dancing to the blowing of a trumpet. We had a happy sing-song and everyone was feeling in fine spirits.

I heard a very philosophical remark that, after all, life's not so bad. We must thank God we're alive anyway. Too true.

Today I had to risk being shot by climbing through the

window and going to the lavatory before the door was opened. And not for a leak either!

Then at 6:15 a Canadian walked round the compound playing the bagpipes. It was the first time I really appreciated them. It was lovely and considering it was a marvellously mild and warm morning, what more could a chap wish for.

At 7:30 I had a glop, then two thick slices of bread, buttered both sides, with bacon in between which had been cooking overnight – wizard, then toast and biscuits with a brew.

At 11:00 we had another brew with toast, biscuit and chocolate. Dinner was good. Stan and I shared a tin of steak and macaroni with mashed spuds and butter and then had Xmas pud with condensed milk. I was so full I couldn't eat all the pud. We had a brew then.

I was eating biscuits, sweets and chocolate during the afternoon when we played solo. We paraded at 5 o'clock and at 5:30 had a brew and a good tea; cake etc. We then sat talking till 7:15 when I cooked Stan's and my chips on the hot plate which we ate at 8 o'clock with a brew.

From then on the boys were dancing etc and at 9 o'clock we had another brew with toast and cheese. A little more talking and then to bed with a well loaded stomach.

During the pm there was a rugger match but I did not go. We had our chains off all day.

The Huns, incidentally, gave us less rations for Xmas than normally. They'll pay for this.

Dec 26th

Very, very cold today.

I had a bad night's sleep with pain in the stomach. Suffering from a couple of boils on the neck and heartburn all day. Ate no breakfast, no dinner just had a little tea.

Played solo in the am. In the evening the final of the ____ _____ was run and the officials donned fancy dress. A most realistic looking number was the highlight who kissed the winners of the races. They were also town criers and random fancy dress. It was very well organised and the winner got 1,280 cigs the 2nd got 500 and the third 250. Very good.

Dec 27th

Still very cold.

Had a wonderful night's sleep and awoke feeling very refreshed. Had a good breakfast.

Rumours that we are moving to Sagan on Jan 16th; that we are in Odessa; that the Russians are 250 miles from the German border; and Churchill's speech "Victory in '43" and heavy bombing etc. A rumour came up during the day; that the Russians had recaptured Minsk and that the Huns were bombing Minsk. Also that Darlan was shot and that we had captured Sfax.

Played Brag in the evening.

In the afternoon had a walk round the various compounds and was amazed at the comfort of the racketeers in 38 compound. 3 fires a brew and a hot plate, bags of food etc. The decorations did not come up to 50% as good as the RAF.

There was apparently a fancy dress dance in the Repat's in the evening.

Dec 28th

Very cold again.

The school re-opened this am. I went down and did private study from 9-10 so then went to agriculture till 12:00.

In the evening we went to the panto. *Aladdin*. It was very good. Costumes picturesque. Mikey Orr naturally stole the show. The band was good but a little slow in the uptake.

Dec 29th

A biting cold blast today.

Too cold to go to school. No rumours or mail. I am beginning to give up hope.

Had a good meal of salmon and mash at night.

Dec 30th

Cold but a lovely day.

Went to school in the morning and afternoon. Had a very interesting lecture on mistakes in agriculture and went to auto engineering in the afternoon.

No mail again. Had a luxury in the form of beetroot at night. Very nice too. Cost 10 cigs.

There are no rumours or news of any sort. It appears that the Russians are advancing 50 miles per day (perhaps!)

An amusing incident during the night when one fellow woke us with a blood curdling scream.

Dec 31ˢᵗ

Last day of the year and still no mail.

We were untied at 11 o'clock. The Hun major was very affable and pleasant with some of the Repats today and said he hoped and thought it would soon be all over. He wished them good luck and Happy New Year.

A *dolmetscher (translator)* said if we were not shaking hands with the folks at home next summer he was a Dutchman.

Tonight we are having a whist drive and then a concert. The lights are to be on till 12 o'clock.

On parade this evening, Joe wished us a Happy New Year and as a New Year concession, said he would have parade at 8 o'clock instead of 7. Kind fellow???

It is certainly amazing the way the Huns have been easing up lately. Maybe we are winning the war, we hope and I certainly think we are.

1943

Jan 1st

Happy New Year John and lots of 'em.

Last night we had a most enjoyable whist drive that started at 7 o'clock and finished at 9. Cigarettes were prizes. There were 72 players and the prizes were 50% to the winner, 25% to 2nd, a snowball of 10% and a booby of 5%. There was also a prize for the last 4 tricks 10%. Altogether there were 20 hands, I did pretty well but the winner got 124 in 16 hands.

We then had a brew and then the boys put on a concert. It was very good but a little crude of course. Bob & Pat's sketches were very good.

We then talked until 12 when Taffy played the New Year in on the trumpet. Then everyone went wild with excitement; tins were banged and kicked around, everyone cheered and of course the inevitable *Auld Lang Syne* was raucously howled out. Then there were the numerous handshakes etc, a little sing-song and so, amidst very excited talking, to bed.

I enjoyed it. May this year see us in a very different position.

Today is still cold and we had a little sleet. We have no bonds today.

Jan 2nd

A very cold windy blast, freezing all day.

Went to school in the morning and read E J Russell's *'English Farming'*. Very good.

Yesterday afternoon, Bill and George on the one side with myself and Stan on the other had a most entertaining 8 hour argument on communism.

This afternoon listened to all the rumours about Turkey, Russia etc. The Russians certainly seem to be advancing about 10 – 20 miles a day and to have taken up, the last 6 weeks, 200,000 PoWs or killed. Turkey has apparently ordered out all Hun diplomats.

In the evening I went to a most interesting lecture by D Armstrong. The second part of his *'A New Yorker in New York'*. Extremely interesting and amusing.

Jan 3rd

Cold again. Some snow in the late afternoon and evening in a howling wind.

It seems to be that Rostov has fallen with about 70,000 PoWs; also we claim to be shelling Tripoli from both sides; also Italy is supposed to have been bombed for 7 days and nights; also there is supposed to have been the heaviest raid of the war on Cologne where the civilian casualties were greater than the German army has lost soldiers.

Jan 4th

Very cold with lots of snow.

Went down to school today. Very interesting.

A good Hun soup today. Had four letters from home tonight. October mail and one November. Makes me feel pretty good. They are now getting my mail OK and there are bags of cigs on the way. Too many weddings.

In the evening there was a fight in the barrack between two chaps who had a row at lunchtime. Good show. No gloves, good entertainment. One bloke almost out. Wizard.

Had a shower today.

Jan 5th

Extremely cold again.

Wrote a letter home today. Bulk day so I had a good woof.

There are rumours that the chains will be coming off next Friday or Sunday.

Today everyone – including those who were previously pessimistic – is very optimistic about the war.

Jan 6th

Very cold again.

Up at 05.30 to get rid of my _____ and empty the *scheisse* bucket. Had another good lecture on nutrition. Apparently 3000 cals are the minimum needed all day to keep the human body going. We are getting 2500 from German rations.

A lot of parcels are in, one posted Nov 4th.

Jan 7th

Very, very cold and snowing all morning.

Had an extra camp roll-call this am. Very cold. The compound gates were closed at 10:00am and not reopened until 12:00.

Feeling very tired at night. Easily the coldest day we've had so far.

Jan 8th

Snowing all day and cold again.

School and very interesting.

Rumours that Hitler advised the German people not to lose their morale over defeats since the British people didn't. Churchill is supposed to have warned Germany that the dogs of war will be unleashed by Jan 31st.

Rumours that the Huns have recaptured Riga and Kiev.

Jan 9th

Very cold again and deep drifts of snow this morning. Snowing all day. These cold dreary days rend very much to despair when it seems as though no news is coming in.

It is very hard to 'keep ones chin up' but we are all trying hard. More food and warmth would make all the difference.

Laurie is pessimistic and does not think the war will be over for another two years.

Heard some BBC news. The war is going very well in Russia, the Huns being pushed back 200 miles in the Barren Steppe area and Rostov being almost in Russian hands by Jan 3rd; Mosquitoes and Venturas raided Oslo; and in Africa the Coldstream Grenadiers and Hamps did very well in Tunisia.

Jan 10th

A little warmer this morning but still freezing.

Nothing at all happened.

Wrote a card home and a card to Mary. Feeling a bit brassed off.

Jan 11th

Had a terrible night's sleep. Very cold feet. I had the most horrible impression I was going insane. It was terrible.

Extremely cold today. I estimate about 20 degrees of frost.

3 roll-calls this morning. A Dieppe boy escaped. It was the coldest am I have ever experienced. There was lots of ice inside the barrack windows.

Some new boys came in today. They brought some excellent news which confirms lots of rumours. Rostov has fallen and the Ruskies are beating hell out of the Huns. Tripoli has fallen. Wizard news altogether. Everyone in good spirits at night.

Jan 12th

Even colder. An icy wind blowing.

A better night's sleep last night. Easily the coldest day I have ever experienced. A very dry cold and what a frost. Lots of ice inside the barrack windows. Couldn't keep warm at all. Last night there were 54 degrees of frost and at 12 noon there were 36 degrees.

In the barrack in the evening we had an entertainment by the *Lamsdorf Melody Makers*, a string orchestra. It was the best barrack concert we ever had. Good singers too.

Jan 13th

No frost today but bags of wind.

I'm now wearing 2 pants, 2 shirts and feel much warmer. Good night's sleep last night.

Went to school. Agriculture. These lectures are all very interesting. Having read *'Hell on Ice'* by Edward Ellsburg, life as a PoW seems comparatively luxurious.

My system of eating is now no breakfast, soup at dinnertime, half my bread with the brew at 4 and the rest of my bread with spuds at 7. Works quite well.

Jan 14th

Very cold wind. Very drafty inside the barrack.

No news at all today.

Jan 15th

Much warmer today. Thawed very rapidly this afternoon.

Missed agriculture for the first time as there were two soups and the bulk coming up.

Lots of rumours today; that Italy was out of the war; Krakow captured by the Russians; that the Huns have landed at Benghazi and that Joe and Puzh have been posted to the Russian Front.

It is very funny, but a bad rumour, eg the Benghazi one, is immediately disbelieved and pooh-poohed but a good one of Krakow is at least entertained. Typical PoW psychology.

One of the boys who has been here 2 years had a letter from his wife very optimistic who says she is cancelling his next clothing parcel and ordering him a new suit!!

Jan 16th

Fairly cold but not too bad.

Spent an enjoyable 2 hours reading Economy in the library this morning. Went to a good concert by the *Lamsdorf Melody Makers* which was followed by a talk by D Armstrong on Hollywood. Very good as usual and most amusing. He told us how they do the kick scenes and a little about the stars. Tyrone Power, ____

Jan 17th

Very foggy and not too warm. A typical, raw English day.

Had an argument in the afternoon about food and pettiness. I simply can't understand the mentality of a chap who says he would rather have ¾ parcel per bed and bulk than the food on the squadron. Or that we are not much less fit than before we became PoWs.

Rumours today that Italy is invaded and that Turkey is in the war.

Jan 18th

Day's raw, cold, foggy again.

I hear that 2 escapists have been brought in suffering from frostbite.

Went to school in the morning. Interesting again.

In the evening, the final heats of the racing were run off. My horse *Pissquick* (crude but quite amusing) won its heat. The entrance fee is 2 cigs and once there were 85 entrants. The first prize is 100, second 50 and third 20. The table have 10 horses of which 3 have won their heats so far.

There was some very good news in the Hun communique today. The Russians are doing very well and there has been a raid on Berlin. Also the fighting in the desert has flared up again.

Jan 19th

Very sharp frost last night. Very cold in bed last night. Couldn't sleep.

Lots of rumours today. The Russians are doing excellently and there have been some very heavy RAF raids on Italy and Germany. The Yanks also wiped out a Jap convoy in the Pacific.

We had half a parcel each man. Stan and I shared a good one.

My horse crashed in the semi-final but Stan's won. He came third in the final with a consequent win of 30 cigs of which I got 12 as we were sharing no matter whose horse won.

Jan 20th

Very treacherous underfoot. It has been raining hard all morning on a super cooled surface, it froze and formed a glazed frost. There were many tip-ups, some blokes have to be carried away.

Went to school again and read an article on food and diets. I now have a list of food calorific values so lots of fun and revelation. It appears we get nothing which the experts deem essential for healthy life.

The Huns claim 25 aircraft on the second raid on Berlin. There is a very persistent rumour that Italy is out of the war or at least that there is some big political move on.

Jan 21st

A lovely morning and not at all cold.

No rumours today. Iraq has declared war on Germany as announced by DAZ. This is a very good sign.

In the evening, we were entertained by Jimmy Howes and his band. They are wizard and played a very good selection from 'Down Argentina Way'.

Today I got a letter from Mary dated Oct 25th and one from Molly at Gunstone dated Nov 11th.

The highlight of the mail was the first parcel due in the barrack to a chap who came in two weeks after us - a Canadian clothing parcel.

Jan 22nd

Quite warm again but very wet and slushy underfoot.

Had a wizard night's sleep after the boys were ridiculing the *Stalag (camp)* oddities as we shall do after we get home. Went to school today. Had a haircut in the afternoon. A sensation of the week.

There is a rumour that the Irish Free State has declared war on Germany.

Jan 23rd

Once again quite warm but wet.

The new guard came in today. Bloody fools.

No news today. A rumour that the Russians have recaptured Vilna near Krakow. The thaw seems to be starting in Russia. I hope this early thaw doesn't affect plans.

Jan 24th

Mild but wet. A howling gale during the night banging all the windows.

Yesterday I had my boil attended to again. Terrible pain. I felt quite ill after it.

Today is Sunday and a dreary day again. Saturday and Sunday are always dreary days.

It seems definite that Tripoli has been successfully evacuated as their radio is reputed to have put it.

Wrote a letter home, a card to Rob and a card to Harold and Veronica.

Turned icy cold and freezing at night time.

Finished a very good book called '*Green Hell*' a story about South America and it is strengthening my determination to do a spot of barnstorming when I've had about three months at home. I'm afraid I shall never settle down until I get older. In fact I'm hoping the war will still be on in the Far East so I can have another crack, preferably on bombers or twin fighters. Let's get at those yellow rats.

According to rumours there is a proper shambles in the desert.

Jan 25th

Very cold and freezing all day today. A biting cold wind.

Went to school again.

Today we had the best news we've ever had. The Hun papers admit the Russians have broken through on practically every front and have vastly superior forces. They also admit the fall of Tripoli and finally there is an exhortation to the

German people to have courage, give everything they've got, etc, etc. It's wizard news and everyone is very excited.

Jan 26th

Terribly bitter, wet and freezing all day with a biting wind but brilliant sunshine. I estimate about 40 degrees of frost.

Rumours today that 360,000 PoWs were taken at Stalingrad. A report in the DAZ emphasises the grave danger Germany is in.

Last night I caused considerable amusement by falling out of bed. It was one of my usual swallowing dreams. A ton of cheese this time. Probably the thought of bulk tomorrow and the good news we've had today. Not so funny for me though, but I didn't hurt myself.

There were three more parcel chits in the barrack all for colonials including one for Sandy on our table.

Jan 27th

A bit warmer but still very cold and snowing all day. And we thought the winter had gone, but if it helps the Russians its good enough for me.

Rumours of an extremely heavy Russian raid on the retreating Hun at Voronezh with a consequent national mourning in Germany.

A fellow in the convalescent compound committed suicide by hanging himself last night.

Went to agriculture again. He is now on stock. Very good too. In 1920 a Scotsman sold a bull to an Argentinian for 10,000 guineas. He died worth 300,000 pounds. Looks as though there's money in farming after all.

Rumours that the Russians have claimed 500,000 PoWs at Stalingrad. Also that the Hun have lost 200,000 at Stalingrad and 60,000 at Voronezh. Also that Churchill and Sikorsky are in America. There is also a rumour that there is unrest in Italy and the Balkans.

Had some mail today. A letter from Rene and a letter from Aunt Maggie. Rene tells me how many trips Stan has done, in plain words of course! Blacked out. Idiotic.

Jan 28th

It started to thaw last night again and is much warmer this morning. A good job too for we were kept for 2 hours on parade while they searched the whole camp for a bloke who had been sentenced to civvy jail and was hiding somewhere in the camp.

No rumours or news today or mail for that matter.

Had the dance band in the billet at night. Very good.

Jan 29th

A beautiful, warm, sunny day.

Lots of rumours about Tunisia cleared up. British and Yank troops land on Kush Peninsular and that Romania has packed in and offered Bessarabia to the Russians.

Bulk today after we had a medical inspection. No news today.

Outside in the afternoon getting the sun.

Churchill, Roosevelt, De Gaulle and Giraud have met in Casablanca.

Jan 30th

Frost last night but nice sunny morning.

Had a most interesting conversation last night with a Canadian from the Hudson Bay Company, working at a post in Baffin Land. I have, previous to then, decided to consider applying for a job there as soon as we get home.

There were rumours at night, two good one bad, that there was a 4hr landing at Dieppe; that there was an 8 point landing between Dieppe and _____ and that the Hun had recaptured Voronezh.

Churchill and Roosevelt have finished their meeting, so let's hope big things happen now. Goering and Goebbels are both making speeches today.

Jan 31st

Last day of month. Raining on parade but fairly warm.

Had a Xmas card from Rene yesterday. Played a wizard game of solo with Stan, Bill and Jock in the afternoon. I was lucky enough to win.

No news today. A rumour that there was a Lepoint landing in Denmark with the capture of an aerodrome.

Feb 1st

A bit cold but not too bad.

Stan and I on tea carrying. Went to school and in the agriculture class a chap mentioned he came from Staffs. I spoke to him after and he came from near the Bradford Arms and strangely enough he was at one time courting Phyllis Nan

Ivetsey. Small world. He asked me to send his love next time I write that way. Shall see him on Wednesday.

Apparently the hold up in the desert was because of the terrific amount of material and provision taken.

Jimmy Howes and his boys played a request programme last night. Good as ever. *'In the Mood'* as expected was the first on the list.

Mac got his clothing parcel chit today. There were 6 in the barrack one of them being for an Englishman taken at Dieppe. Looks good.

It was a wizard afternoon. Sunny and warm.

Feb 2nd

A beautiful morning. Warm and sunny after a night frost.

Had a quarter of an English parcel today. Warm and sunny again. Sat outside in the sun in the pm.

Reports today that there was a 2000 raid on Berlin. 300 by day and 1700 at night. Also that the Huns admit that Stalingrad has fallen – if they ever had it.

Had a shower in the afternoon and heard that Finland has capitulated.

Feb 3rd

Nice sunny day again.

Did some private study on poultry in the morning.

Some new *fliegels (flyers)* are supposed to have arrived tonight. Good show. The news is exceptionally good from the Russian front but there are reports of a gigantic Jap convoy approaching Australia with bags of panic there. There are rumours that Churchill went to Moscow from Turkey and said that the Russians lost 2,000,000 in Nov; that the desert war would not be over before the end of March and that the war would not be over before June 1944.

God help us if we have to spend another Xmas here.

Danny got a 1000 cig parcel from home. I was especially pleased at Danny getting it for he has been down since July last and has not had even a letter. He never moaned or said anything but I could see he felt it quite a lot when we got mail and he didn't.

Contrary to the egotistical selfish attitude of that --- Sandy, who never lets anyone see his parcel let alone the chocolate, Danny gave the smokers 10 each on the table and shared the rest with his cobber George.

Mac was good enough to give me some socks, pants and vest. He, unluckily for him, didn't get any chocolate but I'm sure if he had he would, as the rest of us, intend to share it with the boys.

Felt a bit browned off today for the first time for a long time.

Feb 4th

Cool this am.

Nothing of much importance happened today except that the Huns admit the final fall of Stalingrad.

The new boys came in today, mostly tanks. They were all pretty optimistic with estimates ranging from the middle of March to 18 months. They haven't much information. The Red X committee are trying to get us ½ parcel instead of ¼ tomorrow and are trying to get a general increase for the future.

Feb 5th

Quite bad again. Sleet this am and pretty cold with it.

It was almost a black Friday. At first the Huns refused to let us have our ½ parcel, but later climbed down and we had it. From then everything was wizard. Half a Canadians parcel. It was the first time we had milk chocolate since last September.

There are rumours that the 10th Army is in Turkey in civilian clothes.

Very little mail recently.

Feb 6th

As announced by ACK who makes a public speech of it every morning with *"Quiet Please; the date today is"*, etc, etc.

Cold and dreary.

Had a letter from Mary in the morning.

Heard about the conditions at Sagan today. They have never had less than ¾ parcel, have a wizard sports ground, wooden huts to accommodate 70 men, a very good library, school, cinema, billiards tables and Ping-Pong tables a swimming bath etc, etc. They are living a life of luxury and no one ever wishes to escape. They have bags of food and cigs and know that this place stinks.

Our own food situation is improving; we are promised ¾ parcel next week. Had a bang-on meal tonight. One of the best since I've been here. ½ tin of salmon and smashed spuds. Then a tin containing one broken biscuit soaked in Klim milk with 5 prunes and half my raisins with bags of sugar and butter. It was wizard. Then 3 slices of bread, marg and spread. A cup of coffee and thick milk finished it off. I felt wizard after it.

No news today.

Feb 7th

A very wet morning. Damp and cold most of the day.

Bags of BBC gen that the Hun have lost 5,000,000 casualties in Russia and that the Russians are driving and surrounding the Hun practically everywhere.

Feb 8th

Cold this am.

Wrote a letter to Mary yesterday. School this morning.

Rumours that the Italian cabinet has resigned with unrest there. Also that Churchill gives the Turks 8 days to decide whether to join in or not.

A message has come through from Geneva allowing us to have 1 parcel per week. We are promised ½ tomorrow, ½ on Thursday and ¼ on Sat to make up for last week. We shall have to see what these damn Huns have to say first.

Feb 9th

Very cold and freezing all day but a beautiful and sunny day.

Had ½ a parcel today.

Not much news today. Was weighed this am. I am 10st 12lb in my clothes ie; I have lost about ½ a stone since I came here. Not bad really. Bill has lost 20lbs.

Feb 10th

Cold and windy.

School this am.

Reports that Rostov has fallen.

Rumours that the shots we heard the other night were aimed at escaping Russian prisoners when 7 were killed or wounded and 4 escaped. Also that the Russians at their camp bashed a guard so 14 were picked out at random and shot. The Huns are capable of doing that and wouldn't think twice. The Russians still push on but where is our effort? That is the question that everyone is asking.

There are very strong rumours that we shall be moving from here very soon. I hope that isn't so because of our attempt in March and April. The Yanks are moving out to a special Yank camp. The ground staff here are also moving out on working parties.

Feel rather ill this evening. So do Nobby, George and many others. I think I have a cold in my stomach.

Feb 11th

A fine mild morning. Had 2 letters and a Xmas card yesterday. The card from Aunt Kate, the letter from Turpin and an extremely nice letter from Mr Sheen.

The rumours are very prevalent that the Italian royal family are in England; that there were 240,000 Hun/PoWs at Rostov and that the Russians are advancing on Kiev.

Our barrack at night is like a sanatorium with all the bronchitis cases.

Feb 12th

A cool but nice morning.

Woof day today so no school. Stan and I collected our parcels at 2.30. ¾ per man, less the bully beef. Naturally had a really good feed. It never rains but what it pours. I got the only parcel chit in the barrack tonight. A cig parcel.

Feb 13th

Very windy.

Collected my cig parcel – 500 sent by Mum. Jolly good show. Gave the boys some.

There are supposed to be some more *Fliegen* coming in tomorrow. Rumours today that Italy packed up at 11am yesterday.

Good feeding today. A howling wind and storm all day.

Feb 14th

A snowstorm during the night. Cold this morning.

On chain this am. Had a glorious woof all day.

Rumours that Turkey has been in the war one week.

The guard in here today came in this morning and straight away shook hands with all the Poles. He had been a PoW in a Polish camp for 2 years. He stressed yet again the fact that all the sabotage groups are waiting for the 2nd Front.

Feb 15th

Cold wind again.

I have a very bad cold in my head. It is throbbing like hell. Did not go to school on account of my cold.

Played bridge at night. 95 new fellows arrived today. No one I know. Some reckon the war will be over in 3 months and others 18.

Feb 16th

Warmer.

Stan got a 200 cig parcel today. I got another chit. I am getting very worried about my eyes. Maybe my cold is affecting them a little. I have a very bad headache.

The Huns admit today the fall of Rostov and Voroshilovgrad.

Had half a parcel today. Bought a packet of raisins for 30 and a bar of choc for 60 cigs. The price of choc in some places has gone up to 120 cigs.

Rumours that there is a 10-day armistice and Cripps is in Berlin.

Feb 17th

Quite mild.

Couldn't get to sleep last night for headache, chronic toothache and the infernal noise.

Rumours that Krakow has fallen.

Got 200 cigs from Aunt Kate. Went to school but couldn't get interested because of my cold.

There are very persistent rumours that Cripps, Eden and Halifax are in Berlin with a Hun delegation.

Feb 18th

Very fine and sunny but cold.

Rumours that there are to be no papers or wireless in Germany for 3 days. Also that the Russians have got Sebastopol, Odessa and have crossed the Dneiper in 3 places.

Starting to get organised. Went to a show *'Topsy Turvy'* tonight. Excellent. A laugh from beginning to end.

Feb 19th

Fine and sunny but very cold on account of the howling wind.

We had our half parcel today.

Rumours that the Hun have evacuated Norway and that the line in Russia extends from Riga to Kiev to Odessa. There are also rumours that they are withdrawing working parties from Poland.

Mac got his clothing parcel from NZ today and Sandy got his the day before.

Feb 20th

Cold and windy again.

I can't think what's happened to my mail. I haven't heard from home since November 9th. I suppose it will roll along some day.

This afternoon we were allowed to be on our beds from 12-4pm.

Rumours that the war in the desert is cleared up after the rumour of the Yanks withdrawing and Montgomery following up the Huns, who were driven out into the desert, and wiping them out.

Feb 21st

Windy again but fine and sunny all day.

Strong rumours that there was a 3-point landing in Norway when 1570 of the first landing was wiped out but the 2nd landing was well established. Also that we lost *HMS Rodney*, 2 cruisers and 4 destroyers. Also that the Hun are appealing to the British to join them and stay the Bolshevists.

Feb 22nd

A lovely morning.

We are unchained today as it is 17A's day off. We now have a day off instead of the fortnightly half day.

I wrote a letter home yesterday.

Sun bathing in the afternoon. It is amazingly fine weather, very warm for February with beautiful nights and clear sunny skies with absolutely no cloud at all.

The Hun communique tonight was a little disappointing from our point of view.

Played an amusing game of pontoon at night with Lawley & co.

Feb 23rd

A beautiful day again.

Sunbathing all day. Bulk today. No news at all. Ate 7 ladles of soup during the day.

Joseph Goebbels apparently made a very defeatist speech exhorting the German people to greater effort.

Feb 24ᵗʰ

Lovely morning again.

Did my usual morning preparation exercise. Turned very foggy at about 9 o'clock and remained damp and foggy all day.

Conflicting rumours all day that Hitler is dead; Karkov retaken by Huns; Russians 20 miles beyond Kiev; Odessa in Russian hands etc, etc.

Played a wizard game of bridge in the evening with Bill against Ernie and John Matthews. At close of play we are 3100 points in the lead in a 3-rubber game for 5 cigs each.

A very promising communique this evening.

Feb 25ᵗʰ

A damp foggy day again.

Stan got his clothing parcel today, 2lbs choc. Finished off our bridge in the morning winning by about 3000 points.

A good communique tonight. Was weighed again today. 73 kilos so I have gained 6 kg since the last time I was weighed.

Played bridge again at night.

Feb 26ᵗʰ

Nice morning.

Danny got 3 cig parcels again. The Canadians are getting a comforts parcel, 3 food parcels and a chocolate parcel. The NZs are getting food parcel. Got 2 parcel chits in the evening; one for books and one for cigs.

Lovely afternoon. Played bridge outside and played again in the evening. I am gradually learning.

Quite a good communique again.

Feb 27th

Cold this am.

I am disgusted with the escape committee. I have been to them every day this week for maps to copy and each time they have put me off with excuses and snags, snags, snags.

Rumours that 15 Hun division are surrounded; that the Russians are advancing all down the line and that Eden promises a special front in March.

Got my book parcel today. One detective yarn. I don't know who it's from.

Played bridge in the evening.

Feb 28th

A fairly mild morning.

Collected my third fag parcel today. 200 from Mary. Danny also got one.

Quite a good communique.

Mar 1st

Should have said collected my parcel today. Yesterday I wrote a card to Rene and a card to Aunt Kate.

Mar 2nd

Today I collected my clothing parcel. A wizard one. The

pullover is grand and Mum has had the good sense to send decent summer underclothes, two wizard shirts etc, etc. It was great. About 2lbs of chocolate.

Played bridge in the afternoon and housey-housey at night.

Mar 3rd

The very cold howling March winds persist with snow today.

Pat got his clothing parcel today.

The Huns ordered that the Aussies and NZ's should be unchained but they refused, consequently there is a panic as the Huns class this as mutiny and threaten to put them all in a compound by themselves. All the compound is to be chained up again tomorrow.

There has apparently been another very heavy Berlin raid. Had a very good concert in the barrack in the evening. Jacobs was his usual good self.

Mar 4th

Lots of snow during the night.

Got the second parcel today. Again pretty _____ Got a chit for another cig parcel.

It is rumoured that the Aussies have got to move into another compound where they will remain unchained. It also appears that the Huns asked some blokes if they would like to fly in the Luftwaffe against the Russians.

The Hun announced the fall of **Rzcheve**.

Mar 5th

Mild this am.

Collected my 4th cig parcel sent by Aunt Maggie. 200.

Gen that Churchill said the 2nd Front will be opened before Nov; that the Huns are surrounded at Kiev; that Stalino and Voronezh have fallen.

The Aussies, NZ's & 24 --- numbers are all supposed to be moving out on Monday and there are supposed to be 90 new *fliegen* coming in.

Mar 6th

Wet am. A wet miserable day.

Played bridge most of the day.

The new boys arrived in camp. 97 of them including about 50 Yanks. Their estimates are about 6-12 months.

Mar 7th

Not bad today.

Wrote a letter home thanking them for my clothing parcel. Not a very good Red X issue next week.

There seem to be vague rumours of a landing of some sort in France.

Played bridge at night again.

Mar 8th

A lovely morning after a frosty night.

Did many circuits around the compound with Bill. My

efforts at getting maps are not meeting with much success but I'll get them eventually.

This morning all the Aussies, NZ's & 24 --- numbers moved and to 7-10 compound.

Having very bad night's sleep. Lately always dreaming I'm at home etc.

I have <u>never, never</u>, in all my life, been as browned off as I am today. I feel as though I could burst into tears any time. It's terrible this awful boredom.

Hick and Pat both had to move into another barrack to make room for 47 French Canadians who came into the billet.

It seems to be gen that Kiev fell about a fortnight ago.

Played bridge at night.

Mar 9th

A fine sunny morning but cold owing to the strong wind.

George moved out this morning. Had a chat with the new boys some of whom say Kiev has fallen. It's a treat to talk to them since they are all optimistic and cheerful.

Mar 10th

Bill and Jock moved out today.

A lovely warm day again.

Was deloused in the afternoon. Bridge in the evening.

Stan reckons we are advancing on Kiev and Smolensk. There are reports that the boys have made the biggest raid of the war on Munich. The Huns are supposed have made a special broadcast about it and said the streets were running with blood.

Collected 2 more cig parcels today. One from home and one from Aunt Margaret and Uncle Harry. I now have 1000 in my possession. Bridge again at night.

Mar 11th

Had a good nights' sleep with no fleas. A good walk round the compound on this fine sunny morning. Saved my marg and biscuits from the bulk, stopping the holes up with chewing gum.

The Hun papers are decrying the Munich raid as barbarous etc saying it has shocked Europe etc, etc. There has also been a big raid on Nuremberg.

Had another pleasant chat with one of the new boys. They are apparently using Spit 20s on ops and doing bags of rhubarbs. Damn my luck.

Played bridge at night and got 3 letters one from Mum, Mary and Aunt Alice. They have been I think to Sagan.

Bill and I have decided to make for Turkey.

There are rumours that the British Navy is shelling Odessa and that Sebastopol has fallen to the Russians.

Mar 12th

A lovely day again. Sunbathing as for the past 3 days.

Yesterday an event occurred not, I hope, to be repeated. It was in the shape of meat in the camp – in the form of a rat.

Rumours that the Hun have recaptured Krakow.

We had a concert from Jimmy Howes and his boys. They played a number of very good new tunes.

Danny went down to 7-10 compound and the Aussies think they are going to another Aussie camp.

1943

Mar 13th

A miserable damp day after the beautiful weather we've been having.

I had to hand in my souvenir chains this am to prevent the barrack going on strafe *(punishment)*.

Heard yesterday that F/Sgt James caused a great stir at Sagan especially in the debating society which was despised previous to his entry but afterwards was packed out.

Rumours that the new boys are in the camp. No news at all. We are now expecting the 2nd Front somewhere around June.

Mar 14th

Sunny but cold.

Wrote a card home and a card to Mary. Played a very entertaining game of bridge in the afternoon.

Rumours today that the Huns have evacuated the Channel Isles and that Tunisia is cleared up.

Mar 15th

Cold again but sunny.

Bridge morning and afternoon.

72 new boys arrived. Quite a good communique was put up last night, and much better one today.

The Huns are still screaming about the murderers. The new boys are very optimistic.

Stan – the ace racketeer – had a real egg for supper. Quite a treat to even see one.

Mar 16th

A lovely sunny morning again.

Took a walk down to the new boys and met one of the rare fighter pilots from England. A whirlwind boy from Manston who altho' he has no gen of my particular squadron, was very interesting. He, like all the others, is very optimistic and says England is full of the joys of life. I enjoy talking to the new boys. They seed new rays of hope through a disconsolate spirit.

Parcels today. Spent the whole afternoon washing my clothes.

Received a letter from Mum dated Jan 22nd and a Xmas card from Aunt Maggie. They seemed at home a little upset by my postcard apparently sent in Nov when I told them of the chaining up etc. I hope they don't think this place is getting me down – or anyone for that matter. Far from it.

Got chits for a book and a cig parcel in the evening.

A most beautiful warm day and glorious evening just like summer at home. The fighters flying around stirred up old Gravesend memories and made me yearn for squadron life again.

Mar 17th

A sunny day again but cool air.

Bill and I have almost decided to go on a working party since the advantages of that, distance, ease of escape, food etc, far outweigh an attempt through the wire.

Bridge this morning and a bath in the afternoon or should I say a swill from above.

Received a cig parcel from I don't know who. I wish I did. They are Sunripe - pretty Tennerish. I also had a couple of good books very well bound. One by John Buchan and the other by Hugh Walpole, again I don't know who from.

No news or rumours.

Mar 18th

Freezing today.

Joe apparently pinched my coat yesterday. Was cold in bed at night.

It appears that some of the boys saw 4 RAF lads strung up on lampposts at Munich.

Half a parcel today.

There are very strong rumours that the 2nd Front is on, eg., parachutists landed in S. France and in Holland. This is reputed to originate from a *Posten (guard)*.

Heard rather an amusing tale if somewhat gruesome of the chap who was stopped from cutting his throat with ragged cut throat razor. He is of course *Stalag* happy, as also is the chap who is always painting water colours of Christ on the Cross.

Also of the chap who proudly showed another fellow a photo of a flame of his. It was the other's wife! He chased the other chap around the compound with a razor.

Mar 19th

Cold again.

Got my coat back today. The repeat 2nd Front seems just another hoax.

Bridge in the morning. Got another cig parcel chit at night. The fighting in the desert seems to have flared up.

Mar 20th

Sunny but a cold wind.

Got 200 cigs my third parcel from home. Received two letters one from Molly Johnson and one from Aunt Kate. Watched a good game football in the afternoon.

No gen today.

Mar 21st

Sunny again.

Had a good chat with the escape committee who would like to be helpful but have practically no material to work on.

Beat Alex and Cliff at bridge this morning for the first time.

Wrote home today warning them not to expect too much mail.

Mar 22nd

Cold today.

I also have quite a bad cold.

Bridge in the morning. No mistakes. Stan and I are getting much better.

There seems to be absolutely no news at all.

Mar 23rd

Not much doing today. Sunny but cold.

I had a terrible throat and the smoke in the barrack at night makes it worse.

Bridge this am. Got another cig chit this evening.

It seems that the Aug attack in the desert is on.

Mar 24th

Got 200 cigs from Mrs Fowler today. Also got 4 letters, two from home and two from Mary.

Heard some amazingly revealing stories about certain British bastards on the camp, and about the lengths some chaps go to get off working parties; nails, silver paper, boiling water, _____ in cuts, etc, etc.

Mar 25th

Sunny but cold again.

Bridge in the morning. Another cig parcel chit today.

Rumours that the Russians have taken Smolensk and that we are getting a bit of a kicking in the desert again!

Mar 26th

Mild but not so sunny.

Bridge again in the morning and afternoon. We play 10 cigs for the best of 5 rubbers and 2 cigs a hundred points. Stan and I have so far paid out about 500 cigs each.

60 new boys came in today. No gen at all.

Got 2 letters one from Rene and one from Mum and a Xmas card from the W'ton (*Wolverhampton*) PoW families club.

Mar 27th

A nice mild spring morning. There has been a slight smattering of rain which has freshened the air.

Wizard bridge today.

Watched the final in the knock-out competition of soccer today. A very good game. The high standard of football played is amazing.

There are lot of soldiers coming into the camp tonight.

Mar 28th

Nice and Springy again.

Bridge in the morning and watched rugger in the afternoon.

The soldiers are from Stalag 7a near Munich. They were in a luxury camp where they could barter food (and lots of it) from the civvies and often got into Munich. The could get 14 eggs for 2oz tea, 8 eggs for a bar of chocolate, a cake for 2 cakes of soap etc. The raid they say was terrific.

Mar 29th

Raining practically all day.

No news at all except at night a wild rumour that the 9th, 10th, 11th armies and the Turks had marched into Bulgaria.

Mar 30th

A lovely day.

Half a parcel. Got 4 letters. Mum, Dad, Rene and A. Kate.

Mar 31st

Last night Stan, Mac and I moved into 17B. I needn't have gone but thought it best to keep with Stan.

Lots of news about the prohibited area in England etc., and a supposed battle off Kiel canal.

3 wizard books.

April 1st

Windy cold and wet.

There seems to be lots of shootings going on on the working party.

Saw a wizard RAF concert. Jacobson again excellent and I believe he wrote and produced the whole show.

Another WAFF parcel.

April 2nd

Cold again.

Got a 200 cig parcel from the W'ton PoW families club.
Raining a lot.
Bridge in the am. Stan got his 2nd clothing parcel today.

April 3rd

Cold and windy and wet.

Stayed in and played bridge most of the day.
The army in the desert seem to be doing ok.

April 4th

Wrote a letter to Mary. Bridge in the morning. Watched soccer in the afternoon. Got another cig parcel chit.

Just finished a very good book. *'The General'* by C S Forester. A skit on the army in general.

April 5th

Nice day but a bit windy.

Lovely evening. Got a 200 cig parcel from home and collected 3 chits at night.

April 6th

A lovely day.

Swapped 2oz tea for a tin of jam.

Got 200 cigs from home, 200 from Aunt Doll and Bill and 200 from Aunt Maggie.

Raining most of the afternoon so played bridge.

No news today. Heard that Frank is doing well in the desert and has shot 2 down.

April 7th

Very cold today. Snowing in the afternoon.

Got two wizard photos from home of Molly's wedding. Rene looks marvellous.

I also got a letter from Aunt Maggie dated March 25th which means it has come in the amazing time of 13 days. She tells me Ustie has finally got married.

Officers made a search in the barrack last night after lights out.

I had a bad night's sleep falling out of bed twice due to the bed boards giving way.

Got my 19th parcel chit.

Rene.

April 8th

Cold, nasty day with sleet.

200 cigs from W'ton PoWs families club. 2 more chits in the evening. Bridge in the morning.

There seems to have been a flare up in the desert again and lots of RAF raids. I heard today that one of the chaps who landed with the Canadians at Dieppe was a Hun and is now interrogating people down in the lager. No wonder they knew.

Had a very interesting talk with Irish last night who spent 16 years at sea and is certainly a man of the world.

April 9th

Very cold today.

Bridge in the morning.

A good mail day for me. 200 cigs from Mrs Beech and 200 from Mrs Johnson in Scotland. I also got two letters from Mum. They were old ones but I think they complete my mail up to Dec 31st.

Apparently there is bags of chocolate in my next parcel.

April 10th

Nasty day again.

Stan plays increasingly ridiculous bridge. Although I'm not much good, he's rotten. I played with Bill in the morning and we beat Alex and Cliff by 3000 points in 3 rubbers, which looks like proof.

Extremely good news in communique tonight. Also rumours that Tunis is cleared up.

April 11th

Rotten day again.

I have another cold.

Bridge in the am.

Wrote a card to Rene and a card to Aunt Maggie in the afternoon.

No news today.

April 12th

Not a bad day although a little dull.

A bit better bridge in the morning. Half a parcel today.

News this afternoon that the German radio announced the fall of Tunisia with cessation of fighting there and Rommel in Germany. If this is true it is indeed a notable victory and now we may see further successes elsewhere.

In passing I think a tribute to a very brave and able man is not out of place although he is one of the enemy. I salute FM ROMMEL.

April 13th

Started our bridge league by beating Cliff and Alex.

A beautiful day sunbathing in the afternoon.

The gen about Tunisia seems to have been duff.

April 14th

A glorious day with lots of sunbathing.

Bridge in the morning and evening.

Received a letter from Hazel Fowler.

April 15th

Glorious day again and very hot.

Shower in the afternoon. Half a parcel again.

I am getting on fine with the map but have to do it between 12 and 2 on my bed.

April 16th

Not quite so nice today since the sky has been overcast.

Bridge again.

April 17th

Windy but quite warm.

Watched a good game of soccer in the afternoon. Bridge morning and evening.

No gen.

April 18th

Quite warm again.

Still fighting in Tunisia; we are claiming 100,000 tons of shipping in the med; and the Huns claim 50 a/c during a raid on Mannheim.

April 19th

Lovely day again. Half a parcel. Got 4 letters and a Xmas card today. All Jan stuff.

Stan had done 22 trips to the end of Jan. Damn good show.

April 20th

Wet and dull today.

Just as Bill and I were going to fire up for swap-overs, the compound was locked and a check parade was ordered. We were told that we were again a *strafe* compound for at least 14 days unless the existing swap-overs gave themselves up!! The punishment is for too much swapping over. Again no school, cinema, soccer etc, etc.

Wrote a letter home.

April 21st

A lovely morning.

We had the check parade this afternoon and 75 names were taken as swap-overs. Mine amongst about 50 other real RAF chaps was taken. Joke of jokes! Again we were told the compound would be opened if the swap-overs gave themselves up.

April 22nd

A glorious day.

Half a parcel again. I got 200 cigs from home.

Our interrogation did not take place.

Sunbathing, bridge most of the day.

April 23rd

Sunbathing and very hot sun.

Went through the wire this morning to see Danny. Got stuck going through. Bags of fun. Through again in the evening with Bill. No fire up for swap-over. I have a chap who is a little undecided at the moment but I think he will do it when he gets a pal. Watched the football and then back.

Stan and I played some very good bridge today.

It is thought that the _____ have been caught at last. They were given 3 degrees and I believe a confession was extracted.

April 24th

Glorious day again. Bags of sunbathing.

Went through the wire with Stan in the evening.

April 25th

Lovely day again.

Went through the wire to watch the rugger matches. Almost got caught in a purge. The Lager officer says that anyone caught going through will be shot.

April 26th

Nice day till later in the evening when we had a terrific thunderstorm with bags of lightening.

Went through the wire to see the art exhibition and football match. The art exhibition was excellent. In fact one of them is a picture called *"Dieppe"* sold for 1,250 marks, others sold also.

April 27th

Nasty wet day.

Went over the top of the wire today.

April 28th

Rumours of a 2nd Front of Russians in Gibraltar.

Nothing interesting happening.

April 29th

Nasty day again.

Received 2 letters from home in which they told me Stan has finished his tour and collected a commission whilst Bob has returned from America and collected one also. Their amazing luck, although giving me quiet pleasure, gives me pangs of disappointment to think that I volunteered of my own will whereas they joined because they had to.

Still I suppose that is fate but it makes me all the more determined to escape and get back home.

April 30th

Half a parcel again. Not a very good day.

Played quite a lot of bridge.

Went over the wire in the evening to see the soccer match between the **Hunnich** boys and the rest of the camp. Wizard game.

April 31st

Last day of April. Weather not too good.

Had a round or two with _____ with the gloves. Terribly unfit.

Went out to fix up swap-overs but lots of snags. We now have two agents helping us so we should have a bit more luck.

No gen lately. Watched the French Dandelions in the evening playing some amusing games.

May 1st

Nice day again.

Got a 200 cig parcel from Stan yesterday. Had my few rounds with the gloves in the evening.

No news.

Just one year ago today I joined the squadron. Happy day.

May 2nd

Lovely day.

Through the wire in the evening to try and fix up with swap-overs. No luck again.

The Russians seem to have started their summer offensive.

May 3rd

Lovely morning. Sunbathing and bridge.

Half a parcel today.

May 4th

The gates were opened again today.

Weather not quite so good.

Have at last found some chaps who are willing to swap-over. Now we can get weaving.

May 5th

Lovely day again. Sunbathing and bridge.

May 6th

Lovely day.

May 7th

Not quite so nice.

No news at all lately. Half parcel.

May 8th

Lovely day.

Heard yesterday that Max Wytie the Aussie was shot escaping. Actually it was sheer murder.

May 9th

Lovely day. Wrote a letter home.

News that Tunisia is finished.

May 10th

Lovely day. Bags of sunbathing and tenniquoits.

May 11th

Lovely again.

Watched a wizard 11-a-side soccer match between 7A and 8B. 8B won 11-7 in a game which did not reflect the score.

Very hot today.

May 12th

Received 7 letters today. Bags of new about Ustie's wedding etc.

Tunisia seems to have definitely finished and is heralded as one of the greatest military victories this year.

May 13th

This weather is marvellous and I am getting very sunburned.

Got my 2nd clothing parcel today. A wizard blanket, underwear and bags of chocolate. Marvellous.

Dan has left the camp after advising (I am a member of the escape committee) Bill and I not to escape.... We are consequently leaving it till June to see if the 2nd Front starts. If not........

May 14th

Cig parcel from Aunt K.

Today there were reports that 18 chaps escaped from a wood party amongst them 4 RAF... Consequently we had an additional roll-call after the 5pm parade and the gates on the whole camp were closed.

2 chaps out of our barrack did escape but the rest were out unofficially on the party and could not get back in time for parade.

May 15th

Gates locked indefinitely but do we give a damn?

Bags of bridge, sunbathing etc. Eric, Ron and I seem to have a natural affinity towards each other. Maybe it's in our ability to see the lighter side of life.

May 16th

Today, as we had been warned about 5 days ago, the Gestapo search came off. None of us buried our stuff outside in the gardens. We were kept out in the parade ground from 7 till 12 when the barracks were thoroughly ransacked by the Gestapo while we were personally searched by some guards. I sneaked across from the unsearched to the searched crowd so escaped.

The Gestapo looked just what I expected. Typical Gestapo. Sneaky, slimy, cruel and ruthless. The rats!

May 17th

The war in Africa is supposed to have been the greatest military victory as far as Booty is concerned.

Lovely day again.

Half a NZ parcel today. Very good for spread.

We are still locked in the compound.

May 18th

Glorious day again. No news.

May 19th

Lovely day.

A cig parcel from Mum and one from the PoW club. Making 31 parcels in all.

Had an inoculation for Typhus.

May 20th

Lovely day. No news. The gates were opened.

May 21st

The weather still continues.

News of a raid on Dortmund bursting the dam there, with

great loss of life. Also that Churchill has promised 2nd Front and that Russia is highly delighted over the Africa campaign. Bad news from the Far East.

May 22nd

Glorious day. The boys are looking like natives. I myself am very sunburned.

Got a letter from Mum telling me Frank is missing and that Phyl Crewe has had a baby. Rather startling news.

May 23rd

Lovely day.

The squadron which took part at Dortmund is supposed to have been OC Stan's old squadron. 17 a/c lost.

May 24th

Lovely day although not quite so sunny.

Half an English parcel. Wrote a letter to Mary yesterday.

May 25th

Raining most of the day.

Got 6 more wizard photos including a glorious one of Rene and Rosa and Stan and Rover. I wonder if he will remember me when I get back. Also 2 more letters.

May 26th

Raining in the morning.

There are supposed to be 200,000 casualties at Kassel.

Dad and Rover

May 27th

Not too good again. Half a NZ parcel.

May 28th

Not too bad.

May 29th

No news lately. The weather seems to be getting more wintery. Cold and wet.

May 30th

Cold wind.

Watched a very good soccer game. Wales and Scotland.
Wrote a card to Molly J and one to Jayne.

May 31st

A lovely day again.

Played football in the am for 17B. We drew 1-1. I missed about 3 chances. Half a parcel.

According to rumour the Turks are almost in the war.

NO FURTHER ENTRIES FOR 1943

1944

Sat Jan 1st

Saw the New Year in, in the traditional way.

Received a letter from Pete's father giving me Pete's address and PoW no.

Balmy, Slim & Paul going strong in Oct. Saw Loft in '*Riviera*' and afterwards saw Barney and Ken. Nice bunks.

Razor slashes in full swing. The camp authorities are trying to clear up with menace. Good frat.

Jan 2nd

Raining all day with gale.

Saw Loft again. A little bridge with Mat.

100 new blokes (mostly sick and wounded) arrived from *Stalag*. Some had gangrene after fighting knee-deep in mud. An RAF bloke down 3 days.

In bed all morning.

Negro minstrel band in barrack in evening. Quite good. Lights out, record concert.

Jan 3rd

A cold wind but no frost.

The Germans are making huge claims over the battle in the Bay of Biscay. I think this battle means big things. The rumours of the landing at Brest still persist.

Bridge in the evening with Alex.

Jan 4th

Snowing most of the day. In bed all morning.

In evening saw *'Treasure Ho'* a very good panto with the leading lady the most realistic I've ever seen. Scenery and costumes, excellent.

Received 4 letters, Mum 2, Aunt K & Marjorie.

Tragic news that little Jimmy from Parkside was killed by a milk lorry.

Jan 5th

Freezing all day.

The Germans are trying to tighten up on discipline by inaugurating a *strafe* barrack for late on parade; in bed at wrong time offences etc. I'll probably spend most of the time till the end of the war there.

Mac got 2 years at his court martial for 'attempted sabotage of the German National defence'.

Bridge in the evening. Air raid warning at night. Record concert.

Jan 6th

Very cold and freezing.

Got last night's BBC explaining the naval battle. Also Franco withdrawing the Spanish Blue Division.

Wrote a note to be delivered to Pete. Hope it gets through.

Received some smashing photos from Rene. She gets lovelier every time.

Bridge in the morning with Ron.

Lots of parcels supposed to be in. Maybe I'll get one.

Jan 7th

Very cold all day. In the evening a violent blizzard blew up blowing pots and pans helter-skelter.

In the evening we had a concert by the *Desert Rats*. It was very good, as the last one but as always, the jokes were crude.

Can't make up my mind whether to go out and make a break or not.

Jan 8th

Cold again but a nice sunny day.

An extra roll call at 13.00hrs developed into a pitched snow battle between the RAF and Army compounds.

Bridge in the evening with Ron in the ladder. We were drawn 5th and managed to hold it.

Jan 9th

Mild today, snow melting.

Saw Loft again. Looking very fit. Wrote a letter to Mary.

Roy made another prize crack about racing horses. The dead loss effect.

Had an amazing quiz competition in the evening. Played lots of crib and got through first two rounds in the competition.

Another gramophone recital. Wonderful '*Rhapsody in Blue*'.

Jan 10th

Quite mild again but wet.

Irish recently had a do with Sherriff over Jack Levine. Mentioned the razor slashing.

Had an interesting talk with Freddie Mills who fought Dave McClea for the Southern Area welter championship.

Finished off the bridge – 6640 win.

Received letters from Mary and Marjorie. Photo home.

Cliff and I slid two rungs down the crib ladder.

Jan 11th

Gale and snow during night.

Some aircraft over. Very good news last night. Rumours that Finland is suing for peace & Hun paratroopers land in Spain.

Lost to Johnny Buit in the singles crib competition. Won another bridge match with Ron by 2520.

We hear that Count Ciano has been sentenced to death.

Lots of parcels today but as yet I'm unlucky. Carrying today.

Jan 12th

Quite mild again today. We are getting a much milder winter than last year. Shower today for the first time for a month.

Rumours that the 2nd Front has started again. Heard a mediocre lecture on nudist colonies.

Another gram recital. Did some washing.

Thurs Jan 13th

Lovey day again.

Got 2 cig parcels – 400 in the morning. Got another chit at night.

Rumours of a big air attack on Deutschland losing 123. The commandant is supposed to have said we must be prepared to evacuate within 28 days. The Ruskies are pushing well into Poland.

Bridge again today.

Fri Jan 14th

Got 200 fags again today. The air battle seems to have been pretty gigantic. The biggest of the war claim the Jerries. May be able to get a radio for 3000 fags. Cheap at the price if we can raise them.

Lost in the bridge by 1480 points.

Saw an excellent map of Poland including **Sainy**. Stan is going to make a copy.

Wet today.

Jan 15th

Mild but very muddy underfoot.

An amusing incident happened this am. A fellow tried to walk across the parade ground in clogs. He was bogged on numerous occasions.

The Ruskies ever advance. We are supposed to be ready to evacuate at 24hrs notice.

Ron and I last night bid and got our 14th Grand Slam. Yeach!!

Cliff and I retained our position in the crib ladder by beating Stan and Eric. I'd rather beat those two than reach the top of the ladder.

Jan 16th

Wrote a card home, and one to Mr Dunnford. Also wrote one to Mrs Schofield which I am posting later in the week.

Lost to Winny and Ron in bridge by 700 pts.

Mon Jan 17th

Today I was an idiot. Alex arranged a soccer match with the DEL's v 170. I played (??) RH Harvey (Gateshead) Stevens, Stevens (both Leeds U) and Roberts (Chesterfield) were all in the forward line. A very nice game, very fast in spite of heavy ground. Cliff passed out after 20 mins and had to have attention from the MO. I thought I was going to be as sick as a dog.

Lost by 1940 to Thommy at bridge.

Jan 18th

Dull and a little colder.

In the evening we had a team bridge match against 16A. 4 pairs from each barrack. Ron and I won by 1780 points over 4 ½ rubbers. All 4 pairs from 17B won their matches.

I got a book parcel today. *'The Gentleman of the Party'* and *'The Flaming Stallion'*.

Jan 19th

Snowing in the am and drizzle in the afternoon.

A search for an officer this morning so we had to stay on parade about 2 hrs.

Won at bridge by 2170 pts.

A very interesting talk by a CSM previously in the Merchant NAVY NZ on "a shipwreck", the Pacific Islands and "a Government brothel". Very amusing indeed.

Jan 20th

Quite a nice day again.

Ron and I again lost to Thommy and Pat by 1560 pts. They just seem to get the cards at the right time.

Feeling a little cheesed. I worry too much about my eyes fearing I shall not be able to fly again. Such an event would ruin my whole life.

Jan 21st

Very mild again today.

There is a strange lack of news lately. Let's hope it is the calm before the storm.

Jan 22nd

Very mild again.

Heard some BBC for the 21st. ____

Had a very amusing concert in the evening. In a short

sketch Pete Martine was laughing so much he couldn't say his piece. Real Tommy at Dover Patrol.

Sun Jan 23rd

Wrote a letter home. Very mild.

Got some BBC for the 20th last night.

In the evening had a very amusing cut throat quiz competition Pilots v Gunners. It was a draw at the end of the 10 rounds but one more round gave a win of 3 points to the Gunners. Oh calamity!

Got BBC for the 22nd. Last night's 6 o'clock in fact!!!!

Jan 24th

Lovely day again.

Played bridge for 1713 (3 teams) against the Czechs. Ron and I won by 3980. Just starting the 8th rubber after 2 ½ hrs. Cliff and Alex lost by 2500. Thommy and Bert won by 750. So we won.

The Saree brothers are out for revenge.

Jan 25th

A glorious morning.

The excitement of the morning is that the Canadians, 400 in number, don't know where they are going. Much mystery is attached to it and they are a little worried. The Huns are taking extraordinary precautions.

Jan 26th

The mystery of the moment is the disappearance of the Canadian who went out of his bk at 9.00 pm in pyjamas to take a piss and never returned. The Huns and British are looking for him. He had stomach troubles. The Canadians were told by the *Kommandant* that they are going to a model camp.

Played bridge for the barrack against the Police. All four won. Ron and I by 70!!

Thurs Jan 27th

A lovely day again.

A record concert last night. The best of the lot was Bing Crosby singing '*Song of the Islands*'. Wizard.

Got my 5th clothing parcel yesterday. Got another fag parcel. 200 GF from Mrs F Ross Taylor, pro Harrods. Amongst 'the Soceeitea' at last.

Had a very amusing talk from an ex-Tramp etc. Very amusing.

Jan 28th

A nice day.

Heard some recent BBC gen. Everything seems to be leading up to the 2nd Front. How we long for that great day.

Ron and I lost by 960 to Winny and Ron. We had no cards at all.

It appears the Indians are leaving. Maybe going home with the Repats next month.

Sat Jan 29th

This morning we had a surprise, in fact, very big surprise, camp check parade. A large number of front-line troops from outside were also brought in. They were Jager and Panzer troops who had all seen service in Russia and are going back next week. On being asked *"Wenn ist der Krieg fartig?"* he replied in perfect English *"No, the war is not over."*

Two lads, one 20 the other 21, each had two children, both were unmarried and both had been 3 years on the Russian front!! They were very friendly, very much like us and thought the war a racket, I wonder!!!

Some were very young lads.

Jan 30th

A bit wet.

Heard some BBC for last night. The AM admit the loss of 100 a/c last night. There'll be a chance for us yet.

The Navigators easily beat the Engineers in the quiz this evening.

A good record concert again.

Mon Jan 31st

Wet again today.

Played the Saree brothers in a team match. The barrack won but Ron and I lost by 2040 pts. Ron played like a Queenie. Their bidding is superb. One bid in particular; NB (myself) 2 spades, NB, Grand Slam Spades and he laid his hand in!!!

Received a letter from Mum and Mary. The AM sent home £245.

Feb 1st

A glorious day.

Got more mail 1 Les, 1 Aunt Edie, 1 Mum, 1 Rene. Apparently Mum was very upset about my letter warning them I intend carrying on flying. Rene's reply was very much blacked out. Maybe I shouldn't have sent it.

Ron and I beat Stan and Bingo by 2720 pts.

Feb 2nd

Saw a list of Aussie gangsters today.

Saw that Jerry Jascowski AFM is now a F/Lt with the DFC. Good show.

A glorious day.

Wrote a card to Mum yesterday and one to Rene.

Feb 3rd

Am becoming greater and greater friends with Joe Holder a 22yr old Aussie fighter boy. A wizard lad. Spends most of his time on my bed – like many others.

Played a terrible game soccer for the barrack against 15A. Lost 1-0

Fri Feb 4th

Today volunteers were asked to hand in their names for moving. Apparently 500 are going in two batches of 250 each. I am not volunteering. Stan is.

Had a good walk round with Joe. He's a wizard fellow.

I hope we both stay. Everyone is trying to get the gen on the move.

Sat Feb 5th

A nice morning.

Had a letter from Norman Steele today who is getting a commission in the army. He gave bags of news about various chaps. Mr Bailey killed and Dicky Cooper. He writes or attempts to write like a grown up man. Rather amusing.

Played a nice game soccer. We beat 16B 4-1. I was RH

Sun Feb 6th

Wrote a very mediocre letter to Mary. I find it increasingly difficult to write anything of consequence.

The cold weather seems to have returned with snow and frost.

The Huns are taking volunteers for this moving. They are apparently going to a Luft camp in East Prussia. I am not volunteering.

The navigators beat the gunners in the quiz.

Feb 7th

Very cold again.

We have definite gen that the boys are going to an annexe of Lufts at Meinel. This seems rather improbable and highly mysterious with the Russians so close.

Tues Feb 8th

Got a cig parcel of 200 SS (*Senior Service cigarettes*).

No news today.

Heard a talk on the damage in Berlin. It is devastated with a capital D. The lecturer suggested that after the war they might as well forget about B and build a new city.

The civvies were strangely friendly and the women admirable.

Wed Feb 9th

We were kept on parade whilst the boys move out to the working compound. There is bags of excitement and the barrack now looks once again reasonably habitable – for more reasons than one.

Unfortunately my combine with Stan is now separated.

Feb 10th

Dave and I are now in full combine. He is a queer cove, rather 'eccentric'. His chief attributes are, a large nose, a 'refined' voice, and he attempts to play (???) the guitar. I think he believes he now has me under his wing!!! He is 29.

Feb 11th

Two parties came in today from Lemburg area. They were rushed in at 5 minutes' notice. They came in pyjamas on top of coal wagons etc. They claim to have heard the guns firing with the Ruskies very close. The boys did not move 'owing to transport difficulties'???

Sat Feb 12th

Snowing all day.

Played Joe at chess. Won 1 lost 2. Played 5-suit bridge in the evening. Not bad, but not so good as ordinary. Very difficult to assess the value of a hand.

Heard last night's BBC.

Sun Feb 13th

Snowing again all day.

Won two games chess with Joe. Saw Stan in the afternoon.

In quiz team RAF v ARMY. We won by 2 pts.

Wrote a card to Mrs F Ross Taylor a cig donor and one to Rene.

'Sheify' Cooper broke his leg yesterday.

Mon Feb 14th

Very cold again.

Received a 200 cig parcel today.

There was a very enlightening report in the Hun paper today concerning the coming second front. They seem very worried and expect a big do.

Feb 15th

Played bridge in the evening. It was too easy.

Received a letter from Mum today and one from Aunt K. Mum seems adamant in her efforts to prevent me flying again. That makes two of us; unfortunately opposite factions.

Feb 16th

Snow and cold.

Some 200 Army (British and Yanks) wounded arrived from Italy. The Yanks aren't very impressed by the war but the British are full of good news and can't say enough of the good work being done by the RAF.

Finland is supposed to have packed in and Rome taken.

Feb 17th

Snowing all day and very cold.

Ron and I play two Czechs at bridge in the evening and won by 2920pts over 6 rubbers. Also visited the Latin quarter.

The Finland and Rome rumours persist. Heard last night's BBC. Another raid on Berlin.

Feb 18th

Snow and extremely cold again.

Ron and I lost to Alex and Cliff at bridge. They had wonderful cards, which isn't an excuse. More chess.

Taffy Morgan and his band played some mediocre music in the evening or maybe I'm getting too critical.

No news.

Sat Feb 19th

Received a book parcel which is just about the end! A farming book I already have!!

Very cold again.

Played a little bridge with Johnny Clayden who also today gave me all the gen on tank battles. A tank unit can be compared with a fighter squadron.

No news at all of any importance recently.

Sun Feb 20th

Freezing hard all day but nice and sunny in the morning so Joe and I had a brisk walk round the camp.

Played a little chess and in the evening had an interesting discussion on our outlook on life since being made a PoW. My outlook is definitely much broader.

Wrote a letter home.

Mon Feb 21st

Very cold again.

I have decided to make a list of good books to be read at some future date. One per day.

'Fame is the Spur' by Howard Spring.

Snowing again.

The RAF apparently lost 83 a/c on Leipzig. Heard the story of the siege of Tobruk by an Aussie. Very interesting. They did a wonderful job. Also of the North Fusiliers.

Feb 22nd

Cold with more snow.

Played Gordon Howe and Marty in the evening. We won by 280 pts. They argue too much.

Rumours that the RAF raided Stuttgart. The boys seemed to think their move is definite on 29th. Canadians going on Friday.

'Crowthers of Bankdam' by Thomas Armstrong

Feb 23rd

Very cold but sunny.

Played bridge in afternoon. We were winning by 5690 pts after 3 rubbers so they gave us the game. A little chess in the evening.

Received 3 letters; 2 Mum, 1 Mary one of which, Aug 26th, had been sent to Italy.

'King's Row' by Bellaman

Thurs Feb 24th

A glorious sunny morning altho still very cold.

Played a little chess otherwise nothing happened.

Received a 200 cig parcel and Dave received 500 cigs so the combine is in the money.

'Gone with the Wind' Margaret Mitchell

Feb 25th

Sunny but cold.

Today the Germans gave their interpretations of Mr Churchill's speech. From our point of view it was very disappointing but of course we aren't Germans.

Played bridge with Tommy and beat him by 1100 pnts over 7 rubbers. Received 1 letter from Mary.

'Lust for Life' Irving Stone

Sat Feb 26th

Cold again.

Played Alex and Cliff at bridge. We were winning by 300 pts at the beginning of the last rubber. They got vulnerable and they won by a grand slam!!! Everything happens to us.

Had a good chat with Doug Porteous on Whitney Straight and his escaping experiences and escaping in general.

'Three Loves' AJ Cronin

Feb 27th

Cold again.

Wrote a card home via the Army post-box and with a rank of Sgt. I wonder how long it will take to get home.

In a quiz N v S in the evening. We lost.

Heard Churchill's *pukka* speech. Very encouraging.

A good record concert.

'Anthony Adverse' (Hervey Allen)

Mon Feb 28th

Sunny and thawing.

Had a wonderful snow-fight with the next compound this afternoon. I had 3 destroyed, a few probable and a number damaged.

Saw Ian and the boys who are moving tomorrow.

Played bridge in the evening.

'Without Armour' James Hilton

Feb 29th

Cold again.

The boys did not move as expected. No reason given. Maybe the Huns are shooting too many down. Instead 1000 Army NCOs are going to **Thomesan** Saturday.

Received a letter from Rene. Stan recognised two lads on the photo, Adams & Cheedle, both of whom I have never heard of!!

Saw a wonderful dance band show at the theatre last night. Very, very good.

'*Seven Tempest*'

Wed Mar 1st

Very cold and drizzling.

Received two 200 SS parcels. Apparently the boys did not move as 700 Yanks suddenly arrived at Luft 6 unexpectedly and filled the camp.

There is very little news recently and I am very browned off.

'*England is my Village*' *Llewellyn Rhys*

Mar 2nd

Very cold and freezing.

The highlights of the day from my point of view was an argument in the evening between myself, Ron, Pete Blakeley and Jack Kean and Leo about whether a man should be allowed more than one wife. An intelligent argument is very enjoyable.

'*The Healing Knife*' *George Sava*

Fri Mar 3rd

Very cold again.

It looks as though there will be no hitch in the movement of the 1000 NCOs. We are having no BBC for about 5 weeks as someone is squealing. The bastards.

Started to teach Eric Sannett chess.

Won my first leg in the darts competition by beating George Read. Wonders never cease!!!

'The Sun is my Undoing' Marguerite Steen

Mar 4th

We were locked in most of the morning as the last of the 1000 NCOs were cleared. Got another 200 SS parcel. Apparently Churchill and all *Fliegens* in Hunlands have been sentenced to death for murder. The sentence is awaiting execution!!??!!

I was told that Lord Haw-Haw was really a SS (*Secret Service*) agent and has been shot by the Huns.

Sun Mar 5th

Quite cold again.

Read some more of *'Twilight our England'*. The Rackets the Jews were in, if true as put in the book, are absolutely amazing.

Gave Eric his chess lesson and Stan came up in the evening. Heard about Memel and some of Jerries new air tactics.

'Sorrell and Son' Warwick Deeping

Mon Mar 6th

Snowing hard all day although a little warmer.

Heard that the RAF are now using 12,000lb bombs!!

Ron and I climbed another step up the bridge ladder but I took the dive in the darts competition after winning the first game.

Bags of snow around.
'The Citadel' AJ Cronin

Tues Mar 7th

Thawing a little.

Ron and I were again thwarted at bridge by being 2000 up in the last rubber and then being beaten by a slam. It's a good job we don't take it to heart.

'Hatter's Castle' AJ Cronin

Mar 8th

Thawing again but still miserable weather.

We hear that a *feldwebel (Sergeant)* and 11 *Postens (guards)* have been shot at Teschen by Polish bandits. If true, it's a fine bit of work. The Yanks have made a big daylight on Berlin.

A little bridge. 3 small slams in 2 rubbers!!

'It Isn't' by Geoffrey Gilby.

Mar 9th

Quite mild and dryer.

Had an argument with Dave about religion. The situation between myself, Cliff, Bob and Eddie is becoming very acute. I was in a terrible but amusing stew last night. The gloves are off.

Got a letter from Aunt Maggie.

I hear we are eligible for the 1939-43 star.

'The Earth is the Lord's' by Taylor Caldwell

Mar 10th

Snowing again after a blizzard during the night.

The boys came back into the barrack from 25 & 26 and the Army lads moved to 7 – 10. Now maybe I'll be able to get a decent night's sleep. How they could snore! Old Stan is back in the old spot and seems pleased.

Had a terrific argument on the merits (???) if any of modern swing. I think Glen Miller stinks.

Sat Mar 11th

Snowing again. When will this winter end.

Making a copy of Eric Johnson's talk on the bombing of Berlin. Very interesting. Frank Gillian was telling us all about the PRU. Very interesting.

Played darts for the barrack against 15B. We won 6-4.

There is a Typhus case in the camp. Horrors!!!!

Mar 12th

Miserable again.

Had the FFI and louse inspection today. Everyone ok.

Played bridge in the afternoon when we were licked by Alex and Cliff. Wrote 3 cards to Aunts Maggie and Gladys and one to Mary.

I have rather a bad head cold.

'Enter Three Witches' DL Murray

Mar 13th

Cold and snowing again. It is a very long winter since this time last year we were sunbathing.

No mail again. A little cards and darts. Cliff and I spend lots of our time dodging Bob, the Army lad.

Apparently there were 176 cases of lice in the camp. None from this compound.

'*Green Fire*' *Peter Rainier*

Mar 14th

Snowing again and very cold.

Had a terrific argument with Bob in the evening on the prowess of the Yanks. I think they are so much loud-mouthed baggage!

Bridge in the afternoon in a new league. We lost by 8pts to 1 ½. No cards. Darts in the evening.

'*Dawn*' *Theodore Dreiser*

Wed Mar 15th

Lovely morning but cold.

Trouble on parade this am. The boys won't get out in time. Snowstorm during the day.

Apparently there is something going on because no BBC can be read out and we have to be very careful who we are talking to. It seems there are 4 Jerries in the camp in British uniform.

Bridge in the evening with Lofty. A letter from Rene today.

'*American Tragedy*' *Theodore Dreiser*

Mar 16th

Very, very cold again.

Received 3 letters. 1 Marjory, 1 Mum, 1 Rene. Apparently Jim Shanks an MO has been killed in Italy.

Not a lot of news but we are again getting the BBC but underground.

Bridge in the evening with Lofty.

Mar 17th

Not too good weather.

Received 2 letters from Mum, 1 Marjory, 1 Rene. Bob Boyd is dead. Alfie Humphrey is home from the 2nd Front. Quite a lot of news but Rene will persist in giving her news too openly with the result that most of it is blacked out.

A little bridge with Tommy and Bert. Relations restored with Ron again. I am very pleased.

Mar 18th

Weather not too bad. A little rain.

Ron and I finished off Tommy by winning 3½ - 3 and then in a very unpleasant game, lost to Alex 6-2. Ron and I had very unpleasant ructions and for the time being have scrapped the club convention.

Had a very good show Al Burk's boys in at night. The four goons performed again. They are terrific.

Mar 19th

Windy and cold with snowstorm.

Wrote a letter to Mary.

Played darts in the evening in a competition. Pilots v Navs v etc. We were knocked out in the first round. Ron and

I beat Irish and Len by 7230pts over 5 rubbers in a knock-out competition.

Mar 20th

Blizzards, howling gale and cold.

The Russians are knocking hell out of the Jerries in the Odessa corner of the Ukraine.

Ron and I won by 5830pts over 5 rubbers against Stan and Bingo in the league. Was knocked out of the crib competition.

Our potato ration is being cut down.

Mar 21st

Snowing again with about 1 inch on the ground this first day of Spring.

Wrote a card to Stan and to Aunt Kate. Bridge in the afternoon.

The Russians seem to be doing as well as ever.

'Arches of the Years' Halliday Sutherland.

Mar 22nd

Much snow again and very cold.

Ron and I lost to Alex and Cliff in the knock-out. I find that peoples' small mannerisms which I used to ignore are now annoying me intensely. I become easily irritated. A change would do me good.

'In my Path' Halliday Sutherland.

Thurs Mar 23rd

Very, very cold with snow.

Won in the bridge by 11-1 against Joe Byrne and Wilkie.

Heard that Ernie Mark's first swop is home. Good show.

A little BBC but nothing of importance.

Skip McCabe gave a good record concert last night.

'Random Harvest' James Hilton

Mar 24th

Snowing all day and cold. Will this winter ever end?

There are rumours that Finland is out of the war and Romania suing for terms. Also that the Russians are 15kms this side of Lemburg. I wish they were.

Oliver W is well.

Sat Mar 25th

Cold again.

Some bridge during the day.

No news of any importance except that the Russians are doing excellently.

Snowing hard again.

'Imperial Palace' Arnold Bennett

Mar 26th

Snowing hard and cold.

Wrote a card to Rene and a card to Norman. Sent them via the Army.

A little bridge during the day. Ron and I are 3rd in the league.

Went to a concert in the evening given to the Blackpool and Liverpool associations. I was a guest of Cliff's. It was an excellent show given by the *Lamsdorf Melody Makers*.

Mon Mar 27th

This morning we awoke to just the deepest snow since I've been here – and still snowing. Snowing most of the day.

Bridge again. We beat Lofty and Twig and then Alan Tarkin and Jim Cameron.

The Russians are well inside Romania. The 5th Army in Italy is supposed to be cut off.

Mar 28th

Snowing and cold again. Fine in the afternoon.

There was nothing of importance in Mr Churchill's speech. I am seriously considering another attempt at a break if I can find a suitable partner who can speak German.

'My Son, My Son' Howard Spring

Wed Mar 29th

Snowstorms but fine in the afternoon.

Am very much pondering this escape question. Alex received a letter dated March 14th.

Not feeling too brilliant today.

Churchill is supposed to have made a speech.

'Shabby Tiger' Howard Spring

Mar 30th

Snow in the morning but turned very nice in the afternoon. Maybe the winter has disappeared.

The Ruskies have made tremendous advanced in the last few weeks. It seems to be a complete rout.

Have good gen on an escape.

Fri Mar 31st

Sent off two pc's. One to Bob and one to Marjorie via the Army.

A Canadian was found dead in bed today.

A lovely fine morning.

Bags of flying at the nearby drome. *(Aerodrome)* Do I feel homesick?

Played bridge in the evening. A very even and interesting game. After 4¾ rubbers there were 10pnts in it.

'The Great Grab' Thomas Burton

Apr 1st

We had a wizard parcel chit leg pull on old Stan but Harry Whelan, the stupid old woman, wouldn't let us do it and squashed the post office arrangements. Am I mad?

The Huns are supplying Tannopal and Kowel by air and there is fighting in the area of Stanislav. My. My.

We won against Marty and Gordon.

Terrific snowstorm in the evening after a fine sunny morning.

Sun Apr 2nd

Quite nice today with a few snow storms in between.

The Russians are still driving on. Saw the six engined aircraft – 'The Gigant' the other day for the first time but today had my best view of it. It is a terrific thing, bigger than any aircraft I have yet seen but very slow. Seems to be flying in the Russian front direction.

Apr 3rd

Quite nice today.

Created, I think, a small record by getting two Grand Slams in one rubber. Both were doubled and redoubled.

No news today. Heard some more interesting tales of the treatment of the Dunkirk lads on their march. Some Jerries from the Russian front at the station said "All is lost". They looked worse than the Dunkirk prisoners.

Tue Apr 4th

Lovely day but cold wind. Beat Bob and Dennis by 10pnts to 1.

No news of any importance. A joke in the *Stalag* is now that Stalin made a speech in which he said that if the British and Americans can manage to hold Cassino till Xmas he will go down and take Rome himself next year.

A nice day today with light rain in the evening.

Apr 5th

A glorious warm spring morning.

Lost to Tommy by 6½ - 2½ in the am.

The *Tirpitz* is supposed to have been sunk.

The Jerries found the tunnel in 7-10 and poured *Sheisen* (*Shizen or shit*) down it! The bastards.

I am told Richard Aldington is a good author.

Thurs Apr 6th

A lovely morning again.

Played Alex and Cliff bridge in the afternoon. We won 8½ - 1 in a good game which gives us quite a good average.

Saw the McCrea – Kennedy farewell match on the 8-a-side pitch. Not bad for a start.

Apr 7th

Quite a nice day.

Watch a soccer match in the morning. Quite good but still not up to the standard yet. Everyone must be given a chance to get fit tho'.

Saw *'Charlie's Aunt'* in the evening. Very good.

No news of any import.

Sat Apr 8th

A glorious sunny morning.

At last I received some mail. One from home and two from Mary. Ustie's marriage seems to be rather a comic effort.

A glorious day when I watched two soccer matches. The RAF won 2-1 but both games were rather poor standard.

Apr 9th

Rather cold again but quite fine.

Saw the RAF lose 3-2 in the afternoon in a very fine game. They lost after extra time. Saw another match in the evening. Wrote a letter home today.

The Second Front according to rumour gets ever nearer and nearer.

Mon Apr 10th

A nice day again today.

Ron and I beat Blaskey and Keen by 11-1. We played, I think, the best bridge we have ever played.

Saw the depot beat the bulldogs in quite a good game. 2-1 was the result.

No news of any importance.

Apr 11th

A little light rain but mild.

The important news of today is that the Germans admit the evacuation of Odessa. The Jerries seem to be holding the North section of the front but can do very little in the southern sector.

Went to a very good military band concert.

Wed Apr 12th

A lovely morning.

At last I've been caught. I had to stand with about a dozen others for 2hrs outside A for being late on parade. Quite amusing.

Cliff's statement of accounts came through so mine should be here anytime now. Ron and I beat Byrke and Wilky 16½ – 0 which puts us in a good position.

Apr 13th

A glorious morning again.

Had a little hockey practice in the morning.

Ron and I beat Irish and Len by 8-1 which gave us an average of 250 and a very good position too.

Watched a very poor 8-a-side soccer match.

Fri Apr 14th

A wonderful day. Sunbathing quite a lot today.

According to the Camp the weather in England is glorious after a very mild winter.

The Thompson/Farmer combine has split after a display of fisticuffs over a trivial affair which puts our average to 287.

Rumours that Raeder has taken over Supreme Command.

Apr 15th

A glorious day again.

Played my first game of soccer for the barrack this season against the Slashers. We won 4-1 in a good game. I was lucky enough to score 2 and Bob scored 2. I was OR.

Did some washing in the evening.

The Hitler out of power rumour persists.

Sun Apr 16th

A glorious morning again.

Stan caught 25 fleas on his blanket this am.

Played Don and Winnie at bridge and beat them 8/1½ which puts our average to 296 and gives us a good chance of winning the competition.

Played tenniquoits, the latest craze.

Finished off my first batch of laundry.

Apr 17th

A glorious hot day again.

Played Lofty and Cyril in the evening after tenniquoits. Winning 3 rubbers to 1.

No important news. The flag did not go up. The rumours started in the camp about Raeder etc., seems to be spreading all over Germany. Most amusing.

Tues Apr 18th

Not so nice today.

No news of any importance. Some mail and parcels today but none for me. Did more washing.

I wonder if I shall ever be able to fly again, my eyes are very bad. I worry over them too much.

Wrote my card home and one to Mary, via the Army.

Drew 3/3 with Lofty and Cyril.

Apr 19th

A rainy miserable day.

Played bridge against Gordon and Marty. Lost 13½ /1 which brings our average down considerably.

We hear that no diplomats are allowed to leave England.

Apr 20th

Miserable again.

Played Tonkin and Cameron at bridge and lost 7½/2. Also played Stan and Bingo and won 11½/1½ which puts us in the running again. We had our 18th Grand Slam making 9-9.

Got my 6th Clothing Parcel containing a 'visitors' mug and a plate.

Apr 21st

A thunderstorm during the afternoon after a heavy morning. Should clear the air a bit.

Apparently everyone in England is "breathlessly waiting for the 2nd Front" according to the Germans.

Sat Apr 22nd

Wet again.

Played soccer in the morning when we won 8-0. I played terribly.

Twig got out on a party successfully to Sudetenland.

Winnie and Ron won the bridge competition with an average of 238. We were 2nd with 204. They won 14 lost 6. We won 13 lost 5 drew 2. We had 139½ pts for, 68½ against.

Apr 23rd

There is supposed to be no communication whatsoever between England and the outside world. I hope this is true.

Windy today, but fine.

An argument about unemployment today. Wrote a letter home today.

The civvy seems to me to be an extremely clever sort of a cove trying to create an impression by taking chaps out of bunker etc.

Mon Apr 24th

A nice morning.

6 permanent strafe boys got out last night including Mac and Eric. Through the wire. Let's hope they make it this time. One of the 6 was caught soon after getting out.

A little bridge with Stan against Alan and Jim. Watched Stan play (??) rugger. Most amusing.

Tue Apr 25th

After a restless night with toothache I decided to visit the dentist. This must be marked as a memorable day in my life for it was the first tooth I had extracted and 'horrors' the first time I fainted! After the cocaine. I think it was due to my super objection to hypodermics. It was a dead faint. Actually it turned out best for I didn't have to wait the usual 2 hours but had it out right away. The dentist was a gentleman.

Wed Apr 26th

We hear that some troops from Lager II went to quell the riots in Czecho. Also that *Stukas* were used on a village outside Prague.

Wizard night last night. Finished off the bridge with Stan.

Got a 200 cig parcel today. An argument with Dave about socialism.

George Davison passed the commission. Damn good show.

Thurs Apr 27th

Quite a nice day.

Am reading a very good book *'A Life for a Life'* by Stephen McKenna. He seems to be a man extremely disappointed over the social system after the last war.

The 2nd Front looms ever nearer.

Apr 28th

Colder.

Played soccer against the Gremlins. We won 3-2 in a very hard and good game. I managed to score the winning goal 2 mins from the end. Played a little table tennis today.

Churchill had 2 audiences with the King on Wednesday. Let's hope it's something big.

Sat Apr 29th

Very cold and windy.

The book is impressing me more and more as I get into it. I wonder if the disillusionment of the past Great War will be the same after this. I sincerely hope not.

We hear the 46 officers have been shot at Sagan either escaping or after they had been caught. Very unsatisfactory.

Sun Apr 30th

Not a bad day.

Wrote a card home through the RAF as I hear that Army mail written over 14 days ago is still here owing to the parcel panic.

A little BBC today most of it we heard.

Watched some international rugby. I find it very interesting to watch.

Rumours of a Naval Battle in the Pacific.

Mon May 1st

A bit cold and dull.

Feel a little depressed on this rather dead day. No news at all. I have reached the conclusion that after returning home it will need many long solitary quiet moments to sort out the impressions and ideas that have developed since leaving home. Only then can I view circumspectively *(sic)* my philosophy of life, religion, politics etc.

Tues May 2nd

Regarding this philosophy business, I find that although I have experienced life in many aspects I cannot, in this noisy atmosphere, solidify my jumbled thoughts and impressions.

A miserable day with rain at odd intervals.

Nothing of any major interest. Have finished the book. Excellent, although I feel that he has failed in his main object in that the book is not powerful enough.

May 3rd

Very sunny, but windy.

Had an interesting conversation with Eric Newman's swop. He has made 6 attempts to get home.

Played soccer today for the CT *(Cork Tips)*. We won again

1-0 but were very lucky to win, which makes us still unbeaten. I played terribly but I loathe the position.

No news of any importance.

Thurs May 4th

Very windy and cold with occasional rain.

Got a book parcel today. One very poor book. I would very much like to know who sends this tripe.

The court of inquiry into the pool man seems to have finished.

Volleyball and tenniquoits today.

On looking through my mail I have only received 2 Jan letters and one Feb from home.

Dan says everything is ready.

May 5th

Have a very bad cold and cough.

Got a 200 SS parcel in the morning and a 200 GF *(Gold Flake)* parcel in the afternoon. Cliff got 2 soccer balls in his parcel.

According to the news the 2nd Front looms ever nearer. The Jerries are very apprehensive. Saw some pamphlets dropped on Berlin. Very interesting indeed.

Tenniquoits again.

2 uniforms riddled with bullet holes came into the camp today for identification.

Sat May 6th

A glorious morning after a very hot night.

Many cracks about the unleavened bread which has come in for the Jews. Tenniquoits again.

Rumours that Spain is almost in the war against Germany, massing troops on the Pyrenean border. The new battle cruiser *Black Prince* has apparently been in action in the channel.

Stan's WO came through today.

May 7th

A mild morning again. Very windy again.

Watched a little rugby in the evening. No news of any importance. A good discussion with Dave on psychology.

Mon May 8th

Cold and windy.

Today I was dropped from the Cork Tips. I am very disgusted at the shabby treatment I have received because I told them I couldn't play at outside right. I should have refused in the first place.

A good game tenniquoits in the evening. Very cold.

The Huns are supposed to have marched into Spain.

May 9th

Windy and quite cold.

No mail for me again. I have missed out the last 10 or 12 batches from Sagan.

Played some volley ball today.

A good argument with Dave about Trust.

Wed May 10th

A nice warm day today.

Played soccer for the Weights in the am. We won 5-1. I scored the first goal. Had a much better game at RH. Played two games volleyball and 1 tenniquoits.

Lofty and I knocked out Thommy and Partner in the camp.

No news of any importance.

May 11th

A nice day again.

Played my first game Ruggah *(rugby)* in the am. I played L Wing three-quarter. I was a mild sensation! Scored a try.

A huge but rather crude joke in camp today. After a bet one year ago, a Canadian shat on the chest of another at a ball game tonight. The bet was a ____ ____. Quite a ceremony.

No news.

Fri May 12th

Nice again today.

Played Rugby in the am, losing 8-3 after our 15-6 win yesterday. I feel very tired after all the sport this week. Shall take a rest for a day or two.

At long last I received some mail. 7 letters. Rene has apparently broken it off with Stan. I am sorry for Stan's sake but she naturally knows her own mind best.

'It Was Good While It Lasted' by H Longhouse

May 13th

Nice day again.

I was trying to ponder last night over what I have learnt here. I have learnt nothing material but reaped a fund of experience of life and human nature. I have learnt to think and argue more clearly which is a big thing.

No games today.

Yesterday I ate my first real egg for 21 months. I paid 10 fags for it.

'My Goodness! My Passport' Lella Secor Florence

Sun May 14th

Wrote a card to Rene and one to Molly Johnson.

A very hot but lovely day when we all did a spot of sunbathing.

I played a short practice rugger game in the morning at Stand-off and then watched the Cork Tips trounced by the Shamrocks 5-1.

In the evening we watched two rugger internationals the England ¾ line playing excellently. England beat Scotland 17-6 and Australia beat SA 14-10.

May 15th

Raining and cold today.

Received 200 Players No 3 today.

The Jerries have apparently completed the evacuation? of the Crimea.

Had another egg (poached) for lunch.

I sometimes feel a bitter resentment towards the last few years. I entered Germany as a young lad of 21 looking 17 and will leave an old man of 23 looking 40. But again, I have no regrets for I have a clear conscience in that I did my duty.

Tues May 16th

A rainy morning.

Another 400 chaps arrived from Munich after being caught in Italy. Some were on leave in England in February!! And even March!!! Many have the Africa Star and all have nothing but praise for the work of the RAF. It is noticeable that the standard in the Guards regiment has a deterioration. The number of under 20's is noticeable.

The war should end this year. The big attack in Italy is on.

May 17th

A lovely morning again.

Had a good walk around with Bas. Watched a very good 8-a-side soccer match between Bulldogs (2) and Depot (1). An excellent game.

No news of any importance except that the attack in Italy is pretty good.

Took a £2 bet with Stan the war will not be over by Sept 31st.
'Disgrace Abounding' Douglas Reed

Thurs May 18th

A wet coldish day.

This morning we were 'raised' out at 4.30 by half the German army with bayonets and told there had been a mass breakout. At 8.00 we were all marched out of camp counted and recounted. The joke is that most compounds have too many men.

It was a most unpleasant day for me as I had chronic neuralgia the whole time. Apparently 12 lads went through the tunnel.

May 19th

A nice day again.

Played soccer for the CT's. We won 2-0 in a reasonably good game.

The Irish are moving to another camp, maybe Senshagen. Rumours are that (1) it is reprisals and (2) a prop camp. The Irish RAF are also moving.

Took some laundry in for the first time.

'Insanity Fair' Douglas Reed

May 20th

A glorious sunny, warm day.

Rugger for the BK. Lost 13-0

Went a lovely walk out to a lake with 20 of the boys and the Civvy. I don't know whether we did right. Irish was too talkative. I was very impressed by the number of kids of 3-8, by the very clean neat cottages and by the lovely green of the grass and trees and of the blossom. After confinement for 20 months it was a fine treat; we were out from 2 till 6.15. He took photos outside. A red-letter day. Oh for home and freedom again.

May 21st

A glorious day which ended by a thunderstorm in the evening.

Watched SA beat up Scotland at Rugby in the evening.

A sensation occurred when a guard shot at some chaps up against the warning wire. He hit 3 of them. One in the neck another in the thigh and another in the wrist. The day will come.

Beat up Eric at Cravette again.

Apparently there are two English newspapers in camp. D.Sk of Ap.10 and D.Ex of Ap.10

Mon May 22nd

Raining and cold all day.

In bed most of the day. In the above mentioned papers the Aust. premier said we shall be lucky if the war in Europe is over by next April!!! And here we are hoping to be home by Xmas.

Yesterday I wrote a letter to Mary.

Took on a £5 bet with Shorty Braddock that the 2nd Front will start before Dec 31st.

May 23rd

Very windy and cold.

Played my first game hockey today. We won 5-0 in a very good game. I played R.H.

The big attack in Italy still goes on. I think they mean business this time.

May 24th

Very cold and windy.

Was in bed most of the day with neuralgia. Feeling most miserable it gave me terrible pain. Got up in the evening to play Eric Cravette.

Two MCs from the drome had a mid-air collision. Neither bailed out.

Some Irish moved out today. Rumours that the SA's and Kiwis are also going.

May 24th

Quite cold and dull again.

Neuralgia much better today. Feeling very cheerful again.

Bas and Joe swapped over today. They should and I hope, make it, for Bas has worked really hard.

No news at all today.

May 26th

Not a bad day.

Got a book parcel today. *'John Cornelius'* by Hugh Walpole and *'John Splendid'* by Neil Munro.

Had a very interesting and amusing argument and discussion with the Aussies and Kiwis about accents.

Cravette again.

No news of any importance except that the big attack on Italy makes still more progress.

May 27th

A glorious day.

The first day of the Whitsun sports programme was quite entertaining altho I don't think the athletic times will compare with last year's. The Indians, not being here, shows a marked lack of colour and competition.

Sun May 28th

The Fates really are kind. A glorious hot day again. I got very sunburnt, more than I should have done.

Watched more eliminating sports and then two very good international rugger matches. Aus beat NZ 11-8 and SA beat Eng.

An English speaking Hun in the compound on about the Legion of St George. He said they are traitors, his mother is English. Germany doesn't mind treachery but hates the traitors.

May 29th

A glorious day again.

The Carnival was excellent. The Zulu tableau won first prize (and they deserved it) with RAF and their 'Lanc' model 2nd.

The tableau wire (1) Pearly kings, (2) RAF, (3) Cenotaph, (4) Zulus, (5) Volga Bockam, (6) Palestine and camel, (7) Farming advances, (8) Rhapsody in blue (with Frank Hunt), (9) Anthony and Cleopatra, (10) The Pirate, and (11) Monopoly.

At the finale the Cenotaph was raised to reveal King Neptune the band struck up 'Rule Britannia'.

The Huns certainly were lenient.

May 30th

A further tableau yesterday was the parcel tableau.

In the afternoon the sports took place although the times weren't so good. In the evening a good boxing tournament which I missed. I saw the arts and crafts exhibition which was not so good as last year. A thoroughly enjoyable day, the Hampstead Heath going over very well.

Today was very hot and the cricket match between the two best teams in Stalag was very entertaining. Sheddon bowled well.

Hockey in am. Won 2-1 again. Was offs.*(off side)*

May 31st

Wrote a card to Aunt Edie and Uncle Will and one home on Mon.

The BBC lately has been excellent. There is a bit of a flap about the 'British Free Corps' a 'Legion of St George'. I don't think they will have much success. They have been issuing pamphlets I believe, but I haven't seen one.

Thurs June 1st

A glorious day, a little cooler but nevertheless it was 92F in the shade at 1.45 pm today!!

A tremendous argument on the new Jerry aircraft flying about today. They are either Hs 129s, Fw 187, Me 210 or Me 410.

Received 3 letters. 1 mum, 1 Aunt M and 1 Mary.

No important news. Doubts about the 2nd Front are becoming rife.

1800 new PoWs coming in tomorrow.

June 2ⁿᵈ

Wet and colder today.

The prisoners seem to be from Posen and are in transit having been bombed out.

No news of importance today.

Sat June 3ʳᵈ

Quite nice although not so sunny.

Played my best game of soccer in camp at 1.30 when the CTs beat Potters 6-2. I was CF *(centre forward)* and scored 3 goals. I was very pleased.

No important news.

June 4ᵗʰ

A glorious day again.

Wrote a letter home (Rene).

Cliff took another walking party today. They had a glorious time including a swim!

Saw a very good soccer match. BEF v The Rest. The Rest won 2-0.

Mon June 5ᵗʰ

A glorious sunny hot day.

My week of startling news opened well when we heard at lunchtime the fall of Rome. Apparently certain people were listening to the wireless all day long. Everyone is most cheerful.

Played a little tenniquoits today. Received a book parcel. *'The Shepherds Farm'*

Wrote a card to Bob Henderson's sister.

June 6th

A miserable wet day.

Is this to be the red letter day of my life so far? We heard at lunchtime that the 2nd Front has started with landings at Calais, Dunkirk and on the Seine. Everyone is outwardly calm, but I suspect inwardly highly excited.

The RAF also beat the Bulldogs 4-2 which made the end of a perfect day. This is a turning point in our lives.

(If the 2nd Front hasn't started by this day it will never start (May 13))

June 7th

Mild this morning.

I hear a big Russian offensive has started which puts these Huns in a pretty big spot.

Played soccer in am when we beat the Sparrows 7-0. I scored 2 at CF.

Had a 200 SS parcel. Rumours that Rouen has been taken. The VB has huge red headlines "The battle in the west has begun".

Saw the RAF lose 2-1 in a terrible game in evening.

June 8th

Mild again.

Took up PT *(physical training)* this am. It is very tough at first. I have gone through the usual ragging over it.

The invasion seems to be well established and losses slighter than expected. It appears that the Huns have got the wind up in Greece and S. France.

Read Eric's letter to Stan.

June 9th

Mild again.

PT in am.

The Jerries, the bastards, have cut the electricity supplies so that we shan't be able to get any BBC. But will that stop us? Not much news today tho' till the boys get organised.

Watched the Magpies beat the Depot 8-a-side. What a strip.

June 10th

Mild again.

PT in morning. I enjoy this PT quite a lot.

The civvies from **Krengsburg** gave us a little entertainment last night.

Rumours of more landings in S France and Belgium. Not much reliable gen about tho'.

Sun June 11th

Damp after a night thunderstorm.

No PT this morning. Wrote a card to Mary and one to Stan.

After a dull day there was great excitement in the evening on rumours of surrender by Kesselring; of divs in Italy, paratroops in the Brenner and suicide of Kesselring etc. Everyone went to bed very excited.

Saw a good confiscated book *'Signed with their Honour'* by James Aldridge.

June 12th

A nice day today, with lots of sun in the afternoon.

Watched a little of the cricket. Bob made a very solid 23 and was run out (not out really). Watched a little of a ball game. What unadulterated tripe and playacting.

Dennis is discontinuing his news service for obvious reasons. Alan told me about his bad luck at not being able to get away from Benghazi.

PT this am. I enjoy it very much.

June 13th

A glorious morning.

Heard last night's BBC at 8am!!!

Played hockey at 8.30 am and won 3-2 in a good game. A 200 SS parcel. Played soccer at 11.30am when we lost 2-1 to the Casuals in our best and hardest match to date. I scored the one goal.

Nothing of any importance during the day.

June 14th

A lovely hot morning turned to a thunderstorm at lunchtime.

A 200 SS parcel today.

Joe Byrne last night imagined someone was holding him by the ankles and then worked up to his neck. He shouted out "-- off, -- off" and then called Len Waterson over. Some nightmare. Most amusing.

Very little news.

Thurs June 15th

Quite nice.

The PT is doing me a tremendous amount of good. I feel fitter every day. The boys are very disappointed, I think, as I haven't packed in already. They were hoping I would give them an excuse for pulling my leg.

200 Players and 200 GF.

Heard the story of the Yanks sending home their prisoner because he was "too young to capture".

June 16th

Good PT this am.

Lovely day after a night thunderstorm.

Bad toothache all night.

My W/O came through today in a statement of accounts. It was from Aug 1st 1943. I am quite well off.

No news of any importance. Heard that F/O Pattison is dead.

June 17th

Raining all morning so didn't go to PT as the ground would be too wet and slippery.

The Huns claim to be using their secret (?) weapon for bombing England. A radio controlled bomber or bomb. They are also claiming 1000 a/c in the first 10 days of the Second Front.

Saw the RAF draw 2-2 with the Magpies in an even game.

Sun Jun 18th

A nice mild day.

Played rugger in the morning against 17A. We lost 8-3 in a very good, hard game. I <u>almost</u> scored two tries.

Some quite good BBC in the evening telling us the King has visited the French battle front.

Saw the Mastiffs beat Depot 6-4. Wrote a letter home.

Mon June 19th

PT again this morning.

Received 3 March letters, two from home and one Mary.

The Cherbourg peninsular is supposed to be cut off. Bob thinks it a brilliant achievement. I don't.

Leo has at last married Connie.

Finished the confiscated flying book.

June 20th

Played hockey today against the Bandits. We won 4-2 again. Saw the Ruffians draw 3-3 with the Sanitators and the Fliegen draw 1-1 with the Bulldogs.

A rumour, which I don't believe, that the King has been killed in an air raid. Mr Churchill has made a very excellent speech. His best of the war.

Wed June 21st

Quite mild with a little rain.

Received a 200 Players from the W. PoW club.

A good day for the Cork Tips. Some of our closest rivals were beaten.

A *Fliegen* alarm *(air raid?)* in the afternoon.

Not much news of any importance. Received my photos for 150 cigs. Very good indeed.

Saw an amusing rugger match. Some of the players were drunk on raisin wine.

June 22nd

A glorious day. Very hot and sunny.

Stewart amused us for quite a time with stories of the desert etc. I only wish I had his art of telling a story.

Watched a spot of cricket in the afternoon.

Dad is third from right on the back row

There seems to be tremendous air activity. No papers today maybe as a result of the Berlin bombing.

Fri June 23rd

200 SS today.

Mild but a cool breeze blowing.

The Germans issued a warning to all escapees that they will accept <u>no</u> responsibility for their treatment at the hands of the civvies on account of the bombing and strafing.

I don't know whether it's the PT but I feel very hungry these days.

Lots of bombing in progress.

June 24th

Cold and wet.

Our soccer match was cancelled. A little bridge. A tremendous argument with Tommy on the number of chances of turning up an ace, 2 or Jack in three cuts. It lasted several hours.

I hear that 14 more chaps were taken from Sagan for interrogation and their ashes came back in caskets!! England is giving threats over the Huns treatment of air men.

Sun June 25th

A glorious day.

Yesterday the Huns whipped Smoky Fogg away for interrogation and he hasn't been seen since. He is not in the camp. The authorities are weaving to find out where he is and why.

Saw an SA today collect a swarm of bees.

Wrote a card home and one to Aunt Maggie.

Not a lot of news.

Saw two good soccer games.

June 26th

A glorious day again.

Played rugger in the am when we lost 8-3 in a very poor game.

Sunbathing most of the rest of the day.

No more has been heard of Smoky as yet.

The Russians have started their offensive.

Tues June 27th

A glorious hot day.

PT in am.

Saw a very good dance band show at the theatre '*What's new?*' Al Burke now has 14 instruments in an excellent band.

No more news of Smoky and two army lads who are in the same predicament as himself.

Cherbourg and Finland are supposed to be caput.

June 28th

A lovely fresh day after the night's thunderstorm.

Good PT.

Received 200 Greys today.

Cherbourg has fallen and the Russians are advancing at tremendous speed.

Thurs June 29th

Received 200 SS and 200 Players. My cig parcels are coming through wonderfully well. I now have 1500. Saw a copy of the 'Signal'.

A glorious hot day when I got quite tanned.

Saw the RAF beat Depot 5-4 in evening. A very exciting match. Depot scored 3 goals in 2 mins from 1-3 to 4-3.

June 30th

Nice morning after thunderstorm.

PT again.

Excitement running high over the game with the Stragglers tomorrow.

Won 120 cigs off Thommy at crib in the evening. Raining in evening.

Sat July 1st

A nice day again.

The great game with the Shaggles had between 5000 and 10000 cigs on it. I had 100. We won 4-2 in a great game. I got the first goal. This puts us in a wonderful position for winning the league.

July 2nd

A lovely day again.

Watched the RAF lose 2-1 in the evening against the Bulldogs in a very poor game.

Some very good news lately.

July 3rd

Very hot.

Rene's birthday today.

PT in am.

Watched quite a good game cricket in the afternoon and evening. NZ v SA. SA won by 9 wickets in a 2 innings match.

I am very sunburnt.

The Russians still advance.

200 SS today.

July 4th

A very hot day again.

Played a good game soccer at RH in the am. We drew 3-3 with the Gangsters.

Played hockey in the afternoon. We lost 2-1 against Cosmos B. We had no forwards.

Chicago Bill (Pertoc) says that the Huns don't know whether to keep the army in charge of PoWs or his department take over.

Wed July 5th

The Huns are claiming 2007 a/c in June. They have lost 5 generals in the last two days including General Dietl, C in C Finland. BBC news a bit cock-eyed.

Heard a wonderful record (Brunswick). The Ink Spots singing 'A Java Jive'.

July 6th

A lovely day again.

200 SS today.

PT in am and hockey in pm. Won 3-0. I think I feel fitter than ever before. It's wizard.

Caught 20 fleas on my blanket after an uncomfortable night.

England lost to Aussie at cricket by an innings and 2 runs.

July 7th

A lovely day again.

PT and then sunbathing.

The Russians are rolling on. There was an air raid warning at about midday. We heard the aircraft and they apparently bombed the Blechhammer area.

July 8th

A glorious hot day today.

Am more sun burned that I have ever been in my life before.

Hear that 200 British PoWs were killed and 800 wounded at Blechhammer by the raid. The Ruskies still roll on.

Saw the Mastiffs beat the Magpies 1-0.

Hear that Gordon Brettell was murdered by the Gestapo.

Sun July 9th

Windy this morning.

According to rumours 1100 fellows are coming into camp tonight. The first of some all-week batches. Also the Russians are supposed to have started a push in the Lemburg *(Lviv)* area.

I saw the RAF beat Wolves 5-2. Wrote a letter to Mary.

July 10th

Received 200 Players.

Not so nice today.

It seems that there is something going on internally. The deaths of 25 Generals in under 3 weeks seems more than a coincidence to me. I think the Nazi party is cracking.

No bread today. Rumours that the bread store at Oppeln *(Opole)* was bombed.

July 11th

Not so warm today with a little rain.

Received 200 Players.

Saw the RAF lose 3-0 to Magpies. Poor game.

The Russians have taken Wilna *(Vilnius)*.

Lost 5-1 at hockey. We gave a very poor display.

June direct mail is coming through OK.

July 12th

Mary's birthday today.

Cooler.

Played soccer in am. We beat the Threshers 3-1 in a poor game.

Rumours that the attack in France is going well. Discussed England's social problem. My solution is mass emigration.

Warsaw was mentioned in the news for the first time.

July 13th

Mum's birthday today.

Rainy so our hockey was cancelled.

Not much news of any importance.

Saw the Fliegen lose 5-3 to the Wolves and the Depot and Bulldogs draw 2-2 in the evening.

July 14th

A bit warmer today.

PT in the morning.

Met two Yugoslavs whose names I don't remember and can't pronounce anyway! They were Air Force cadets at the beginning of the war. Very nice lads. 25 & 22.

Sat July 15th

Colder today.

PT in am.

Saw a good soccer match in the evening. Magpies v Bulldogs. Bulldogs won 4-2 and I won 60 cigs as a result.

Played a spot of tennis for the first time today.

The Russians seem to be almost on East Prussian territory.

July 16th

Not so warm again.

Had a very bad night with toothache.

Taffy and Serg were very amusing last night after their drunken (raisin wine) birthday party.

Saw the RAF lose 2-1 to the Depot.

No news of any importance. Wrote a card home.

Mon July 17th

Quite nice but storm in the afternoon.

PT in am.

Watched some of the cricket Australia v NZ. There was an extremely exciting finish to the first innings, NZ winning by 6 runs. At one time they had 12 to make 9 men out.

Rumours that Germany is suing for peace terms.

July 18th

Raining most of the morning.

The Huns are pepping up morning parades by bringing up 2 *Feldwebels* to get us out. They are making copious use of the bayonet.

Played cricket and knocked 3 and then soccer when we beat the Mosquitoes in a very poor game 2-0.

The Japs are going to shoot all airmen shot down over Japan!! The rats.

Wed July 19th

Dull and cold again.

PT this am.

Big moral victory. The Huns after many threats have eventually given up trying to stop us making holes in the wire and have put in a small gate between blocks V and II.

Played some bridge today.

July 20th

My birthday today and the boys forgot all about it.

Quite a nice day.

After PT watched the cricket. SA beat England on the first innings. It was a very good game, conspicuous for some excellent fielding. We beat the Diggers 3-2 at hockey.

200 SS today.

July 21st

Lovely day today.

PT in am.

Rumours today that an attempt has been made on Hitler's life when at a military conference. The room was dynamited and he is hurt but we don't know how badly. It has caused a great stir in Germany.

Played a spot of tennis.

July 22nd

Glorious day again.

PT. Received a book parcel today. *'Young Ames'*.

Played some crib and watched the Depot beat the Mastiffs 2-1.

The great news is the revolt inside Germany. Goering and Donitz have called on their commanders for support. It seems much more that at first we thought.

Sun July 23rd

Terrific thunderstorms.

The revolt is outstanding. High Hun officers are the main ones including SS officers and men!! If only it can gain momentum. Keitel has been dismissed and the German workers have been called upon to strike now. The Ruskies advance on Lublin and Lemburg has gone.

Wrote a letter home.

July 24th

Nice day again.

Yesterday we were deluged with rumours. They were;

Keitel dismissed

Fighting between SS and army in S. Germany

Cease fighting in Italy

Cease fighting in France

Himmler dead

Hitler machine-gunned and killed

Army appeals to British for support against Nazis

Start fighting in Berlin, Frankfurt and Munich

5500 Hun officers arrested

Martial law in E. Prussia

German sub capitulated and crew gave 3 cheers for British navy etc, etc.

It was amazing.

July 25th

Mild again.

The Posen boys had to get out as a *panza* div took over their camp. There are now ___ efforts in camp. Lublin has gone. Brest, Litovsk and Bialystok surrounded. **Lembon** outflanked and on the road to Warsaw. The Ruskies are now 230 miles from here.

Beat the Wolves 2-1 in quite a good game. My best game of the season.

July 26th

A lovely day.

PT in the am, bar work at 11am and hockey at 1. The bar work is very good and interesting and I surprised myself.

We lost 4-0 at hockey in a good game.

Received a March 31st letter from Mum.

Thurs July 27th

A very hot day.

Bar work this am. It is very good.

Played hockey in the afternoon when we lost 3-1 to the Swallows. Garry played very badly and gave a very poor display of sportsmanship.

July 28th

A glorious day after early rain.

PT.

Everyone is getting excited over the match for the league with the Pitmen tomorrow. We are playing in the Magpies strip.

Jim told me of some of his experiences in hospital in Italy. Of the chap who went mad over food, died of starvation still holding tightly a bag containing 5 days rations.

Sat July 29th

A lovely day.

The big game ended with a win for the Pitmen of 3-1 in an excellent game. My ankle gave out 3 times and I thought the second time I would have to go off. The Pitmen thus win the league.

Our casualties were Wally Hedges, broken ankle; Smithy, broken wrist; myself, sprained ankle and pulled groin muscle.

The RAF lost 3-2 to the Bulldogs in the evening.

July 30th

Lovely morning.

Rumours that Rommel is dead; the Ruskies are outside Warsaw and advancing on Krakow.

If the Ruskies get here, the Hun are going to scram & hoist the Swiss flag over the camp thus making us neutral, according to rumour.

Terrific thunderstorm in the evening with brilliant lightening of a bright purple colour.

Joe Orvill has been caught but nothing heard of Bas.

July 31st

Reasonably nice day.

Aug 1st

Quite a nice day.

Some bar work this am. Played crib most of afternoon and evening and lost to Tommy.

Aug 2nd

Raining all day.

Bridge with Tommy. We lost over 10 rubbers to Boris and Bert Hadley.

News that Turkey has broken off diplomatic relations with Germany.

Aug 3rd

Raining all morning and thunderstorms during the afternoon.

Played crib most of the evening.

The news is very good with big advances in France and Russia; Finland on the borders of packing in; and Turkey cut off diplomatic relations with Germany.

Aug 4th

Raining and dull again.

A little chess in the morning.

The news is very good with a tremendous push in France and the Ruskies 1 km from the East Prussian border.

Bas came in today and related his experiences. The SS and Gestapo are out and out bastards. He saw 7000 Jews marched away to their deaths in the gas chambers.

Aug 5th

A glorious day.

The Russians are advancing on Krakow which brings them much nearer. We are also advancing very well in France. At night we hear tanks and AFVs *(Armoured Fighting Vehicles)* on the road below and many trains in the station etc. Bags of activity.

Quite a good boxing tournament this evening.

Aug 6th

A glorious day. Not a cloud in the sky.

The Carnival was excellent. The best were;

Things to Come

The Chinese Mandarin

Industrial Scotland (model prima)

Palestine's Noah's Ark

The whole thing was very good indeed.

Bags of activity last night again.

Was weighed today. Only 10st 2lbs meaning I have lost 20lbs in the last 12 months.

Wrote a letter home.

Aug 7th

A wonderful day again today.

In the morning we had a very exciting interlude of bombing. We <u>saw</u> some bombers on decoy and then heard lots of bombing and AA *(anti-aircraft)* for about ¼ hr over Blechhammer. Then we heard an a/c going down out of control, rattle of m/gs *(machine-guns)* and then a parachute. We don't know whether he was one of ours.

The sports was good. Wood did mile in 4 min 9 secs. Rest of the camp beat Magpies 4-1 in the evening.

VB day.

Aug 8th

Glorious morning again.

Played hockey in the morning when we lot 5-2 to the _____. It was an excellent game.

England lost by 9 wickets to NZ. They gave a very poor display.

Aug 9th

According to Dan the war should end today (June 10).

A very hot day with practically no water at all in the camp.

Lofty Marta is going into the Lazarette tomorrow with Niffritis *(sic Nephritis)*. I saw him tonight. He looks very ill.

We are advancing very well in France but the Russians seem to be reorganising.

Aug 10th

Raining in the morning and very hot and sultry rest of day.

Feeling very lethargic and have a mild dose of flu so stayed in bed all day to try and sweat it out. Imagine lying on bed boards, between rough blankets, crawling with fleas, on a hot sticky day, sweating pints, feeling greasy and sick, pains in the stomach, no water for a wash – that was me today.

Aug 11th

Very sultry again.

800 more lads from Posen.

It seems the Ruskies have stopped to reorganise. This is unfortunately giving the Huns a breathing space.

Cold much better today but still sweating profusely.

We are doing very well in France.

The water situation is very acute.

Sat Aug 12th

Very hot and sunny.

Played hockey in the morning when we lost 2-1 in a very good game to the Smugglers. I find centre half much my best position. Unfortunately, just before the end of the first half, I trod on the ball and badly twisted my weak ankle.

Saw England beat Scotland 5-1 at soccer in the evening.

Doing very well in France.

Aug 13th

Hot again.

Played my third round in the tennis tournament and beat Dennis Horne 9-7. I didn't expect to get 3 games. He is an infinitely superior tennis player. I won my first round 9-4 against Joe Byrne and 2nd won 9-0 v Hawke. Played Garry Hemmings in ¼ final and beat him 9-2.

Saw the Allies beat Wales 2-1.

Wrote a card to Rene and one to Mary.

Some rain this evening.

Mon Aug 14th

A glorious day with a highly entertaining cricket match between Australia and S Africa. After Australia's 1st and 2nd innings SA were left with 48 to knock in their 2nd innings and win the match outright. They won 1st innings. They were all out for 39 runs. I had 100 fags on Australia.

The most exciting ballgame I've seen in the *Stalag*.

Aug 15th

A lovely day again.

Bar work this am. A little cricket.

The British are closing the gap in France and there is a tremendous air offensive in progress. Recent news of a landing in S France at about 3.30pm. They landed this morning. I prophesised a landing in S France only at lunchtime today.

CT's won 3-1. No injured.

Wed Aug 16th

A glorious day again.

Beat Chris Maltley in the tennis semi-final 10-8. A very tight game. He was winning 8-7!!

The invasion of S France doing very well. They are 30kms inland with no opposition.

Chicago Bill almost admitted he was in Gestapo and SS and brought up a Count to see Cliff today. Discussing conditions.

Aug 17th

A glorious hot day.

Received 4 letters. 1 from Mrs Schofield, one from Rene and two from Mum. Bob Hunter is missing and probably dead. Tough luck.

Vera, Bob Barnes and Eileen will all probably be married shortly. Good show – the less family parties the better.

Aug 18th

A glorious hot day.

Played the tennis final and lost 9-1 to Bill Thomson. He was much too good but the score was not to the play.

British doing well in France.

Played Ned at tennis and beat him 6-3. My tennis is very much improving.

Aug 19th

Glorious hot day again.

Played Thommy tennis. Beat him 6-1 and won 40 fags. The bet was that he would not get more than 2 games.

British advancing wonderfully in France and on outskirts of Paris. Russians in Prussia.

Two years ago today I met my doom. God, how I hate that day!! And that engine!!

Sun Aug 20th

A glorious hot day.

Wrote a letter to Mary. Played 3 games tennis today. I won the first two 6-1, 11-8 and lost the last 6-2.

Aug 21st

A very hot, lovely day.

A new long-range ME 109 squadron arrived at the drome today.

PT and bars in am. Australia beat NZ in quite a good cricket match.

We are pushing hard in France. Montgomery is supposed to have said the war in France is all over, bar mopping up.

Aug 22nd

A glorious day again.

Played Jack Williams in the tennis tournament and beat him 12-10. A very good but gruelling game in blinding heat.

The Russians appear to have started their push in the South.

An air raid this am on Odatol again. 37 killed in the raid on Sunday including a Rhodesian swap from this barrack.

Aug 23rd

Very hot again today.

Bar work in the morning.

I hear that about 15 people (PoWs) were killed in the raid yesterday with many more wounded than in Sunday's raid.

Slept outside under the stars last night. Wizard. Before I went to sleep about 15 of the boys got in my bed singing etc. On the appearance of dogs a terrific panic ensued.

Thurs Aug 24th

Beautiful weather. Very hot.

An air raid warning in the morning. Heard that Romania has unconditionally surrendered to the Allies.

Got up at 5.15 to go for a walk and swim. Unfortunately about 40 of us were turned back owing to **bludgers**. Lovely at that time of day tho. Very nice and cool.

We hear that Bulgaria is trying to follow the example of Romania.

Aug 25th

A very hot day.

Played Joe Holden in my second round of the tennis and beat him 9-4. Easily my worst game to date.

An air raid warning about midday. Played soccer in the evening for the Cork Tips. We beat the Robins 4-2. I was CF and scored 1 goal.

Sat Aug 26th

Very nippy early morning but glorious throughout the day.

Another warning today.

Aug 27th

Gloriously hot again.

A big raid at about noon today. Distinctly saw about 300 bombers glinting in the sun. Pamphlets floated over the camp and much tinsel was dropped in the camp itself. Supposed to be the biggest air offensive of the war today.

Saw England beat the Allies 2-1 in the evening.

Mon Aug 28th

Very hot again.

The big thing of the day was the England v SA cricket test. SA batted first knocking 93. England knocked 107 and

SA then knocked 144 leaving England 131 to knock in 2 ½hrs.

Bob H and Laurie Page batted beautifully taking the score up to 93 for 3.

England eventually won in a very exciting finish in bad light 10mins before time. Webb finishing with a six.

Received 1 letter from Rene May 6th.

Aug 29th

At last the long expected rain came in the evening. Everyone waited for it almost with bated breath. A sigh of relief went up as it came down.

The CT's lost 4-1. Did not play owing to bad foot.

Wrote a card home and one to Mrs Schofield via the Army.

Wed Aug 30th

Nice but cloudier. Very much fresher after the rain.

Received 1 letter from Mr Dumbell and one from Rene (June 22nd).

Had severe stomach ache today.

Saw the RAF lose 4-3 to the Wolves.

Hear that Russia has refused to accept Bulgaria's neutrality; and that there is tension between England and Russia over supplies to Poland.

Aug 31st

Warm but cloudier.

The big talk today is the rumoured preparation for the

use of gas by the Germans. There was much speculation as to whether they would use it or not.

The Huns dropped a search on us this afternoon after finding a set in block 4. They are apparently also looking for men.

Fri Sept 1st

Another big search this morning with dogs etc looking for men.

News excellent. Monty a Field Marshall; fighting inside Belgium; Russians taken Bucharest etc.

Some bar work in the afternoon. Played a little tennis today but my foot is still bad.

Sept 2nd

A lovely day again today.

Saw the Bulldogs beat the Mastiffs 3-2 in the evening.

Also heard a most interesting talk by S/Mjr Tilliard of the SAF who has just returned from a 2 month visit to Genshagen.

Very poor news.

Sun Sept 3rd

Very poor day. Raining most of time.

Wrote a reproduction of Sgt Major Tilliard's talk.

Played some crib. Saw the Depot beat the Magpies 4-3.

Learnt today that 98 lads have gone haywire since the invasion started.

Very good war news today. In Belgium and on the German Ruhr border.

Sept 4th

Nice day today.

News excellent. Crossed into Holland; Finland packed in the war; rumours of risings in Norway and Greece.

Played soccer for the Weights.

Andy the PTI had a most unfortunate accident on the horizontal bar today. Doing an upward somersault he dislocated his neck. Very bad luck. The ___ hits the deck.

Tues Sept 5th

Glorious morning again.

Hear this morning that at 2 pm they were 30 miles inside Holland and that American columns have crossed the German border at two points 150kms apart.

Yesterday some bomb-happy lads were brought in from Blechhammer.

England easily beat Australia by 10 wickets today. Ferraro for Aust, D Peters and Butterworth for Eng batted very well.

Sept 6th

Glorious hot day again.

News today that the rats are leaving the sinking ship and going to Spain. It is believed that Aachen has either been entered or taken. A rumour from **Stackholk** is that the war will end within 72 hrs.

Andy is progressing very favourably. Reports left yesterday.

Sept 7th

Dull and colder this morning. Turned fine towards afternoon and evening.

Bar work again.

South Africa beat New Zealand by about 6 wickets in quite a good game. Wade and Savage batted beautifully, whilst Sibley's bowling for NZ was excellent.

The news is good altho progress in Holland, France and Belgium is slowing up, as expected, before they attack the Siegfried.

Sept 8th

Wet this morning.

Hear that we have landed in Yugoslavia and are fighting with Tito's forces. We are still mopping up the pockets in France and Belgium and massing for the big attack on the Siegfried.

Dave managed to purloin a few more lettuces from the Hun garden.

Sat Sept 9th

Fine but windy.

Played for the CT's in the morning and lost 4-0 to the Pitmen. Bar work later.

Nothing startling in the news apart from the declaration of war by Romania on Hungary and Bulgaria on Germany. Seems to be the fashion these days.

Saw England beat Wales 2-0 in the evening.

Had a big argument on the size and class of the *Prince Eugen. (Prinz Eugen – German warship)*

Sept 10th

Quite a nice morning.

No news of any importance.

The new *unteroffizier* in the compound is a typical Hun bastard. I only hope he's here when the war ends.

Wrote a letter home via the Army.

The discovery of the radio had an amusing aftermath. When the owner told the commandant he only had it to get music from Breslau the C said "I'm disgusted with you. Take it away."

Mon Sept 11th

Very cold again this am.

Today England drew at cricket with NZ after losing the 1st innings by 1 run, the last man being stupidly run out.

Played Bill Thompson in the tennis tournament and lost 9-1. My foot gets worse and worse.

Hear that the Huns are going to try and stop all sports and entertainments as part of their total war effort.

Sept 12th

Lovely day. I think we may have an Indian summer.

The British and Yanks beat the Russians to it by being the first to capture a German town. They have captured **Tries.**

Got some gen on the Sagan affair. One fellow suffering from frost bite was taken out of hospital and shot; W/C Day got home; Some were dressed as prisoners being taken to **Czechu** by others dressed as *Postens* etc. others had dinner suits, evening clothes etc.

Sept 13th

A glorious morning.

What a day. The sirens went at about 11am and at noon the a/c could be seen flying towards Blechhammer. Then we heard the bombs explode and bags of flak went up. Two a/c were seen to explode in the air. The formations, 3 in number, then came right over the camp at about 15-18th. What a sight. Fak leading 61, followed by two lots of Libs all in tight formation. In addition we saw their fighter escort. 120 bombers in all.

At last, one of my *Stalag* ambitions has been realised. It was the most majestic night I've seen since I came here.

The 1940 boys went mad.

Sept 14th

Lovely day again.

Watched quite an interesting cricket match between Australia & SA. The SA won by one wicket. Again an exciting finish, SA going into their second innings with 61 to knock. They were 58 for 9 and just made it although the last man could have been caught at 60.

Fri Sept 15th

A lovely day again.

Am becoming much more proficient on the bars. Managed the upstart quite well today.

Our forces are having a good crack at the Siegfried around Aachen.

Dave is becoming more and more temperamental which annoys me intensely altho I say nothing. I hate anyone who sulks.

Sept 16th

A glorious day.

Played for the CT's v Stragglers when we won 2-1.

Did a little bar work.

Heard an amusing story about the fellow whose face was very swollen going to the dentist, seeing him extract without gas and cocaine and stuttering that his fillings were out!!

News that we have broken through the Siegfried east of Aachen.

Sun Sept 17th

A glorious morning.

Awoke to rumours that we were moving later in the day and receiving 2 food parcels. Received a parcel per man in the afternoon. What a day for rumours.

The gen seems to be a big break through the Siegfried.

The reason for the parcels and all Red X food having to be got rid of is a Hun order 'for reasons of National Security'. They are sharing them and issuing no Hun food till the Red X has run out.

Sept 18th

A glorious day.

So they've landed two more armies in Holland.

Saw the Magpie draw with the Bulldogs last night 2-2.

Received another parcel and 100 cigs today. The cookhouse racketeers should be ok now for the rest of the Red X stuff is going there. That's a good idea as far as the meats are concerned but the rest…

Had excruciating toothache from 3pm to 12pm. It was terrible. I thought I should go mad.

Sept 19th

Toothache better when I woke up.

Played soccer for the CT's v The Dodgers. The ref stopped the game just before half time as he couldn't see!! We were winning 1-0 against the wind.

The news is very good indeed.

I have decided that a diary should be not so much a collection of events but a record of thoughts, impressions and moods. This I have tried to do when my mood is anything other than normal.

Sept 20th

A lovely day altho windy and dusty.

Alan saw the Aussie in block IV. A tragic penalty for indiscretion. Apparently, he gave away the Dutch people who sheltered him and his conscience has driven him completely mad. He wouldn't believe Alan and Mac Currie were Aussies but told them they were Germans.

Received a 200 Players parcel today. One of 20 in camp!!

Had a letter from Mary (May 1st) and one from Rene (May 1st). Stan's 34th birthday today.

Sept 21st

A lovely day again.

Yesterday the Hun walked up to the tunnel without warning. It was given away by some bastard.

Today was the first day of the big game SA & Eng v NZ & Aus. The 1st innings was a draw 162 runs each, Wade knocking a glorious 76 not out. In the second innings Wade and De Freytas put on a 100 partnership, the first in camp and at close of play were 47 and 46 not out respectively.

Sept 22nd

Colder this am.

Received a 200 SS parcel today. Apparently it had been to Luft 6.

Watched the end of the cricket match. England won. Wade knocked 60 and De Freytas 68 in the second innings. Beautiful batting.

Did some bar work in the evening.

Received some news of rises in pay and demobbing plans.

The airborne troops in Holland are having a tough time.

Sat Sept 23rd

Nice day again.

Bars in the am.

The gen is we are getting an extra 2/- a day and we do not come under the demobbing plans till we are 25 so I shall have at least another 3 years in the service. Extra pay for Far East service.

We had a search in the afternoon when the Huns took 15 wireless sets from 15B who were taken by surprise. The rest were luckier.

Sept 24th

Rain during the night freshened the air considerably.

Wrote a letter home and a card to Mary via the Army.

Watched England beat Scotland 4-2 in a poor game in the evening. Did some bar work.

The airborne troops in Holland are having a very tough time but the position seems more hopeful.

Sept 25th

Raining this am.

Last night witnessed a very amusing booze-up which ended with a nauseating exhibition by Oscar Powers. After keeping us amused for some time he was sick over 3 other people's beds and finally moved his bowels in the middle of the barrack. It was disgusting.

Played soccer for the CT's v The Dodgers. We lost 3-1 in a good game.

The airborne troops seem to have had a bad mauling.

Sept 26th

A sharp but sunny morning.

Saw today another typical example of Hun hot-headedness. From what I made out a fellow tried to run off a working party. He was stopped by the shout of the guard and rattle of the rifle bolt. The guard went berserk, pointed the loaded rifle at his heart then bashed him over the head with the butt twice and whizzed him off to the boot. He was white as a sheet – who wouldn't be.

Wed Sept 27th

Quite a nice day.

Played soccer for the CT's v the Gangsters. We lost 5-1. Our defence was like a colander. We are suffering considerably from casualties and unfitness.

Wrote a card to Stan via the Army. Had a good sesh (*session*) on the bars today.

Apparently the Huns are looking for a bloke who bashed a guard with orders to shoot him on sight!

Sept 28th

Cold today and overcast.

Played hockey in the am when we drew 1-1. Afterwards did some bar work. Did not see very much of the day's cricket.

How I wish this war would end as for one reason, I find I dislike Dave more every day. He is unbearable in his egotism.

Hear that some airborne troops have been withdrawn from the S bank of the Rhine. Has it the Dardanelles touch??

Fri Sept 29th

Very cold today.

The cricket match ended with a win by 4 wickets and 2 runs for Australia. Ferraro batted extremely well in the 2nd innings to make 76.

By what we hear of Winnie's speech we shall be here over Xmas. It was not very encouraging. The boys are not a little disappointed.

A good bar morning. I wish I could dispense with this obsession about my eyes.

Sept 30th

The evenings and mornings are becoming very cold. The winter seems to be making an early approach.

Today, by order of the Huns, the compound had a big clean up. Probably because they wanted to look for tunnels and radios etc.

Saw the RAF draw with the Mastiffs 2-2. A good game. The news is still unentertaining but maybe next week is the big week.

The Huns loudly acclaim the paratroops of Holland.

Sun Oct 1st

Cold again.

Bar work.

Hear that the big attack has started.

Wrote a card to Dad and one to Aunt Kate and Uncle John both via the Army.

Watched some football in the evening when once again the Welshmen displayed their total lack of sportsmanship.

There is not much news of any importance.

Wet during the afternoon. My bets with Stan cancelled out today.

Oct 2nd

A dull, dark, cold, wet, miserable day.

I can hardly think of words to describe these conditions as the epitome of *Stalag* misery. Nothing to do, nowhere to go, cold and wet.

Fortunately, our tendency to *Stalag* idiosyncrasies help to keep us reasonably cheerful.

Played an amusing game of bridge in the evening.

We are hoping the attack may have started.

Oct 3rd

Very cold and wet.

Last night, since the wind and rain blew in our window (?) cardboard and wood was fixed in. Consequently, the barrack was as near the Black Hole as ever. Pools of water lay on the floor beneath each window and everywhere was damp and bitterly cold.

The order of the day was back to bed after breakfast (one slice of bread and a cup of tea). 11am tea and 2 slices of bread and then a couple of hours on the parallel bars. 3pm coffee, spuds and M&V.

The personal parcels have arrived just in time.

Oct 4th

Much nicer this morning.

Out of 3 successive lots of Sagan mail I haven't received a letter.

The Huns kept us on parole this morning until someone returned the *Feldwebel's* windows!!

Alex and I whizzed through the wire down to Ken's place.

Recently I have been afflicted with an appallingly large appetite. Unfortunately supply does not adequately cope with demand.

I see that the Civil Service is offering quite good opportunities for air servicemen straight from school.

Thurs Oct 5th

Quite a nice day today.

Last night Bill Russell was most amusing when pulling our mad Kiwi's leg. His mimic of a cockney is excellent. The Kiwi has an obsession for gongs *(awards)*. Bill told him he won the DSO and HM in the last war and is bringing up some photos of '*Journey's End*' tonight to show him.

Hear that we have landed in force in Greece.

The RAF lost 4-1 to the Navy 8-a-side today.

See that the birds are in the final stages of congregation preparatory to migration.

Oct 6th

Cold and dull.

I am convinced that this war is a big political wrangle and naturally as a PoW I feel that I belong to the aggrieved party.

What with the seemingly unnecessary landing in Greece, the affair over Poland and Warsaw etc, etc.

The news indicates that the fighting is speeding up all round and not before time if the war is to be over by Xmas.

Oct 7th

A hot sunny day.

Good bar work. A very exciting day. Watched the finest display of soccer I've seen in camp when England beat the Allies 4-2.

A little luck in the evening when Ron and I bid our first Grand Slam NT *(no trumps)* which Ron played. The game was interrupted by a terrific explosion and then all lights and blowers etc were put out. An air raid was in progress and either a bomb had been dropped or an aircraft gone in just outside the camp. There was quite a lot of panic especially in the theatre where, on boxers night, they fought their way out.

Watched the flak, gun-flashes and flares over Breslau way and Blechhammer. Two fellows got down the sewage hole!! Two ME's went in earlier in the day. All highly exciting.

Oct 8th

A dull morning after the night's fun.

We are supposed to have broken through the Siegfried and had 7000 a/c over Germany yesterday.

Wrote a stupid letter to Mary.

It appears that the a/c last night were Russian. I was told that 14 blokes went crazy and had to be taken to hospital. Others passed out and had to have injections etc.

Saw Wales beat Scotland 1-0.

The warning and lights went out again this evening but it was a false alarm.

Mon Oct 9th

Raining all morning.

The Ruskies have started another offensive in Lithuania.

Cliff's brother is having a marvellous time in Bahamas and Bermuda, holidays in New York, Washington etc now in Mexico.

Received a May letter from Mum. A little bridge in the evening when I bid and got another Grand Slam - my second this season. Bar work again.

Quite amusing when Bob came up in the evening. Cliff was in hysterics.

Oct 10th

Dull, wet morning.

Was first down to see the letter on Civil Aviation. It was quite encouraging and I have decided to embark on quite an extensive programme of work in preparation.

A very pleasant stroll round with Alan in the evening.

Oct 11th

A mild day again.

Played soccer for the Ct's v the Shamrocks in the am. Our best game yet and no one minded losing 2-1. Very hard and fast.

Bob heard that my card to Jean Henderson got through. Some bridge in the evening.

Oct 12th

Quite a nice day.

Received 200 Greys. A good bar morning.

I wonder why the Huns are attaching so much importance to Oct 15th. Everything seems to be either starting or finishing by that date.

Sent a remittance of all outstanding credits home.

Went on a stroll in the evening with Bob.

Fri Oct 13th

Mild day again. Warming at midday.

Heard of conditions in the Russian lager. There is a closed TB barrack where the TB cases go till they become open cases when they spit blood etc and are put in an open TB barrack. There they die and are then carted to a trench and buried 5 deep. The death toll is tremendous.

Very little grub. Another bloke went mad today.

No news of any importance. I certainly don't think the war will end this year.

Oct 14th

A nice day again.

Played for the Battlers v the Dam when we won 3-1.

An air raid warning at noon. Saw fighters streaking across the sky and 4-engined a/c probably Fortresses flew over in very tight formation. About 300. Saw one go down.

At night a bloke was shot dead trying to get over the wire. The chap who hit the Jerry.

A little bridge in the evening.

Rumours that we are going to get ⅟₇ of a parcel a day.

Sun Oct 15th

Mild again.

Wrote a card home and a card to Marjorie via the Army. I made the address in the card home pretty plain.

An air raid warning in the evening. A little bridge. Saw the Magpies beat the Mastiffs 3-0.

Hear that the Huns are going to open all the tins in the parcel issue. The war in the Far East seems to be increasing in intensity.

Did a little bar work today.

Oct 16th

A sunny but cold morning.

Some bar work. A little bridge in the evening when we were once again interrupted twice by air raid warnings. Nothing happened altho flak could be seen over Blechhammer way. They seem to be getting regular occurrences nowadays.

No news of any import except that the Huns have lost two good men. Field Marshall Rommell and Lieutenant Colonel Helmut Lent.

Oct 17th

Cold today.

Air raid warning at noon which stopped our hockey which

we were winning 3-0. We saw through ⁹/₁₀ cloud some fighters and bombers dead overhead.

Received 1 letter from mum, one from Aunt Maggie and one Mary. Nothing of importance.

Played a little bridge in the evening.

There are indications that the Jap war may last till the end of 1947 and even into 1948.

Oct 18th

Cold but not too bad.

Played soccer for the CT's v the Gremlins and lost 4-2. I was disgusted with the forwards.

Played a little bridge in the evening.

No news of any importance whatsoever. Received 2 more letters both from mum, one August and one Sept. I now have 1 April, 1 May, 4 June, 4 July and 3 August letters missing.

Thurs Oct 19th

Raining all night but mild this am.

I have a slight head cold.

Reports that there is going to be a stricter check on incoming and outgoing RAF mail.

There is news that the Ruskies have broken through in the Hungary Check (*Czech*) Slovak area.

Played soccer for the CT's at CF when we beat the Slaphappies 3-0 in a good game. Good tumbling around with Cyril.

Oct 20th

Cold and wet.

My boots are in a terrible state. Some bar work this am.

Received my July 27 clothing parcel. Mostly chocolate. Good tho. In the evening received 9 letters. No news of any importance.

The Huns have massacred a large number of people in Poland.

Hear that Andy the Kiwi has been killed. That leaves only Evan.

Sat Oct 21st

A cold wet day.

Received a 200 Greys parcel. I don't like these Greys a bit.

The news today is excellent. Hear that we have some Hun celebrities in camp. An international soccer player, a trumpeter who was with Jack Hylton for 3 years and one of the best baritones in Germany.

Tennessee was very amusing this evening after his dose of jungle juice. He doesn't like to be associated with Yanks. He is a Rebel!!

Oct 22nd

Cold and wet.

An excellent night's sleep last night.

This morning Vey tried to commit suicide for the 2nd time in 48 hrs. The first time by rope attached to goal post, the second in the pool.

A fellow was shot dead on the doorstep today when trying to run away from guards taking him to strafe. I saw the Hun shoot and then saw the fellow afterwards.

Wrote a letter home today.

He was the fellow they were told to shoot on sight.

Mon Oct 23ʳᵈ

Foggy, wet and cold again.

An amusing side issue on yesterdays attempted suicide. Vey was in his pyjamas and a passer-by said "Go on, you b…. fool, jump in" and he did!

The Yanks landing on the Philippines seem to be making good progress and the Balkans are getting very quickly liberated.

Played bridge in the evening with Alan in 7-10. We won by 3700 over five rubbers.

Oct 24ᵗʰ

Foggy and cold again.

Received a 200 Greys parcel. Read George's letter to Danny. Very good. He seems to have had a good journey back and the RAF certainly got cracking when he arrived in England. He was home within 3 day of landing.

Did some bar work today.

Sun Oct 29ᵗʰ

Cold and wet again.

I must admit that living (nay, existing) in the dank misery of a cold, dark, damp barrack I have a secret dread of the coming hungry, winter. It is with a great effort that we manage to keep cheerful but surely that is part of the British temperament. I now know the real meaning of the words 'cheerful in adversity'.

Oct 30th

Very cold and dull again.

I have just finished reading '*This Above All Vol I*'. I feel incapable of doing anything but think about it. A truly marvellous book and even from my limited experience I realise it's very true. I haven't been so deeply moved for a long, long time.

Played a little bridge in the evening with Alan.

There isn't much news of importance nowadays.

Oct 31st

Cold and wet again.

Sent off my cards to Mum and Mary via the Army. I don't know whether they'll get through. There seems to have been a bit of a purge on.

Played for the CT's v the Palace. We won 2-1 but should have lost.

Churchill says the war may go on for another 7-9 months. God forbid!

Nov 1st

Cold and wet again. We seem to be having an early winter this year.

Dave may have to go into hospital for an operation.

Finished *'This Above All'*. Excellent.

We seem to have cleared Greece up quickly. The Swastikas have definitely been wiped off the aircraft and the flag no longer flies. Eddie was telling us of the time in France when the officer told him not to fire at a/c till the RE's fired. They had gone 2 days.

Thur Nov 2nd

Wet but milder.

Received a book parcel *'The Square Peg'*. I suspect a subtle innuendo.

When Col. Crawford and RSM Goodey made their inspection the other day, a chap was hammering heartily on our window when he should have been quiet. Goodey innately asked him what he was doing. He contemptuously turned around and said "I'm not exactly waiting for a bus. ….. off!"

Received 2 letters 1 Mum, 1 Mary. Had a chat with Ken Ainsworth in the evening.

Nov 3rd

Wet and not too warm.

Dave is in bed with stomach trouble.

Very dark and dreary most of the day.

Played bridge in the evening and Thommy and I beat Alex and Cliff by 5000 pts over 10 rubbers. Some of the rubbers were played by candle light as the fuses continually go. In one hand T & I had 13 hearts between us. I had AKQxxx he had the rest.

Very good news. Intense air bombing going on.

I think the war should end somewhere about this date
(June 15)

Nov 4th

A lovely morning. Bright and sunny altho a little cold.

It looks as tho my prophesy above is very, very much out.

Received 200 Greys from the W. PoW Club. Also 3 letters
(2 Mum, 1 Rene).

Nothing of very great importance in the news except that
the air war is reaching stupendous heights.

Played bridge in the evening with Alex against Marty and
Gordon.

Mac has asked me onto an advisory committee for a series
of lectures for the winter.

Nov 5th

Quite a nice day.

Wrote a letter home and sent it this time via the RAF.

Watched a good soccer match England v the Rest. England
won 2-0. There was some delightful football.

The air war is reaching tremendous proportions. Hear that
FM Sir John Dill is dead. The Ruskies are almost in Budapest.

Mon Nov 6th

A glorious, sunny and quite mild day.

Rumours that 80,000 more food parcels are in and that we
are going on to a full parcel again.

In my last letter Rene tells me Norman Smith is dead and
Foggy wounded.

500 new chaps came in today. All captured about a month ago in Italy. They had very rough treatment from the Hun and were forced to clear away bomb damage, lay railway lines etc at Munich. They had 2 drinks on a 5 day rail journey here and practically no food.

Nov 7th

Very, very cold and wet.

Some of the new chaps fainted (one was out for 20mins) when they had a cigarette. One asked a fellow where he was captured and when told Dunkirk, said "Ok, the teacher told us about that at school"!! Exit Dunkirkiam. *(sic)*

Did a little bar work today. No news today as the effort is under repairs.

Wed Nov 8th

Very cold and wet.

Stayed in bed all morning. In the evening played a little bridge with my new partner Alan Tonkin. He is improving with every game and given practice should make a good player.

The news remains pretty stationary nowadays. We have almost cleared the Schelt estuary which, when completed, should hasten things up somewhat. I believe we have had pretty heavy casualties in Holland.

Nov 9th

Very cold all day. I think we shall have snow in the near future. Wet.

Our new blower stove was fixed in. A super effort. All we need now is some fuel!! Our coal issue from the good kind Germans works out at ¼ of a bucket per man per week!! A bucket is 6 in long, 2 ½ in wide and 2 in deep. So we should keep very warm.

Some more bridge in the evening.

Fri Nov 10th

Very, very cold and our first snow this morn.

Rumours that we are going on to a quarter (¼!!!) of a parcel next week.

Received a book today.

We hear in the news (not without some little trepidation) that the Russian Prime Minister and Government have resigned.

Heard of the use by the Hun of the V2 reaching the tremendous height of 60 to 70 miles and having a speed greater than that of sound.

Nov 11th

Very, very cold, wet and a little snow.

The barrack was very dark all day.

In the evening we had a lecture (the first of a series of 26) by Capt Knowles on Birth Control. An excellent lecture, humorous without being crude and very instructive. Something we all should have been told years ago either at home or school.

Arguing most of the day on the V2 whether a rocket would work in a vacuum.

Sun Nov 12th

A nippy but nice sunny morning.

Since Hitler did not make his customary Munich Speech rather strengthens the death theory.

Yesterday we observed the 2mins Nov 11th silence.

Turned extremely cold in the afternoon. It is much colder than when this time last year or the year before.

Some competition bridge in the evening. We are 2400 down last rubber to play. We can't pick up any cards at all.

Sent a card to Aunt Maggie and a card home via the RAF.

Nov 13th

Cold again but dryer.

Moving rumours are cropping up again. A Hun *feldwebel* is willing to bet 200 fags to a ducking in the pond that there is a move of some sort within 10 days.

Churchill has as good as said that France is to be a buffer state after the war. The SS are taking over the administration of the camp tomorrow.

Lost in the bridge match after a valiant struggle against brilliant cards.

Nov 14th

Extremely cold. I was shivering the whole of the day.

In the evening we received report that there were 550 Gestapo in British uniform in Lager 2.

The Hun have standing jokes; 1. That every member of the RAF compound has a bed lamp; 2. That all the time he's been here, Mr Sherriff has only had one argument with the Huns - that was about his personal supply of coal.

A little bridge when we got excellent cards.

Wed Nov 15th

A little warmer and snowing.

I hear some very disparaging reports of the fighting qualities of the Yanks.

Today I did my long postponed washing. A horrible job. No wonder laundries thrive.

There have been no developments from the SS as yet. There is no news of any importance. Bridge in the evening when again Alan and I got wonderful cards.

Nov 16th

Cold again and very windy but since it was dry I managed to get my washing dried ok without hanging it in our *'Mr Wu's Paradise'*.

The moving rumours are that all prisoners taken before Aug 1st 1941 are to go to Sweden; German prisoners (in the ratio of 85000 to 40000) *(sic)* to go to Turkey.

Just when I wanted to finish off a book I was forced to listen to anecdotes. I still find it hard to be callously rude but wouldn't that be more honest?

Nov 17th

Cold and wet.

A day of the best news since the opening of the second front. The news of the opening of a range of offensive on the Western Front. People are again beginning to think that it may yet be all over by Xmas.

It is a good thing that the news is getting brighter again for we are running mighty short of food.

Some more bridge in the evening when we won again.

Sat Nov 18th

Cold but dry again.

I see in the Hun papers that the Kamikaze squadrons have been at it again against our shipping. They seem to be quite formidable.

Thommy & I were partners in a partner whist drive. Very enjoyable. We had moderate hands and scored 165pts in 24 hands, the winners scoring 183. A good change from bridge.

There was a smash and grab in 38 where the lights suddenly fused and when they came up again, two of Scott's cases were pinched. A pity such bastards can't stay here the rest of their lives.

Nov 19th

A lovely warm day. I have never experienced such rapid changes in weather conditions from one extreme to the other. Let no one moan about changeable England.

Wrote a letter to Mary mainly philosophy. Via the RAF again.

Saw the RAF and Navy lose 2-0 to an Army team. Very poor game.

Alan & I won in 7-10 by 5000pts again.

Excellent news.

Mon Nov 20th

Mild again.

I feel I must write something. I have been thinking of what my future is to be. I find it takes, from me at any rate, more courage to face the realities of the life ahead of me than to face a battery of flak or a squadron of *Focke-Wulfs*. That is a courage born of desperation, of exhilarating excitement, of self-preservation; the other needs a much deeper courage – calm, pre-meditated, decisive, enduring. One can laugh <u>with</u> life, but a fool is he who laughs <u>at</u> life.

Yanks over again today. Saw two a/c go down. One blew up and the other went down in flames.

Nov 21st

Quite mild today.

I have thought a lot recently of the philosophy of life. My mind is full of conflicting ideas of conventionalities which have been bred and instilled into me; of morals, religion, justice. I pray for the day when I can have a quiet moment by myself, when I can really sort out my confused brain. I only hope and pray I shall not disappoint Mum and Dad.

Played a very poor game soccer for the Battlers when we lost 3-1 in a putrid game.

Won again at bridge in the evening against Bert Farmer and partner with their new loser system.

Nov 22nd

Quite mild.

Spent most of the day trying to solve the ladder problem. In the end I gave it up after arriving at most complicated expressions for x & y.

Bridge in the evening when we won once again against better cards.

The attack in France seems to be slowing up slightly. Let's hope it doesn't stop altogether.

I have come to the conclusion that Anthony, the subject of the book I am reading, is a lazy, spoilt, dissipated, conceited, extravagant pug.

Nov 23rd

Wet and a little colder again.

Received 2 letters today, one from Rene and one from Molly T. both Aug letters. Molly T writes an increasingly intelligent letter and I now imagine her to be quite vivacious. She has a good style.

We tried to have a whist drive this evening but after 10 hands the lights were fused for the rest of the evening. This has become so much of a common occurrence that we have got beyond the 'used to it' stage and are demanding some action.

Fri Nov 24th

A day of wind, wet and a little sunshine.

We have taken Strasbourg and have supposed to have crossed the Rhine there.

Played some bridge in the evening when Cliff and I beat Alex and Ken. The Hun replaced our fuse without any argument at all which is, I think, a calculated gesture!

Dave is most amusing with his friendships. One week he is the deadly enemy of someone and the next they are the best of friends and Dave can't say a bad word about him but goes out of his way to cultivate his friendship.

Nov 25th

Quite mild again.

Today we start on the no food parcel era. It has been suggested that instead of the Red X we will maybe have to inaugurate the organisation of the White X?!?! Efforts are being made to get 90000 parcels here.

Heard a lecture by a fellow called Backelandte, a Belgian. This quite interesting lecture was on Belgium.

News at the moment in the camp is very confusing. Hear that Tito's forces have crossed into Austria.

Sun Nov 26th

Quite a nice day, very sunny altho a little cold. A good day for flying.

In the evening Alan and I received our first licking for a long time at the hands of Alex and Cliff. There were some very interesting hands out. I again had brain fog after the session!

No news of any importance. The attack seems to be making steady progress.

I am very interested in the biography of Conan Doyle. My choice of books is flying books, war stories and biographies.

Nov 27th

A glorious day. A sharp frost during the night and early morning, afterwards turned to bright sunshine. Quite warm in the sun with a cloudless sky.

Alan and I fixed up another pane in the window.

Received a July letter from Mary.

Hear that there is a tremendous air offensive on.

Finished off the Conan Doyle book in the evening.

Nov 28th

Very cold, sunny after morning fog and freezing hard all day.

Received a 200 Greys parcel today.

We hear that astronomers have prophesised the hardest winter for 100 years. Heaven help us! Maybe he was an astrologer!! It's certainly making an early start anyway.

Rumours that there may be some sort of a Red X issue late this week.

Played bridge in the evening against Gordon and Monty. Again we got a licking. Alan is a typical Aussie, a brilliant victor, but wicked loser!

Nov 29th

Very, very cold again and freezing hard.

Was busy most of the day making a cupboard. Rather ironic I should do this when we have nothing to put in it!!

Bas and I argued with Dave over man's object in life. What is it? He has some very peculiar and I think fallacious ideas. We stumped him at almost every turn.

We had a most enjoyable little band concert in the evening.

Thurs Nov 30th

Very cold and freezing.

We were remarking today on the fact that there is no flying whatsoever from the drome here, very few a/c about at all altho the weather has been admirable for it. It looks rather significant.

Working parties are now unable to get sacks of bread or any food from the civvies they are so short themselves. And they work 12hrs per day on it!! Hear that the Russians have started a full-scale offensive south of Budapest and are advancing well towards Vienna. Maybe they will out-flank us.

Finished the locker.

Dec 1st

Extremely cold.

Once again the sight of men searching out thrown-out potato peelings for bits of spud is in evidence. They are mainly the new prisoners from Italy. It is, I fear, inevitable in a way, but oh! how low will men stoop when they are hungry – and they must be really hungry!!

I very much enjoy conversations with Bas. To compare Bas with Dave is to compare intelligence with inanity.

An entertaining whist drive in the evening when I never picked up such an atrocious run of cards. I was booby, but no prize.

Big raid today. I estimate over 500 a/c. The bombers came, in beautiful formation directly over the camp to Breslau. The Blechhammer crowd were badly split up by flak.

Dec 2nd

Very cold, but sunny.

I forgot to mention that on 23rd Nov, I saw a Daily Mail of 24th Sept 1944. Very impressive. I could have sat down and read the thing from end to end including the adverts!! But I'm beginning to wonder whose propaganda is the most ineffective. The Huns certainly make their people think over theirs but ours is so childish and ridiculous that a kid wouldn't be convinced. Who's ever heard of Hun generals digging trenches! Even an *unteroffizier* wouldn't do that!

Owing to so many spuds being stolen by the racketeers etc and complaints being made, the Huns have decided to weigh all spud issues and give us the correct weight which means less than we've ever had. Poetic justice!

Dec 3rd

Very cold wind.

Dad's birthday today. I wonder if he's remembered it himself.

Last night we had quite an interesting lecture on Technocracy – the age of potential plenty. It means the science of the control of industry and planned economy for the good of mankind. I could not agree with the speaker, who was one of the New Britain organisation in its infancy, because he seemed to dissociate internal with external politics. I cannot conceive that any single country today can regard itself as a self-supporting entity.

Had to stand down below today for being late on parade.

The laundry and tin shed were burnt down yesterday.

Mon Dec 4th

Cold again.

Wrote a letter to Dad yesterday.

The first reports of the raid on Blechhammer on Sat reveal that a bomb landed on a shelter killing 26 of our boys. More casualties are expected. What a tragic end, to be killed by your own men, after being a prisoner for 4 years. I feel deeply grieved for their families.

We hear that there are riots and disturbances everywhere. First France, then Belgium now Greece (more serious). Always it seems to be the Left Wing element. I am afraid I am rather pessimistic about the future of world politics after the war.

Some bridge in the evening when Cliff and I beat Alex and Ken.

Some rain today.

Dec 5th

Cool but fine.

According to the news the boys in Italy and on the Western Front are to be given leave according to a systematic plan. It seems obvious to me that the plan is to increase the birth-rate as much as possible!!

Lofty picked up a hand last night; Diamonds A, K, Q, J, 10, 8, 4, Spades A, Hearts A, K, Q, J, 8. He opened Grand Slam D. His partner had 3 D's and 10 of Hearts!! An ambition realised. Some bridge in the evening when Alan and I beat Jim and Cyril by over 1000 points.

The affair in Greece seems quite serious and the Japs are doing too well in China.

Wed Dec 6th

A glorious morning; frosty, but sunny.

I have been checking over the grub stakes and at the present rate we have got egg flakes, porridge and fruit to last us about 33 days which isn't at all bad.

Apparently, the coal mines are cluttered up with coal at the pithead and the sugar beet factories are packed out with sugar, the Huns having no transport to get the stuff away.

The situation in Athens seems very serious.

Everyone is rather melancholy about the war which seems fraught with political differences. At this rate it could go on a long, long time. We are making the appearance of fighting stubbornly in the West whereas really I think we could go through in no time if we wished to.

Dec 7th

Nice morning again, but cold.

I am reading a book on spiritualism by Sir Oliver Lodge. I find that when reading any deep book on religion, philosophy etc I can only read a little at a time, to really appreciate and try to understand it.

We have been inundated with rumours about Red X parcels lately, all of which are unfounded.

Played bridge in the evening against Jim and Cyril when we easily beat them by 4000 pts.

Bill Russell almost convinced me tonight that it would be a good thing to go in for farming after the war. I don't know.

Fri Dec 8th

Very cold wind in the am which dropped at midday whereupon it was warm, heralding snow or rain. Actually it rained and the air was sweet afterwards and a treat to breathe.

Mr Lowe has received a note from Geneva informing him that we are now off the ½ parcel standard. How true!! We are – right off!!!

The Hun are asking women to volunteer for operational work. Surely this is their last resort.

We are supposed to be going on to no jam, ½ marg, less spuds and ¼ loaf bread at the New Year.

Bridge in evening when we lost to Alex & Cliff by 100 over five rubbers in the first league game. Result 1 ½ - 1.

Dec 9th

Wet, snowing and quite cold. It cleared up about midday. I am very interested in the weather because I believe it has a substantial effect on military operations.

There seem to be definite indications that some Red X supplies are in the offing.

Listened to a very good tho' short lecture by Leo Krasnakowski on the Foreign Legion. He gave a true picture as he saw it having been in for 15 years. He was almost a fully qualified doctor in White Russia before he joined. He didn't say why he joined. No one does!!

Sun Dec 10th

After a sharp night frost it was quite a decent but very cold day.

Wrote a card to Mary and one to Norman Steele. I wonder if I've made another correspondental *(sic)* error!!

We seem to be battering hard on the Western Front and the Russians appear to have made another break through.

Played Gordon & Monty in the evening when we lost after some most peculiar but interesting hands. They seem to be our hoodoo.

I hear that the boys at Blechhammer are in a terrible state due to the bombing.

Dec 11th

A glorious day, frosty but very sunny.

Did a spell of air-raid trench digging in the morning. Quite enjoyable.

Later did a huge amount of washing. 2 prs pyjamas, 3 shirts, 2 towels, 4 hankies, 1 pr underpants, 2 vests and a woollen pullover. I was very tired at the end of the day. I imagine the food – or lack of it – has a big effect.

Another Roy Gilbert crack. With the digging in view he said today's call was "NO BED", "ONE SPADE". *(A bridge reference.)*

Tues Dec 12th

Windy and cold.

Put my washing out.

A/c over again today.

Had argument with Dave over the relative merits of Tractors, hired and bought, v horses. I'm afraid if I go in for farming I shall be rather revolutionary.

In the evening we played Thommy & Lofty in the competition and won 1½ - 0.

Alan seems to have reached a certain stage where his bidding, leading and playing has improved 100% but he cannot concentrate sufficiently to appreciate the fine value of a hand. Maybe with practice.

Dec 13th

A miserable day. Wet and drizzling. Unable to get my washing properly dry.

Dave last night managed to get a loaf for a bar of York chocolate and 40 fags. Not bad.

In the evening we had a very entertaining whist drive (practice). I partnered Tommy and we were leading two hands from the end but in the last two hands got 5 tricks each.

Winners 148 next 147 we 146. We had a tough fight all evening. One grand slam.

Thurs Dec 14th

A miserable morning again. Wet and drizzle.

I see in the papers Erich Hartmann has shot down (?) 318 a/c.

News of a Red X issue on 19th (½), 23rd (½), or 30th (½) if they come in!!

Rumours of a break through on the W.F. Tunnel.

Very cold this evening which may herald some snow.

I have decided to send home a sort of questionnaire with regard to the future of farming and my special relationships towards it. I really can't make up my mind what to do in the future.

Dec 15th

A terrible day. Awoke to find about 3-4 inches snow and snowing most of the day.

An argument today on the merits of the Public School (boarding) v Home Life. I strongly support home life up to the age of 13 or 14. Then boarding school.

5000 parcels (Can) came in without warning from Sweden.

Bridge in the evening when Alan played much better. We beat Bert and Tom.

Sat Dec 16th

A glorious day. Frosty, snow on the ground but bright sunshine!

Rumours that another 26,000 parcels are on the way from Sweden.

Bob's letter to the Windmill has at last borne fruit – a photograph of 'Veronica'. Hot stuff!!

A very interesting lecture in the evening on '*The Psychology of Crime.*' He tried to avoid the harder technicalities and present a lecture intelligible to the layman and he succeeded.

These lectures are receiving very poor support from the boys. Some people must think they are <u>very</u> well informed.

Dec 17th

Gloriously sunny. 9 below 0!

If only I could concentrate. I find when reading any technical book or book requiring much thought that I can concentrate for a few paragraphs and then my mind wanders and I suddenly find that I've read two or three more without the slightest idea of what I've read. There are so many mental distractions.

A big raid today. Saw 3 a/c come down two by fighters 1 by flak. There was plenty of fighter activity, 5 lads bailed out.

Alan & I beat Stan & Bob 10-1 in the league. A great improvement from Alan.

Dec 18th

Two of the chaps that we saw bale out yesterday were frozen dead when they reached the deck. They were 32 minus in air.

Freezing hard but gloriously sunny.

Wrote a letter home yesterday re farming in the future.

A raid again today. The finest sight we've seen yet. The formation of bombing crossed over each other immediately over the camp and above them, making distinct vapour trails, were the fighter escort, weaving over and around them. A glorious sight. Leaflets and tinsel landed in the camp. The leaflets said the biggest attacks on the Western Front were starting today. Let's hope it's true.

We hear that the Huns have made a big counter attack in S Belgium and have pushed the Yanks back 45kms on a 60km front. Which I don't believe.

Dec 19th

Cold and not sunny.

I have been thinking of various parting regrets I have had at various times and wonder if the parting regret, this strange reluctance at leaving ancient tradition to accept our new inheritance, our new assignments is a relic of Old England. I fear so.

Played some bridge in the evening when I've never played against such bad bridge for a long time. They were constantly underbidding and missed at least one Grand Slam. But still manage to be 3000 up after 4 rubbers.

Hear that the position on the W Front is serious.

Today we got ½ Canadian parcel per man. What jubilation. We certainly appreciate the parcels especially after being without for so long.

Wed Dec 20th

Bitterly cold, foggy and frosty.

We went on parade at 7.00am and didn't get off parade till 12.00am. The Hun made the most secret and systematic search yet. Lots of guards about. They were looking for the fellows hiding up. Eric was recognised and taken away unfortunately. We had nothing to eat or drink. Chaps were fainting right and left. It was terrible.

The worst day we've had for a long time and then there were no spuds, bread or soup up.

Hoch II was out till 5.00 pm. We managed to get some news over to them. 35 lads were taken away of whom about 11 were wanted.

9 chaps got into a hole, in one barrack, made for 2 men. Just as the Huns were going out of the barrack one fellow screamed with hysterics. 5 gave themselves up but 4 stayed in and got away with it.

The long-term men got caught. They were all almost suffocated.

Dec 21ˢᵗ

<u>Bitterly</u> cold altho' a cloudless sky, freezing very hard.

We thought we were due for another stand out this morning but it fortunately didn't materialise.

Hear that the position on the W Front is still serious but we have conflicting reports at the moment.

The Huns got much wireless equipment etc and of course, their usual quota of tobacco, fags and chocolate. The bastards.

Received three letters from home and learn that Humphrey has been killed on the Western Front in a lousy accident. Very tough luck, but once again the fortunes of war. That leaves me the last surviving member of the family still alive in the services.

According to reports the Huns got 22 hide-ups out of 37 suspects. Not a bad haul.

Played Pete & Eric in the evening and won 9½ - 0. Lost to Jim & Cyril by 6-0.

Dec 22ⁿᵈ

Very cold but I think we shall have more snow as soon as the weather gets a little warmer.

I hear that the chap the Huns beat up in Block II died yesterday afternoon.

I waited for 2½ hrs in the freezing cold today to get a shower and then couldn't get one.

There are tremendous arguments going on about the Jerry offensive on the W Front. I think we have made a mistake in underestimating Jerry. He has taken advantage of it and realises that if this push is a success, he will be able to prolong the war and perhaps get a negotiated peace or hope for a split in the Allies, but if it fails then Germany is lost anyway.

It is a do or die effort.

I refuse to believe as Bob, Bill and Dave, that it is a trap on our part and we are luring the Hun in. Do they think they are more intelligent or better tacticians than some of the finest German military brains?

Dec 23rd

Extremely cold again. I estimate the temperature is well below 0 F *(-17C)*. Altho there are cloudless skies, my feet haven't been warm all day and to walk around is to court disaster in the shape of a gargantuan appetite.

Managed to get a shower this morning after waiting from 7.15am to 8.15am. But it was well worth it. One thing we are all looking forward to is a luxurious Turkish bath.

Received two 200 Greys parcels today. Most opportune arrival.

Hear that the Huns on the search the other day got away with enormous quantities of stuff.

There seems to be a general apathy towards Xmas this year which may be the result of thwarted ambitions or disillusionment, or what was more probable, the initial grim prospect of no Red X which has now been relieved, which shows that an empty belly breeds empty spirits.

Dec 24th

Christmas Eve and extremely cold. Our average temperature is 10 – 16 degrees of frost. Thank Heaven there's no wind.

Alan was telling us of the Kiwi battalion who bayonetted their way through a Jerry hospital in the desert. This was a result of our discussing the Huns use of sulphuric acid on the W Front. And now the strange case of Jerry Jerome. Caught stealing, he was missing and is now located in the *Lazarette* ostensibly with appendicitis. He was very much implicated with the Huns and rackets.

Alan said today that Monty and God will see that the boys in France have a good Xmas, if I am permitted to quote jocular cynical sacrilege. That was after sob stuff speeches we have heard from the Allied leaders lately.

Wrote a card to Rene and one to Aunt Edie.

Dec 25th

Sunny again. Warmer altho still very cold.

Xmas day not quite in the workhouse!!

Rose at 6.45am. Lit the fire and made porridge. Washed and made my bed with parade at 8.00am. Breakfast; porridge, 2 slices bread and coffee (Jerry). Prepared lunch. Brew and biscuit 11.00am. Started cooking 1.45pm and finished 2.30pm. Mashed spuds, Jerry soup, egg flakes and fried spam (½ tin). Tea. Shaved, washed and changed into best clothes complete with collar and tie. Read until 5pm when ate pudding (chopped raisins, prunes and apricots with porridge) and *Klim* milk and a slice of bread and marmalade. Tea. Read. At 7.00pm partner whist drive (with Tommy) when we got 129. Winners 145 (80 cigs) (2nd 48). Supper 2 slices bread and jam and cheese, biscuit and butter and jam and some chocolate. Talked till bed at 11.30pm.

News improving considerably.

Dec 26th

Glorious day but very cold again.

Raid at noon. Saw fighters and bombers very high.

Yesterday I had a queer feeling of contentment all day. Whether it was because our visitor Ernie seemed to enjoy himself and is a very pleasant cove; of the improving news or the food, or a combination of all three I don't know. Anyway, I felt quite happy but thought continuously of home. I wonder what they did?

There was a terrific amount of racket food in the camp yesterday. Meat, spuds, carrots etc. I am not jealous as I realise that they may be having a big meal now but I will certainly be having bigger and better meals than them for the rest of my life when I get home.

I also realised to the full yesterday what a horrible thing communion at home would be when I sat at table, with their visitors round a barrel of hooch, dirty mugs on the table, a dirty table and themselves looking dirty and untidy.

As I said to Bas "_The TUES proletariat entertains_". It struck me recently what shallow depth of thought has the average man.

Dec 27th

The average man has very little depth of thought. He fails, as far as I can see, to appreciate the real and concrete values of life. Truth, Honesty, Goodness (and I don't mean goody-goodiness, but a real, honest Christian outlook) and Character. They seem to think more of a dandy with pointed toe caps etc who would rob his own mother than a scruffy individual, overflowing with goodness of heart and moral honesty.

An air raid warning but possible only a recce.

Played some bridge in the evening (league) and had to finish before the lights went out and with only the last rubber to go. We are 1700 pts up.

Alan will never make a bridge player because he seems to find it impossible to grant it that full unqualified attention which is so necessary. The slightest little thing distracts him.

Dec 28th

Extremely cold again. I think this is the longest spell of continuous cold we have had since being taken prisoner.

I was thinking that the special glamour attached to air warfare and especially to fighter pilots maybe due to the reintroduction of the single combat of the Knights of old, 'the heroic age of single combat'.

Lots of parcel rumours around but nothing concrete. Rumour has parcels arriving at the rate of 1 truck load per minute!!

The news is quite good today. Budapest almost taken and the W Front is proceeding more favourably.

According to a tank navigator Captain in the *Lazarette* they almost bombed the camp the other day when they took a wrong pinpoint due to haze. They just took a correct p.p. in time, but all the same he didn't know the camp was here!

Dec 29th

Snowing and a little warmer.

Yesterday saw an innovation in the camp in the shape of the first talkie film. I saw it this evening the first being '*Life Begins for Andy Handy*'.

What a strange, wonderful almost intoxicating sensation of hearing a woman talk again – the first for 2½ years. Altho I had seen the film before, and altho it was cut here quite badly, I thoroughly enjoyed it. The strange thing was that after watching the film for 30mins it seemed perfectly normal again, which proves the old platitude 'the anticipation is greater than the event'.

I have decided to try and read *'The Social Relations of Science'* when I get home. I could, I think, assimilate it much better.

Sat Dec 30ᵗʰ

Freezing hard again after the snow. The temp is now round about 24 degrees of frost. I hear they had 55 degrees of frost at home on Boxing Day!!

Ron & I got in a little practice for the match on Tuesday. I am rather looking forward to it.

I was looking through Government white paper on Education after the war. They seem to be offering quite a good deal of University training for ex-servicemen after general demobilisation. I think I may take advantage of it, but it will need an amount of investigation and work before I make a final decision. I think I will do some work in maths and science next year.

200 Greys again.

Dec 31ˢᵗ

Cold again after more snow during the night.

The Aussies today got their Xmas parcel via the Huns.

Hear that Von Kluge has committed suicide and Von Rundstedt preparing for the new offensive. The news actually is on the upgrade again.

Snowing in the evening. From the news it looks as tho' they are having a very severe winter at home.

We had a very quiet day with a whist drive in the evening. Tommy and I were again winning in the last but one hand but only got 6 in the last and were beaten by 3 tricks. The second beat us by one, we actually scored 148.

Jim wrote an excellent New Year poem. Goodbye '44 and good riddance!!

1945

Mon Jan 1st

As an opening to the New Year, I think it appropriate to outline a programme as far as possible. I am not making any resolutions as my previous ones have all fallen flat.

We saw the N.Y. in very quietly, no singing, not even '*Ould Lang Syne*,' no shouting, just a hearty handshake with the boys.

I must admit, I still felt a little excitement at the prospect of fresh hopes for this year. But this time, one minute past 12 was not characterised by our previous "Well, home this year for a cert" which has been the popular phrase of my last two Jan 1sts. There has been some apathy and a great deal of conservatism over the celebrations this year after the disillusionment of last year.

Anyway, as I said, why should we sing '*Ould Lang Syne*' etc. which is a token of the enjoyment we have had in the previous year, when after all, we had had very little to be thankful for or joyful about. Certainly very little material gain. Pray God I'm not just becoming a cynic.

But why do we celebrate the New Year? Is it because we are glad the old one is through, with its trials, tribulations and disappointments? Or excited at the anticipation of another year, better, brighter, fuller, than the last? Or are we merely being conventional?

As usual, today had its usual round of Scotch bagpipes. In the evening Alan and I won our bridge match 3-0 and then I had some more practice with Ron.

Yesterday there was a big raid on the cookhouse, so today we had less spuds. I would shoot all these blackguards for they are not robbing the Hun of anything. No punishment is too bad for them in my opinion.

No news of any importance and the weather was cold and snowing.

My outline of a programme is this. I will attempt to read 104 books made up of the following; 20 novels, 10 on Maths, Science and Astronomy, 10 on Economics and Politics, 15 on war, 5 on Psychology, 8 on Philosophy, 12 Biographies, 6 on History and Geography, 10 on English Literature and 8 on Sociology. I will attempt to study some Maths and Science with perhaps a little History. As for the physical side, I will attempt to keep fit, food and God willing, with soccer, hockey and PT.

On my return home, I shall have to decide quickly what my future career will be. Whenever I think of this, I am in mental conflict. I am torn between two opposites. Shall I resign myself to a quiet, sober, married home life, which I should love so much, or shall I pursue that which seems to drag at me, at my very heart-strings; a life of gay adventure, travel, excitement, seeing the world and life. Strange travel allures me, strange people intrigue me, doing strange things fascinates me. From whom do I inherit this accursed wanderlust? Or is it youthful exuberance, or repression?

Jim Cameron, lying on his sickbed, a strange illness too – a chilblain on his nose, and what a size – added a spice of humour today, by his witty poem on the cake. It came from the parcel donated by the Australian Prime Minister to all Aussies.

They gave each member of the table some cake including the Kiwis (minority problem) on table 6. I quote the poem here. Dedicated by Jim to -

> **Table 7 and our Minority Problem on Table 6**
> *In olden days the Bible says*
> *The Throng were fed and loosened their stays,*
> *With two small loaves of 'curvey bread'*
> *And one-sixth of a tin of 'Fancy Red'.*
>
> *You have no Jewish appetite,*
> *Sated with such tiny bite*
> *But we are paupers, same as you,*
> *(A chilblain does not make a Jew).*
>
> *We share with you our half-bread bun,*
> *Out of Switzerland by the Hun,*
> *A two-year-old; Helvetian born,*
> *We trust it shows no Epsom form.*
>
> *Be of good cheer, this is the year,*
> *Of cakes and ale or fish and beer,*
> *Enjoy our cake (there are no fishes)*
> *But with it goes our four's good wishes.*
>
> *A bright New Year to all of you,*
> *Regret I am not down there too,*
> *And yet I wish with all my heart,*
> *That next New Year we're far apart.*
> **James Nose**

Tues Jan 2nd

A very cold day again today freezing hard in the evening.

I received 5 letters today. 2 from Mum, one Mary, 1 Aunt Maggie and one Mr Schofield. Tilly is still going strong in the Middle East. Betty seems almost married to the S African.

Sam Crutchley had a letter from home in which his mother said he would be home for Xmas and they would wait at the station for him. His comment was typically cynical, "I expect they will be bloody well frozen to death by now!!" The letter was written in Oct.

Nine trucks of parcels arrived today. In the evening Ron and I were part of a team of 6 pairs from the barrack opposing 6 pairs from 33A in a duplicate bridge match. We lost by 230 points. Unfortunately, there was a mistake in the distribution of the hands at Alex's Offs table (they lost by 2000) so we can't tell who won the match. Of the remaining 5 pairs as a total, we won.

From the news it appears that the Huns have started a new offensive on the W. Front.

Wed 3rd Jan

Extremely cold again.

I was very cold in bed and had to get up twice.

In the evening I played a little bridge.

We have information that tomorrow there will be a search of some sort.

Thurs 4th Jan

A glorious day but very cold.

We went out on parade prepared for a long stay. I had some grub and cigs in my pockets, a drink before I went out and was clothed by a vest, shirt, underpants, pyjamas, two pullovers, two pairs of socks, scarf, tunic, trousers, balaclava and overcoat and gloves. Clogs as footwear. We only had to stay out 2 hours when the Huns made a fanatical search.

In 38 they were directed to the hole by arrows saying "to the hole" and over the hole was a placard. "Here it is".

Our parcel today was English and is quite average. 2oz tea, 3oz sugar, tin evaporated milk, 3oz cheese, 12oz biscuits, 12oz jam, 5oz marg, 3oz egg powder, 6oz rolled oats, 16oz mixed fruit pudding, 8oz peas, 12oz meat roll, 16oz meat pie, 7oz pilchards, 4oz chocolate, 8oz cocoa and bar soap.

This is to last 2 of us one week as we are only on $\frac{1}{2}$ parcel per week.

Today our Hun rations were a cup of coffee in the morning, a mixed veg soup, $\frac{1}{7}$ loaf of bread, 2oz marg, $\frac{1}{4}$oz jam, 3 spuds and mint tea also $\frac{1}{2}$oz fresh cheese.

This is a normal days' issue.

A little bridge in the evening.

Fri 5th Jan

Very cold and freezing hard.

We have rumours, quite strong I fear, that RAF will be moving to a new camp. I personally think that there is a 50:50 chance of going but my tendency, if anything, is that we shall not move. Maybe this is wishful thinking, for although a move will certainly be a change, it would be unfortunate in this weather and also the parcels etc are coming through nicely again and everything seems to be getting organised.

There are also rumours that a repatriation is in the air again which seems to have some validation according to the BBC news. I hope so for the boys' sake.

In the evening we played some bridge, finished off the match with Gordon and Monty, which we won 1½ - 0 after being 1350 down at the beginning of the last rubber. This now puts us at the top of the league, an achievement we are proud of, considering the length of time we've been playing together and Alan's standard of bridge when we started. He has improved his all-round bidding and play 500%. As I told him, he is now playing BRIDGE and not CARDS.

Sat Jan 6th

Cold with a little light snow.

Hear that F.M. Monty is now Supreme C in C the Field on the W. Front. This, in my opinion, is a big move and can, I think, be compared with the appointment in the last war of F.M. Foch as *Generalissimo* in the last 6 months of the war. If Churchill's flipping around from one country (Eng-Greece-Eng-France-Eng) to another is any indication, things may be a little 'dicky'.

Actually, I have no qualms about present military operations but I think we have underestimated the Hun. For his present stand, I certainly take my hat off to him. He knows how to "make the *Krieg*". We now hear that they have retaken one of the islands in the Scheldt estuary. Their general advances in the west are really remarkable achievements considering our immense superiority in the air.

It seems that there has been a lot of trouble in our High Command at home. Let's hope they have cleared the situation up now. Roosevelt is making a speech tonight which I am keen to hear and we are also anticipating big events after the meeting of Stalin, Churchill and Roosevelt which is coming off shortly.

This evening Alan and I played Ron and Winny in the competition. We won 3½ - 0 after a gruelling game. We had the best of the cards but the distribution was so extraordinary that at the beginning of the last rubber, we were only 120 points in the lead after winning 3 rubbers. We finally won by getting 3 spades doubled and a small slam in spades. Alan played the S.S. to a gallery of about a dozen spectators. We were trembling like leaves. How silly it seems to get oneself so worked up over a game of cards.

Sun 7th Jan

A little warmer tho snowing.

Dave seems to be cultivating many friendships with an ulterior motive. His own gain after the war. I sincerely deprecate anything of this sort. It is despicable and dishonest. Honesty is to me one of my dominative principles. I hate and abhor anything, no matter how small, that has any relation to pettiness, deceit, theft, untruthfulness and all the other characteristics that make up dishonesty. This is due to the severe upbringing I have had in irreproachable honesty, due to my mother and father. I thank them deeply. This experience, where dishonesty has its greatest possibilities and advantages, has certainly as far as I know, stood the test, for I can honestly say I have not committed one dishonest act, no matter how small, the whole time I have been here.

The other night two Huns, an officer and gestapo were searching 17A, but someone fused the lights so everything turned out OK. A Hun was in the barrack doing some trading and the amusing spectacle was seen of a Hun jumping, white-faced, through a window and running for his life.

We had quite a good record programme last night. My appreciation of sopranos has gone up 100% since I have heard such singers as Joan Hammond, Isabel Bailey and Mary Ellis.

There have been some tremendous repercussions to the suggestion by Lowe that the Red X issue next week should be ⅙ payable on Tuesday & Thursday and ⅙ bulk on Sat. The RAF, as usual, is taking the lead. A petition has been sent to Sherriff with 5 points:

- That a statement of stocks be issued each week;
- That we know on which day an issue starts, Tuesday, Thursday or Saturday;
- That bulk be held over until a full parcel can be issued or existing stocks run out;
- Whether parcels can be issued in ¼'s or ½'s instead of ⅙ths;
- A statement regarding exchanges.

If a reply is not forthcoming further action is being taken via Geneva and London.

Wrote a letter home to Mary.

Alan and I played return duplicate bridge match v 33A and at the end of the game were dead level with 2040 each. This is the first time it has ever happened to me. Remarkable. We did very well, for we should have lost by about 900.

Mon 8ᵗʰ Jan

Cold again.

In the afternoon Alan and I played Eric and Peter in a

duplicate match, the hands exchanged by Alex and Cliff. The hands were rather poor being much too tricky. Periodically, every one was a trap. We did very well again only to lose by 1200 points. They caused tremendous arguments and Tommy was very cheesed.

The results of the Red X discussions are that next week we are to have ½ bulk each week.

No news of any importance.

Tues 9th Jan

Cold with quite a lot more snow. But there is still a pile of it to come yet.

At the moment, there is a tremendous purge on the racketeers in the camp and about time too. This camp is rotten to the core from the British point of view. The racketeers, which includes a large number of Army, yes and some RAF too, NCO's, who are supposed to set some sort of example of decency. So far they have shown a singular disregard of the elementary principles of decency, and the hackneyed 'esprit de corps'. Their one obsession has been their own selfish betterment at the expense of their fellow prisoners. They have committed unmitigated crimes in respect of food, clothes, coal, and, in fact, all the necessaries of merest existence.

My own opinion is that the various leaders and organisers (I should say dis-organisers) of the camp are all too deeply embroiled in the rackets themselves to even want to do anything about it. Previously, especially in warm weather, these rackets have been grossly overlooked but now, when food is scares and the weather cold, they are much more ostentatious.

I believe that if the camp leaders had made any determined

effort to stamp out rackets they would have done it. Now certain British fellows and the Huns are having a big clean up.

According to the **Volkisbher Becbachter** the Huns destroyed 1879 a/c in December and in the raid on the dromes in Belgium they are claiming 579 a/c destroyed. We claimed 193 Hun a/c. The leader of this raid was the now famous Colonel Rudel, 28 year old hero of 2400 trips 'against the enemy', who claims to have destroyed the Russian battleship Marat and 453 *panzas*. He now leads the *'Immelman'* squadron which I believe are *Dorniers*, but previously he was on *Stuka's*. They claim he is the world's greatest airman and I believe he is. He is the holder, the only one so far, of the golden iron cross, with oak-leaves, swords and diamonds. I should like to meet him.

Montgomery has recently played glowing tribute to F.M. von Runstadt who he believes is better than Rommel. He must be good with a capital G.

A number of new people are in the camp. They bring the reports awaiting their departure. Some are RAF, others Army, including some caught in Anaheim. It was undoubtedly a remarkable achievement but it looks as though Army Intelligence made a slight boob. It would have been a brilliant manoeuvre if it had come off.

According to the RAF lads, Kreuzbag Luft 7 is an ideal camp as far as PoW camps go; decent huts, 12 to a room, 14lbs of fuel per day, communal feeding, cinema etc, etc above all, no rackets whatsoever. They say there is a glut of aircrew in England and even Sgt Pilots are flying as gunners. Looks as though we are back numbers.

Had a good shower today. The significance of this remark is the fact that it even warrants an entry in a diary!!

No news of any importance.

Wed 10th Jan

A lot more snow this morning but it cleared about lunch time.

Whilst on the subject of rackets I will here enumerate some of the rackets going on, although I don't know some of them. They are:

1. **Cookhouse rackets** – Spuds being handed through the window to a) friends for nothing; b) others who sell them for cigs. The same for soup. Practically no meat goes in the soup, it's finding it's way onto the cook's barrack tables and also being sold for cigs. The price at Xmas was 30 fags a pork chop. In fact, half a pig was found in a barrack in 10 block 3 days ago. Sugar being sold, not only by the British but also by the Huns. So much per biscuit tin. Coffee sold at 100 cigs per packet. All this stuff should go to the chaps in camp as part of a Hun issue. The spud racketeers collected their boxes of spuds and then had to walk past the rubbish dump where they hypocritically criticized the new fellows they saw there scraping, nay grovelling in the rubbish for spud peelings etc. That only increases the magnitude of their crime.

2. **Post office racket** – I believe that parcels are given by the PO workers to their pals after taking what they want themselves. I know that one official was in a position to buy 3 x 2½ kilo loaves every week even whilst the great shortage of cig parcels was on. They forge signatures on chits and just take

241

the parcels. This especially goes on with swap-over parcels as an inquiry revealed. They buy grub off the Huns with cigs they get out of other peoples parcels.

3. **Clothing rackets** – Here I am very much in the dark.

4. **Coal rackets** – Our issue is $\frac{1}{6}$th of a bucket per man per week. The rest of our issue is sold to us by the British and Huns who work in coordination. The present price is 300 cigs per kettle ie., one to each barrack. Friends of workers can get coal free from the coal store staff and cookhouse staff. Elsewhere it can be bought at 50 cigs per Canadian Red X box from these same workers.

5. **Red X rackets** – Here again I have not very much data but I believe the extent of them is enormous. Friends of the Red X store workers can get, and do get, articles from time to time, even invalid articles and Yank parcel articles when it is not known that there are Yank parcels in camp. I know a fellow who gets a parcel of tea, sugar, chocolate etc <u>every</u> week without fail. When, at odd times, the stuff had to go to the cookhouse, they took untold quantities of stuff – milk, meat, tea etc. At one stage the racket in invalid parcels was terrific and it was all covered on the books by having their issue stopped one week.

6. **Miscellaneous** – Small, petty rackets such as free, good seats for the theatre, cinema etc. Books repaired for a fee. Wood sold from the carpenters shop. Washing done for a fee at the bathhouse etc, etc, etc.

7. *Reveir (infirmary)* **and** *Lazarette* **rachets** – which are all in the food and white bread line.

All these rackets are my own opinion of what goes on and would probably be vehemently denied but nevertheless…

Last night we were warned, with the warning coming from the *Feldwebel,* that the RAF here are on stand-to. We must have our kit packed in bundles easy to carry, have a good pair of boots, always carry our disc now, and generally to be ready to move at a moment's notice. A list is to be taken of all aircrew, paratroops, cleaners, ground-crew etc in the compound.

Indications are definitely that something is in the air and a move may come off. I sincerely hope not in this weather. I am very unfit and I'm sure that if we had to walk any distance, half of us would never arrive at our destination. We have been given 8 days in which to get ready. Anything can happen after that.

In the evening we had another partner whist drive when Tommy and I managed to pick up even worse cards than in our previous games. Even so we got a Grand Slam in the last hand which makes one each in the last three drives. Without fear of boasting, I think I can say that we certainly know how to use cards when we get them. We only scored 133 tricks, the winner scoring 155 in 20 hands.

We had good news in the evening concerning the Red X issues. On the 20th we are to have ½ a Xmas parcel and a parcel a week for the following fortnight when we return to ¼ parcel. A big meeting with the Red X commission in attendance cleared up a lot of points, amongst which it was made clear that Lowe is subordinate to Sherriff and can be kicked out if the camp think, so a great deal of the trouble in the camp is in the process of being cleared up.

After lights out Oscar Powers gave us a wonderful aside. Gordon, Peter and Monty were talking about various favourite dishes etc, the usual topic, and after about a quarter of an hour of this Oscar said "For Christ's sake, bring out the biscuits and cheese and let's get this bloody meal over". Superb!!

Thurs 11th Jan

Much warmer, in fact thawing a little and some rain.

Received 2 letters yesterday, one from Mary and one from Molly Johnson who seems to take Victorian delight in her mild flirtations.

Bridge in the evening when Ian and I played very well and after 3 rubbers are 4000 points in the lead. We were top of the league last week.

No news of any importance. Apparently the whole camp is on stand-to.

Fri 12th Jan

Warmer and thawing. It is very miserable outside nowadays. Foggy, overcast, damp air with intermittent snow or rain, whilst inside it is cold, dark, smoky, the floor perpetually wet.

The room is already festooned with wet, dripping washing.

There has recently been a very interesting, though disgusting, sidelight on human nature. The repats, who should be home within a fortnight, have demanded that Xmas parcels be issued to them before they go.

Bunny, Stan's Army friend and Jo, Alex's Navy friend, are very, very depressed and low spirited recently, hard to cheer up, easy to depress. Life seems to have been knocked out of them. Rather an interesting psychological reflection on Army and Navy average mentality. It is noticeable that the RAF, although disillusioned, have sufficient intelligence not to let it get them down but can take a much more philosophical attitude towards their confinement. Their attitude is one, not so much of despondency, but of anger at the political intrigue which we believe is holding up the termination of the war.

Alan and I finished our final game in the league, winning handsomely by 9½ - 0. This concludes, for us, a highly successful tournament, all the more creditable in light of the length of time, a shortness of it, we had been playing together. I am very pleased with Alan's progress but we still have some polishing up to do. In the tournament we played 11 games; won 7, lost 2. Our points were 39½ for, 7½ against, giving us a score of 526.6.

No news of any importance but rumours came up at night that the Ruskies have started an offensive in the Cracow area. If they have, it is – tramp, tramp, tramp along the highway....! I fully believe that Budapest is another Stalingrad.

We had quite an interesting lecture this evening by S/Sgt Ford on soccer. He is a veritable encyclopaedia on the subject and has a remarkable memory stored with dates, scores, gates, games and numbers. It was only spoiled, I thought, by his droning away, non-stop, in a sepulchral voice like an alltonation *(sic)*.

Sat Jan 13

Cold again and freezing hard.

The rumours of the offensive in the Cracow area are confirmed from German sources. In fact, no less than three new offensives have started, East Prussia, Cracow & the Czech-Hungarian border, this last with 24 divs and 3 *panzer* corps!!

Naturally, the Cracow one affects us most being about 80 miles from here. The news taken as a whole is definitely on the up-grade. The Yanks are claiming to have sunk a Jap 45,800 ton battleship in Oct and their new landing on Luzon is doing well.

These Huns are amazing people. I can't understand certain aspects of their character and temperament. When the reports came in from other camps recently, the Commandant boasted how many men there were from Anaheim and when told, gave each one of them some cigarettes. They place heroism in action very high. It is a German ideal.

The Germans are a mixture, as far as I can see, of Teutonic racialism, Prussian domination and Mediterranean (ie Latin) infiltration. Their character is bombastic and domineering in victory, snivelling in defeat. They lack the Englishman's stolidity, that being replaced by a highly irascible temper. Vicious. As far as I can see, they are essentially honest, hardworking, thrifty and have a terrific capacity for endurance. They are good fighters but their morale needs numbers to keep it strong. But their big failing is that they definitely have a sadistic streak in them which they will use when every opportunity presents itself.

Sun Jan 14

A glorious day today, sunny but freezing very hard.

The news is very good in many respects, but in one respect it is a little disturbing. The push in the Cracow section is making rapid progress in this direction. There are various rumours of our moving but as yet nothing concrete.

We had a blanket parcel this morning.

Joe Holder made a crack last night typical of our lights-out ribaldry. Tommy, Dave etc were engaged in their usual repartee and Dave was instructed to call Tommy 'Daddy'. Someone else said "No, call him Pappy" and Joe said "Yeah! Slaphappy".

Wrote a card to Molly J and a card home.

In the evening, Alan and I played a little bridge against Cliff and Ron. A Hun *Posten*, a Pole incidentally, considers the Huns have had it, in 2 days they have no defences in Poland.

Mon Jan 15th

Very cold and frosty. Last night was the coldest night in Germany since 1938.

Today, Bas and I were engaged in a terrific argument against Dave concerning Psychology. Dave seems to look upon 'the mind' as something real and tangible which, in my opinion, it is not. The exact nature of the mind is an unknown quantity. Pavlov was a psycho-pathologist and not a psychologist pure and simple. We later had an argument about marriage and true love, with all its implications, sexual relationships, happiness etc.

In the evening we had another duplicate bridge match v 17A. The barrack won easily altho Alan & I lost. Without making excuses for myself, I must say that Alan played his worst for a long time.

Preparing my kit and kit-bag for a march. News very good.

Tues Jan 16th

Very cold and frosty, but a lovely day on account of the brilliant sunshine. The power of the sun is becoming more noticeable.

Dave becomes increasingly useless and objectionable. I am beginning to hate the sight of him. I realise now how much he has played on me up 'til now. I have been an absolute idiot and he is an absolute rat. I sometimes despair of human nature altho I still believe there is some inherent good in man but the trend of present day economic and social tendencies seems to have sublimated the good for the bad. Again a cynic!!

The repats left for Switzerland and home yesterday. The Huns here are on stand-by and have to keep their uniform on at all time.

Russians still advancing.

Wed Jan 17th

Very, very cold. An extremely sharp frost last night. Inches of ice on the inside of the windows this morning.

I am inwardly terribly excited about the Russian advance. They are coming straight for Opole and very quickly too, we should hear the guns anytime.

Bert Farmer says he heard a dull rumbling last night but it may have been imagination. I shall go out and listen tonight. The latest rumour is that they are 15 miles from the border. I have got all my kit ready in case we have to move. The British have also started an offensive in the West.

No arguments or discussions today just news – news – news. I think there must be permanent listeners-in.

The RAF received 24,000 over from Sagan. There was terrific air activity last night a/c flying very low over the camp.

Hear terrible tales of the Konigsberg evacuation. They were made to run up and down with full kit on until they had discarded nearly all their kit. 68 of them suffered from bayonette and gunshot wounds, two of whom died.

The lights nowadays are very unstable: every night without fail they go out for periods saying between 1 minute and 3-4 hours. If it's not this barrack's light fusing, the phase goes, if not the phase, half the camp goes; if not half the camp, the whole camp goes; and if it's not a technical defect, it's an air raid. We quite often have to finish a hand of bridge, spread our bread and get our brew with the aid of little magazine lamps.

This entry is terribly disjointed, but I do feel very excited, altho I am trying to supress it.

Just heard a rumour that the guards have been told to be ready to move and they are having a skeleton staff here. Pray God they do!! Even Xmas parcel issues on Saturday have been forgotten which means a great deal.

Since I wrote this about 3 hours ago, news has come in that Warsaw has fallen, as announced in an order of the day ordered by Stalin and that Krakow has fallen. Altho in a 2nd order of the day that another offensive has started N of Warsaw.

The Russians are at Tschenstochau *(now Czestochow)* which is 15 miles from the border and is about 50 miles from here. The only main road from there leads to Opole which at their present rate of advance they should reach in about 24hrs to 2 days. It's terrific!! Absolutely!!

Everyone this evening has certainly lost his equanimity and we are all wildly excited. I wouldn't be at all surprised if we are moved either tonight or tomorrow. It strikes me that after then it may be too late. By now, Luft 7 at Kreuzberg should be liberated as they are between Tschenstochau and Oppeln.

This has been the greatest day of the war for news.

This evening we played 17A in a return duplicate match and Alan & I lost by 1330, which was about right.

The barrack lost.

Thursday Jan 18th

Very cold, with a little wind and frost.

The news is very much quieter today tho the rumour has it that (1) the Russians have crossed the border about 50 miles from here and N of Breslau; (2) that Stalin said that Breslau and Berlin are his next stops; (3) that Litzmannstadt has been reached; (4) that the Huns have halted the push; (5) that Budapest has fallen.

Practically all the Huns in the camp say that we shall not move but of course they know no more than we do. A Gerry Lieutenant said that the only people to move would be wearing given uniforms. Have a drink on him in Moscow!!

The civvies around here today were given six hours to get moving. The trains and stations are apparently crowded especially ____. Oppeln is also being evacuated.

Churchill is also supposed to have made a statement but according to first reports he doesn't know very much about the war – according to us of course!!

It was very amusing last night, and ironical too, for the lights didn't go out at 10pm as usual, but stayed on for a considerable time after 10pm. Instead of the usual "You square-headed bastards" which is the usual accompaniment to darkness, everyone was saying "I wish to Christ they'd switch their bloody lights off". Which was exactly how I felt about it. There was a sigh of relief when eventually the lights did go out.

A/c were again heard flying over the camp during the night. Today flak was seen going up quite close to the camp, but I believe it was practice. I am told that the drome here is packed with fighters, MEs, FW190s etc.

Recently the small soccer pitch in 38 compound was flooded and next morning, Hey Presto – Earls Court in the raw. A considerable amount of skating has been done but as usual skates are almost a nonentity.

We have been issued a considerable amount of toilet paper recently for the first time almost since we've been in camp! I wonder if it's a reflection of the Huns personal needs?

A rumour in the RAF compound today is that the Air Ministry consider that anyone who has been a prisoner for more than 12 months is fit neither mentally nor physically for any further flying. Consequently we shall all be discharged when we go home. I think this is a product of wishful thinking on the part of some (nay, many) tho I myself will be bitterly disappointed. I might almost say broken-hearted, if I have any heart left after 3 years here, if I cannot fly again. I honestly and truly pray to fly against the Japs. Flying is my very life-blood, the only thing where I can say I have been happy to saturation point.

The recent excitement has doubly brought home to me the terrible, I am tempted to say fatal, realism of the hackneyed phrase 'Civil Service Complex'. Our few members of the clan have exhibited a truly hypocritical solemnity and nonchalance, almost bordering on apparent disinterest. Why don't they wake up to themselves and step down from their smug, complacent, self-appointed pedestal. Who do they think they are deceiving?

Fri Jan 19th

Bitterly cold with a biting wind.

News from the front very scarce. Rumours are rife that (1) some of the cook house staff are moving to Gorlitz to be followed by half the camp; (2) that Teschen admin staff are coming here which means that the infamous Major Birkhalf will be here again; (3) that the Huns are evacuating the drome nearby; (4) that 400 more fellows are coming into the camp.

The Huns are obviously feverishly evacuating this area, in fact, they allocated some transport to us today for the Red X but later commandeered it again with no apology.

Rumour (1) has now been squashed with the information that the cook house staff are going to cope with workers who will be going into 5A at Gorlitz.

Rumour (4) has some information in that 200 RAF lads came in at 4pm. They are from Kreuzberg and are the sick and wounded who came by open lorry.

The rest, 1500 of them, are on the march, 3 guards to 35 men. If any escape they will be shot – 5 men for everyone to escape. They are on their way to Sagan.

These lads saw some terrific sights on their way here. Civvies in horse carts their luggage and women (crying) and children on top. Troops are coming back in horse and carts etc, anything they can get hold of and some marching, in fact jog-trotting, along the roads.

They saw a few small tanks, motor-cycles, lorries and one Tiger tank. This they saw slide in a ditch, crash into a house and turn on its side. The crew just got out, got into a horse and cart and on their way.

The chaos is indescribable. Even Lamsdorf station is packed with civvies. Women and children hanging on to couplings to try to get away. Some were crying their eyes out.

One of the new boys was shot down in Jan '44 in Berlin. He was grabbed by the civvies and suffered a broken leg, broken nose and fractured skull. The rest of his crew were lynched by the irate crowd, he being rescued by the Gestapo above all others.

Chiefy Cooper was talking to another engineer and Chiefy asked him what course he was on at a central station. He said 84, Chiefy's jaw dropped and a glazed look spread over his eyes. Chiefy groaned "I was on 1 course" and he felt 50 yrs older!! Another lad didn't sign up 'til May 1943.

What struck me most, and it struck everyone else, but it hit me very startlingly, was how old we look in comparison with these lads – and I am only 23 when I saw them put 3 or 4 years on to me, I feel it most bitterly.

I also noted how the arrival of new faces put a different atmosphere into the barrack. It shows just how bored, fed-up and sick we are at heart of each other's company. The same faces, the same voices, the same stories day in day out has deadened our senses until the advent of new things brings out in relief our true feelings.

We have become almost numbed into the acceptance of each other's idiosyncrasies with a seemingly grim resignation and endure each other with an apparent cordiality. It is a very good thing we do this, for our lives here would be a continual discord if this were not the situation. But this age business!?!

When I arrived in January I was a young lad of just 21 and looked, so they tell me, 16 or 17. They really thought that, the boys at Dulag. Now I feel, God how old do I feel? I really don't know.

To break this subject I will say that the news is still excellent but Parliament seems a little tired of Mr Churchill's meanderings on Greece.

Alan and I won the bridge league with an overwhelming lead. Our score was 526-6 the second being 287-9!!!! The bottom questioned a score of 10! I am very pleased.

Sat Jan 20th

A lovely day, sunny and a little warmer tho still freezing.

The lights did their usual fading act last night again but we are getting our supper ready early nowadays so they can do what they like.

The raid the night before last when we saw flares and heard bomb and gun fire was on Breslau. Last night flares were dropping all over the Silesia area and many a/c were about.

We were told today that we may have to move (i.e. the fit (?) men) if the camp gets overcrowded. The Huns can give us nothing definite with regard to sleeping accommodation, food etc. The only thing they can give us is that if any man escapes they will turn the machine gun on the rest. This while on a march if we get one.

Rumours today are that the Ruskies are 63 kms from Breslau (10 o'clock BBC).

The lights nowadays are being officially turned out at 9pm.

This evening they are 35 miles from Breslau so the day's news 60 miles – 40 miles – 35 miles. We hear rumour that the marchers from Kreuzberg were turned back by the police as the roads were too packed with civvies. Some chaps came in today from Rozenberg in Czech and they left the town as the Russians were shelling the other end. The Russians occupied the town 2 hours after they left.

Mj Sherriff came in from outside and says the conditions are lots more chaotic than we realise. Worse than France in '40. Some fellows came through Opole station which is the most cosmopolitan station imaginable. Luftwaffe in flying kit; Hun troops going to the front; wounded, their bandages still dripping with undried blood, coming back; Russian PoWs with Italian guards, the Ruskies, huge chaps, very well equipped and their clothing mostly ___ stuff, coats, collars, boots, caps, gloves etc.; Serbs, Croats, French workers etc., Russians in Hun uniform going to the Front; British PoWs coming here; and of course the usual conglomeration of stunned, stupefied, bewildered, weeping civvies. Out of all this lot, no one knew exactly what the score was!!

To get away from the war (but who wants to?) we this afternoon received our belated ½ Xmas parcel after an initial setback. After the setback, Cliff in his anger and disappointment, went back into the barracks, threw his gloves out of the window and spit on top of his bed! Most amusing – worthy of Laurel and Hardy – but it only shows our state of mind. The compound _____ eventually did the trick for us.

In the evening we had a wonderful lecture, amusing, enlightening, highly interesting and topical on 'This Vitamin Business' by Captain Knowles. It strikes me we are very much in need of B2 and B6 and make no use whatsoever of the sun for absorption of D, for we usually wash it all away.

Just heard that Tilsit has gone.

Sun Jan 21st

A glorious morning, sunny but freezing hard and very cold.

News this am is they are 30 miles from Breslau and 15 from Opole. Rumours that Sosnowitz has gone and that 15 parties have been liberated.

We are expecting 40 more chaps in each barrack today. Bas last night asked one of the new lads, a reasonably intelligent and thinking individual, if he noticed any appreciable difference between ourselves and people in England. He has not been a prisoner long. He was very embarrassed and said "without any personal aspersions of you, yes there is a difference, a very marked difference, not only in looks, which are apparent, but also in general demeanour and habits." Our humour is childish and our outlook on life is altogether different to the normal outlook. All of which I fully believe to be true. This probably explains the newcomers' apparent diffidence and incomprehension.

Our Xmas parcel contained; 1 tin roast pork & stuffing (16oz), 1 tin stewed steak (16oz), 1 tin chopped ham (16oz), 1 tin Heinz baked beans (10oz), 1 Xmas pudding (16oz), 1 tin cake (16oz), 3oz bar sugar, large tin condensed milk, 4oz bar blended chocolate, 2oz tea, Yorkshire pudding mixture, 3oz tin sardines, 8oz honey, 8oz butter.

Today we had our antedated Xmas dinner. Roast pork and stuffing, spuds and barley soup, Xmas pudding and custard. Tea excellent.

This afternoon saw part of an ice-hockey match. It is the best Canadian game I've seen. Very fast and very exciting.

Have just seen a squadron of 15 *Stukas* go over, heading towards the front and not 5 minutes ago we heard bombs dropping. The Hun 3 o'clock radio says the Russians are all along the German – Silesian border and so far their counterattacks have been unable to stop them. The Russians claim to be 40kms from Breslau and the Huns say they are 28kms. They are also supposed to be 15 miles from Oppeln.

Our water has gone off and we've been told it's unlikely that we will get any more. Also the Huns say that there is no more bread in the camp but they will do everything possible to get some before tomorrow. It is unlikely there will be any light tonight. This means that either we have had it 'til we are liberated or moved.

The Hun *Abwerk* officer says the war will end this week and the guards, when not on duty, are not allowed to leave their barrack. The Russians are claiming the Huns have lost 65,000 dead since Friday. Also 250,000 PoWs taken and 500 tanks in one place.

I went for a walk today in an effort to find a quiet spot and eventually succeeded and then heard a distant rumbling but was unable to tell whether it was distant gunfire, tanks moving, distant a/c or train.

We are disappointed. The 15 *Stukas* have just returned this minute without loss!!

The lights came on after all. The news this evening is that the Russians are about 36kms from Oppeln ie., 68kms from here. The Russians are claiming Kreuzberg, Rosenberg and another Silesian town. They have made a penetration of Silesia 40km deep and 60km wide.

Alan & I beat Cliff & Alex in the evening after getting our 1st Grand Slam.

The Long March

Mon Jan 22nd

A fairly good morning but cold.

And now the story of the <u>GRIMMEST FORTNIGHT OF MY LIFE</u>

I am writing this from notes taken on the march.

At 12 noon we were told to be ready to move at 1.45 taking no kit, only toilet gear and blankets. We hurriedly made our meal, packed a few sandwiches and in great confusion and excitement made ready to go. Everyone was hoping the thing would be cancelled and when, at 1.45 it was postponed 'til 2.45, our hopes ran high.

Rumours flew around thick and fast even to the extent of paratroops surrounding the area. Eddie Cush, when told this made a typical comment "I don't believe it" but our informant was violently vehement so Eddie said "well, tell 'em to do it again; we didn't see them the first time".

We finally moved off at 2.45. I was wearing 3 vests, 2 pants, 2 pullovers, 2 shirts, 2 socks, trousers, tunic, greatcoat and boots. In my pockets I had toilet gear and _____ and diaries etc, and in my kit bag 2 blankets, 1 towel, plate & cup and a tin of marg. I carried a box of sandwiches, fruit, porridge and some bread. I also had a balaclava, scarf & gloves, such as they were, and some soap in my kit bag.

Amid jocular ribaldry from the fellows staying in camp, we marched through the gates at 3.00pm; blocks 5,4,3,2. The sick of these blocks were left in camp.

After numerous counts and recounts we were issued with ½ loaf bread and a Red Cross parcel plus ¼ block of marg per man, all of which greatly but necessarily increased our load. Everyone was quite cheerful but apprehensive.

We waited around 'til about 6.30pm whilst everything was settled and finally moved off along icebound roads on a clear, bright, frosty moonlit night. Our first troubles were slipping and sliding over the ice. Alan Tonkin fell 5 times before we reached Lamsdorf village. I almost fell many times but during the whole march never hit the deck once.

Before we reached L village, Dennis Toombs threw away his kit bag, blankets and Red X parcel.

Completely demoralised, onwards we raced, the sound of Russian guns in the distance, slipping and sliding, trying to keep together. Then one or two fellows collapsed unconscious which gave the rest of us a brief respite. After an hour or so we were becoming quite exhausted, our packs getting heavier and heavier.

At one stage I asked a Jerry *dolmetscher* how far we were going and exhausted, he lay his head on his arm and said "God knows". That made me feel better.

Still we went on, mucous pouring from everyone's noses but no one bothered to blow it away. It just dribbled. I was alternating between sweating and freezing. My feet were numb. No one spoke - that took too much energy. I tried thinking of everything in an effort to take my mind off the march, but I couldn't concentrate.

Onwards we went, jogging and bumping each other, someone would fall down; the rest just went passed him with hardly a glance. After about 4 nightmare hours of this we were all too mentally and physically exhausted to bother about anything.

At about a quarter to two we eventually arrived at a barn which was our billet for the night. Amidst yells from the Huns we flopped down anywhere, on top of each other, sprawling about helpless on what little straw there was. Cliff, Alex and I eventually summoned up enough energy between us to lay out our blankets, wet with frost, and get in – myself in the middle.

Tues Jan 23rd

Last night I was much too mentally and physically exhausted (I had never been so washed-out in my life) to get any sleep at all. My groins ached, my hips ached, my shoulders felt as tho they had been cut in two, my legs ached and oh! my feet. My toes were absolutely numb.

Against advice, I took my boots off but still I didn't get a wink of sleep.

At 9.00am we got up and had something to eat and a drink of cold water and at 10.00 we were off again minus George Brassey who was really ill and had to be carried away.

Yesterday we did 25km. This day we did another 30 gruelling kms. I actually felt quite good and found chocolate and sugar good marching rations.

Towards evening everyone prayed for a halt but the Huns egged us on with only 1 more km, only 2 more km, the next village etc. I finished the march in a trance. Unfortunately the pace was made for us by two old women!! But I can swear that the boys were as near _____ as any I have ever seen.

We arrived worn out at a brick works, where Dave and I managed to pick as bad a bed as imaginable.

Wed Jan 24th

Last night was ghastly.

We slept on hard rocks in an open shed. It was bitterly cold and the draft came up through the stones whistling through my ribs. Our blankets were wet through and I was shivering all night. I thought at the time that if it went on much longer like that, I should have either pneumonia or rheumatic fever.

On top of all this, when I tried to get my boots on, they were frozen absolutely solid and with my feet so swollen and painful I had to put them on top of a fire to thaw them out before I could get them on. Again not a wink of sleep in this my worst night ever.

Up 'til today I was too exhausted to even feel hungry and only today managed to move my bowels for the first time since leaving camp.

Dave, Alan and Bill all packed in this am ostensibly with bad feet; so far about 200 lads have packed in. I set off feeling worn out and very footsore.

I was trudging along at the rear of the column with Bas, Lofty and Turig after receiving ¼ of a loaf when we had the offer of a *Posterns* sledge. This was a Godsend for me altho this day was one of the worst for sledges. It was through a hilly range in deep snow. Very picturesque scenery. We took it in turns pulling and got along fine.

Last night was spent at Prieborn and we passed through Habendorf, Rummels Berg, Geppersdof, Steinkirche and Wammelwitz before being herded into barn at Prauss at 8.00pm after doing 23km since 8.30am.

So far it was noticeable that there was no military traffic whatsoever going <u>up</u> to the front; some coming away. The civvies were also entirely evacuating by any means available, mostly sledges and covered wagons hauled by horses or cattle, their picturesque sleigh bells jingling. It certainly put me in mind of Xmas.

The villagers are quite good to us, giving us water as we pass through.

Thurs Jan 25ᵗʰ

For the first time last night I managed to get some sleep and when we set out at 8.30 I felt much fresher.

So far the weather had been cold but fine.

I now became obsessed with the dread of frostbite and lice. My toes were still numb, no feeling at all, and remained so for the whole march, but fortunately it wasn't frostbite.

Today we passed through mountainous scenery in sleet and snow, sometimes 1ft and more, up steep hills. It was very hard going. We had an issue of 1½ packets of *Knackebrot* biscuits i.e. 6 biscuits. I lost 4 of mine!!

So far we heard gunfire every day but today it was only desultory. We still entertained hopes that we would be cut off by the Russians. I was optimistic.

We arrived at our barn at 7.45 after passing through **Jolheita,** Grobkniegnitz, Senitz, Heidersdorf , Langenols, to Zobten.

I feel rather better today, my appetite returning. I think we are getting used to it.

Still lots of civvies evacuating.

Fri Jan 26th

20kms yesterday.

The weather was still very cold.

I had a good drink and wash this am and we started at 9.30 after a good night.

Heard no guns today.

We passed through Marxdorf and Klein Mohnau to finish 15kms at Domanze at 4pm. A short day.

We brewed in a yard and it was a remarkable sight to see all the camp fires going in the dark. Almost like a Wild West yarn. We had no ration today.

We heard that the rest of the camp was evacuated the same day as ourselves by 12.30 at night and have gone to **Stalz**.

Today we passed a column of Hungarians / civvies with male civvy police guards. They looked brutish and carry truncheons to deal with miscreants (?) some of whom show traces of their use. Some were pregnant and all looked pitifully thin and cold and starved and weak dressed only in rags. Some smiled woefully and then lowered their eyes. It was a terrible sight. Just after them, we passed Russians pulling a huge heavily laden cart reminiscent of the chain gang. These Huns have certainly got something to pay for.

No rations today.

Sat Jan 27th

After a decent night during which it snowed heavily, we set off at 9.30 after receiving 6 biscuits.

Not a very eventful day just the usual – tramp, tramp, with aching legs, feet and shoulders.

Again we heard distant gunfire after passing through Ingramsdorf, Pitschen, Bertholdsdorf, Gabersdorf, Beckern, Kuhnern to Damsdorf where, after 22km, we stayed the night.

This evening we waited in deep snow, with wet frozen feet for 1¾ hrs before we could get into our billets at 6.15.

Sun Jan 28th

After last night's fiasco I had my best night yet.

We heard rumours that 7 Block IV men have died and 2 RAF lads.

It was extremely cold today, freezing the whole time. My boots were frozen solid all day with the result that my heels were bleeding badly and my socks soaked in blood.

We finished our 21kms at 6.30 after passing through Tschinschwitz, Merzdorf, ___ and Jauer to arrive at St Peterwitz. Again we had no rations.

It was noticeable at this time that the boys were breaking out in sores on their lips. I had one small one. Everyone looked dirty, unshaven and dishevelled. I forgot to mention that in the first night when slipping, I kept knocking my left insole and by now it was very painful and swollen. Nevertheless everyone's spirits were much brighter.

Mon Jan 29th

Today proved to be my worst day so far and in fact the whole trip. I had a very bad night last night: no sleep at all. All I had to eat the whole day 'til the evening was 1 biscuit and 1oz of sugar. On this we ploughed and shuffled through deep snow in a blinding blizzard and bitter cold. I am sure that if any man had fallen on the march, he was a dead man. That is certain.

We started at 9.00am and finished at 5.00pm when we did 20km to the sound of guns all day. We passed through **Heldinsdorf, Pramsnitz,** and **Loblitz** to spend the night at Goldberg. We had to attempt to make our beds in pitch dark in a barn on top of a rick of straw.

Tues Jan 30th

I had a very poor night, slipping towards the precipice all night.

Today we remained here for a rest, much needed I must say. We spent most of the day eating whatever we could. We ate like pigs. I ate raw wheat, carrot and sugar beet pulp. Absolute pig food. But what matter. All our food is covered with dirt and dust, hay and straw and all manner of stuff but no one seems to mind much. Today we had our first issue of hot spuds and 4 days bread and marg rations. 4/5 loaf and 1/7 stale marg.

We hear that 1600 sick are left living like lords at Lamsdorf with 10000 parcels. We expect to arrive at Gorlitz on Fri or Sat.

Wed Jan 31st

We started at 08.00 in snow. I felt terrible early on but improved later. I find that when I start off well I finish very badly, but if I start bad I finish very well. A sort of good wind.

Today we did 19km through picturesque scenery, woods and hills when I find the kms seem to slip by much quicker. The civvies are still with us and constitute a great nuisance to our walking. Whilst we were having a 10 minute (the Huns watches go 5 times as fast as ours) rest some women passed us singing "It's a long way to Tipperary". How terribly true!

We passed through Hennersdorf, Pilgrimsdorf, Hockenau to arrive at Lauterseiffen. Everyone tells the guards now to 'wrap up' just when they feel like it.

Thurs Feb 1st

Last nights proved to be our best billet yet. A small stable, there were only 50 of us at the farm, complete with bags of straw, electric light all night (luxury personified!) and two horses! We had a hot brew within 2mins of arriving and hot spuds were issued. There were bags of rackets with the guards, we managed to get biscuits and bread for soap.

In the morning, after everyone had had a brew or two, I had a wash in Hot water. What a treat! It felt wonderful. On top of this I made acquaintance with the finest lavatory I've seen since I left *Dulag luft*. Whitewashed and with proper seat. It was lovely, if that designation can be given to a lavatory.

We finally started off in wonderful spirits at 8.30, in warm weather it having thawed all night. We did our 21km through slush often 1ft deep and water, passing through Plagwitz, Lowenberg,

Hartelangvorwerk, Neuland to arrive at Giefsmannsdorf at 2.45. It was very strange walking on solid road again.

We heard rumours that Frankfurt on Oder has fallen and Breslau surrounded. Today was remarkable for the rapidity of the thaw. This has been the most rapid thaw I have ever seen.

Fri Feb 2nd

We started at 8.30 to march along dry, hard roads. My feet and legs were very painful due, no doubt, to the hard roads.

We passed our second Gorlitz signpost today in Lauban. The first was some days ago and said 141km but this was much better. 25km. We passed another about 2km further on which said 26km but no matter, we were reaching our destination.

Today was gruelling in the extreme. 27 long weary km. We passed through Siefersdorf, Thiemendorf, Bertelsdorf, Lauban, Lichtenau, Geibsdorf, to arrive at Heidersdorf at 5.15.

This was our worst billet. Pitch dark and so crowded that some lads had to sit up all night! It was a sort of granary and my bed was this shape *(image on p.269)*. There was no straw just hard boards and cold too.

We heard rumours today that Stettin had gone and the Russians were 60km from Berlin.

Sat Feb 3rd

After that ghastly night we started at 8.45 and after fast going saw the *postam* boxes outside the camp at 1.15. Happy hour! How ironical that we should love to see barbed wire again. But it was true.

Today we passed through Nikolausdorf, Schonbrunn and Gorlitz *(Stalag 8A)*.

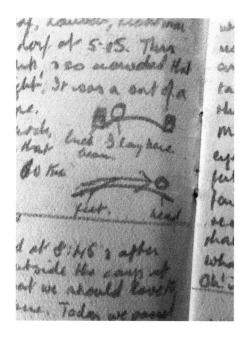

Dad's bed in the
Granary

We were greeted by the inevitable reception committee but I didn't know anyone.

We had no search and after waiting around for a time were herded into a barrack 400 strong! The barracks are dirty, damp and cold. Alex, Cliff and I are on bottom beds and lucky to get those. We were issued with spuds, soup, bread and tea which relieved our distress a little. This is a small but cosmopolitan camp of British, French, Poles, Belgian, Yanks and Russians. The guards are very itchy on the trigger and if we go outside between 9.00pm and 06.00am we must expect a bullet. Also if anyone as much as pokes his head out of the window during an air raid – Bang!!

The weather was quite mild when we arrived but turned cold at night. We have no paillasses or straw but sleep on hard boards on the floor.

Sun Feb 4th

Cold and damp.

I had a terrible night. The draught was howling over my body and I was frozen. Hardly any sleep at all.

Today was spent in trying to get a little more organised and especially in getting cleaned up. A disappointment is that it is unlikely that we shall get any shower but today the magic transformation took place. We painfully scraped our growth away in cold water. But I felt 100% better after a shave and good wash and am surprised at how clean my body is. It really is quite clean but I must have lost stones in weight.

When I first went into the latrine at VIIIB I was nauseated. Here I have no words to describe the state of this shit-house (I can't call it a latrine). The Russians who occupied this barrack previously must live like animals.

Today our barrack strength was brought up to 500. It is disgusting, owing to our being so full, we are unable to even boil up a brew. Consequently we have to get up at 5.00 am to drink our hot mint tea and enjoy it.

The boys' morale is at its lowest I've ever seen. There are rumours that we shall be moving on Wed, but I feel this is just wishful thinking. The rest of 344 should be moving tomorrow. God knows where they will be billeted. From what we can hear, they had much better organisation behind us; hot soups, spuds, bread issues and brews.

My general conclusions about the march are these. I tried hard to take my mind off the discomfort by thinking of various things. Mainly HOME. My thoughts were constantly with Mum, Dad, Rene and Rover. Always there. Mum would cry her eyes out if she only saw us. I plotted and planned my future career which I think will now definitely be farming. Oh for those home comforts. I reorganised the Hollies, redecorated the house; I took over Wrottesley Farm and reorganised that. I thought of all the food I will eat when I get home. What I shall cook up for myself – my own special dishes. Oh! in this misery how I long for home.

Mon Feb 5th

Wet, cold miserable day; just the opposite to what it should be for cheering the boys up, altho I myself don't feel too bad at all.

We have just heard some pukka BBC news and it's good. An offensive on the W Front; the Ruskies 60km from Berlin, with fierce fighting all along the Oder, she looks pretty good. I don't see how the Huns can carry on without their arsenals. Silesia, the Saar and the Ruhr.

I have got a book from the library which makes things better. The English barracks in the camp are quite good. Warm and clean tho a little crowded. But it is easy to see they have been living well at one time. Further to this camp; the water is rusty, and the washroom is flooded ankle deep!!

Well, enough of the gory details. We must now make the best of a bad job, try and acclimatise ourselves as much as possible to the conditions and generally cheer up. I feel quite cheerful today. We now await, not without some trepidation, the next item on the programme.

Played a little bridge in the afternoon.

We hear that there is a big breakthrough in the Breslau area and a big one on the W Front. V good news. I am terrifically optimistic.

I am convinced that the only people who really appreciate the fewer things in life are the ones who have undergone suffering and hardship. They certainly learn a deeper appreciation of the smaller luxuries; a fireside, good bed, good plain food etc, which others accept as their due and as a natural sequence of inheritance. I have certainly learnt how little I previously appreciated a good home life.

Tues Feb 6th

Wet and miserable again.

This morning we had an unexpected but pleasant surprise when we were deloused and consequently had an excellent shower. But what terrible sights we saw. Some Russians were going through and I was almost sick at the sight. Some were crawling and some couldn't even crawl but had to be carried to the shower. They were nothing but skin and bone and I'm sure one was on his last legs. Some had open wounds which the Huns don't seem to bother about at all. It was a terrible sight of absolute suffering and maltreatment and I shall never forget it. These Huns have a lot to pay for.

Hear that the civvies in Gorlitz have orders to evacuate so we should be moving any time. This place absolutely reeks with rumours, most of which are unreliable, but I believe on the whole that the news is excellent. I have heard that our mail did not leave 344 for 14 weeks before we left. In that case it is 17 weeks since my last mail went home. I am very worried for they must be extremely anxious in these unsettled times. I only hope Mum doesn't worry too much.

We hear that Blechhammer was surrounded as the SS

turned machine guns on the Jews, set fire to their barracks and told the British lads to get out into the woods.

The column from 344 following us had a much easier time; bags of soups and spuds and much better all-round organisation. I'm sure our officers could have done more for us.

Wed Feb 7th

A much nicer morning with promise of some sunshine today.

I am amazed at the depth of gloom some of the lads have let themselves slide into. In my opinion this is idiotic for I believe when a man loses his sense of humour he loses all. Life is only what we make of it, no matter where we be and it is up to every man to make the best of a bad job. Undoubtedly, my outlook on life has changed over these past 3 weeks and, altho I still have a small trace of wanderlust still in me, I have almost definitely decided to go in for farming. If I do this I shall invest all my money in poultry, about which I think I know a little, and perhaps a few pigs. This will give me an added interest whilst working under Dad. Of one thing I am certain; that Mum and Dad will be delighted over this decision.

Spent this am having a soak and since it was my duty day, I managed to boil up two brews and soak our egg-flakes. One thing I notice here, no matter how little I do during the day I feel terribly tired and weary at night. This is perhaps a good thing for, altho we go to bed at 6pm, I manage to get a really good night's sleep on hard bed boards 4 and 5 inches apart.

Our food now is no Red X at all; a hot mint tea at 5am, spuds and a small soup one day, a large soup and no spuds the next, $\frac{1}{7}$ of a loaf and $\frac{1}{20}$ of a block of marg, hot sweet coffee *(ersatz)* at 5pm. This is what we have to live on. Major McLeod has promised that if any Red X comes into the camp, the men of the 1st 344 column will get it. Also the Red X authorities have given orders to the Huns that no more PoWs are to be moved under the conditions of the 1st column.

As for the war, I have a sneaking feeling that the Russians may consolidate for a few weeks or couple of months and then everyone make a concerted attack in late March or early April.

Thurs Feb 8th

Miserable again.

The authorities in camp are going to send a letter to the Red X demanding that they send a representative up, and that if the Huns cannot do something about better conditions, that we be sent to a neutral country. What a hope!

The Commandant says we shall be moving within 3 weeks to a new camp distance 240km away. God forbid that we march it.

Bob and Dave arrived today. I was hoping I wouldn't see Dave again. He would ruin my nerves here.

I am amazed at my state of weakness and weariness every evening. I am really ready for bed at 6pm. I have never felt so weak in my life and my legs are far from better yet.

Fri Feb 9th

Weather much better today.

A Russian officer captured at Breslau talking to Dave says the war should end in 14 days to a month. We hear that

Leignitz *(now Legnica)* has gone. We are sure that they are only 74km away so it looks as tho we'll be on the road again any day. Also that there has been a big breakthrough in the West.

Played a little crib this am. We are now completely out of smokes.

This evening whilst engaged in a card game with Tommy, George and Roy, when we were told we should be moving tomorrow with 2 days rations.

One thing is certain, I shan't have much trouble packing my kit.

Sat Feb 10th

A nice morning but with a cold wind blowing.

We were ready to go at 9.30 and after dishing our ration of ½ loaf and ¹⁄₁₀ tin of meat paste, we eventually left the camp at 12.15. So ended exactly 7 days stay at 8A.

I felt very weary and listless when I set out and my worst fears were later confirmed. After 5km I could hardly move my leg for severe pains in the groin and also had bad pains in my left shoulder.

On and on we went passing through Gorlitz, Kunnerwitz, Friedersdorp, to arrive at Reichenbach at 8.30 in pitch dark and rain. It was absolutely terrible. It was worse than my first night; weary, exhausted, almost sick staggering all over the road. And then we were cramped 8000 into one camp. No sleep at all.

Our guards are the old *Volksturm* and were as fatigued as we were. What a set! God Damn these Blasted Huns. 24km

Sun Feb 11th

A glorious sunny day but a bit cold.

The Huns have issued special orders that they will hold a full Court Marshal for any man caught stealing or making a nuisance etc, and if found guilty, the men will be shot in ½ an hour. This is because last night the cows were milked, chicken millet and stuff stolen. I got a brew up this am and we moved off at 9.15.

Passing through Schops we did 10km to arrive at Weissenberg at 1.15. We had ½ a mug of coffee and got into bed.

I felt much better today and would feel happier still if I knew where we were going.

Mon Feb 12th

I had a terrible night, no sleep, shivering all night. I think I have a chill in the stomach for I have bad stomach pains. I said to Alex and Cliff "I don't think I'll make it today" whilst waiting to draw rations of ¼ loaf and ¹⁄₁₆ tin of meat, I had a severe 4 minute black-out, but didn't go unconscious. After having my pulse and temp taken by an MO I felt ok again. Anyway we had a loaf between 3 and a tin of meat between 3 so it did some good!!

I really did feel terrible.

Nevertheless, we started off in bitter cold and a blinding snow storm in what promised to be a terror of a day. It cleared later. We started at 05.00hrs and did 22km passing through Maltitz, where we spent last night incidentally, Kotitz, Wurschen, Neuperschwitz to arrive at Bautzen which seems to be a garrison town, at 2.30.

We waited on a Hun barrack square 'til 3.30, then moved to another barrack at 4.30 where we spent the night in a riding school, on a hardened floor of sand. It was very cold. We had a soup issue for which we queued up for 2hrs and which eventually arrived at 11.30. It was good soup, but I was disgusted with the lads. Each man seemed to be drawing about 4 rations. I only drew one and was glad I stuck to my principles. I felt happier for it. Some lads didn't get their soup. Also the Huns were doing a lot of racketeering but I think it was with our bread which should be issued tomorrow.

Rene Kemp heard the 5 o'c BBC in a hospital and the Ruskies are between **Leiguitz** and Gorlitz and hold a line from there to a point 25km S of Berlin. A commentator said the next 40 days will be critical for Germany – and I think for certain prisoners in _____.

Saw more defence preparations yesterday than any day so far.

Tues Feb 13th

A very wet morning.

I crave now for home, good food and good cigarettes. I have decided that nothing will be too good for me when I do get home. I will make up in food what I would normally have spent in drink if I had stayed in England. Drink doesn't worry me one iota.

We started at 4.15 in good mild weather, but did not leave Bautzen 'til 12.05. It was a terrible march of 30km to a tank barrack in Kamenz where we arrived at 8.15. I have never been so near complete and absolute demoralization in my life. I must confess I was almost in tears at one time with thirst and pain in my foot.

The officers did the usual trick, told us first we were going to a church where we would get coffee "just down the road" and when the church did not appear it was a tank barracks the other side of the town, where we would get soup and coffee. Someone asked if we would get lilos too.

We eventually got a very good helping of soup and coffee at 9.15 and were then kept waiting around for billets. And then an air raid started. To the accompaniment of flashes, flames, gunfire and bomb blast we eventually got into a gymnasium.

It was a terrible day.

Wed Feb 14th

Yesterday we passed through **Niedlitz,** Rattwitz, Bloaschutz, Prischwitz, Lehndorf, Siebitz, Kuckau, Panschwitz and Kamenz.

Started today at 10.45 after a boring wait for coffee. There are a tremendous amount of SS troops around and very fine looking chaps too. I hope they haven't got too many of them.

Terrible day again on account of foot. Extremely painful. Did 15km to Konigsbruck passing through ? and Neukirch to arrive at 4.00. We waited hrs to collect some soup and then didn't get any as they said it was too dark to issue it. We then bedded down in a tent. Here again we saw lots of fine looking SS.

According to a pamphlet that a Russian worker had here, Russian tanks have got into the suburbs of Berlin and appealed to them to pack in the war. We have been passing through the outer defences of Dresden the last two days.

Thurs Feb 15th

What a terrible night. The only night we really needed a good roof over our heads - we were in a tent. It rained cats and dogs and of course we inside were drenched for the tent wasn't water-proof. I moved my bed 3 times but still the eternal drip, drip, drip on my blankets. We had soup (an ____ porridge) at 6 and the ration of ½ loaf and 1/15 tin meat and 2 slabs cheese per man for 2 days.

Hear rumours that Berlin is surrounded and that an air offensive is in progress.

I was in great pain today from the inflammation in my left shoulder.

We did 23km passing through Laussnitz, Tauscha, Thiendorf, Schonfeld to Kalkreuth where we arrived at 5pm. Here after the usual 2-6hrs waiting around whilst everyone catches pneumonia, we had a good issue of spuds. I then managed to get a most cramped and uncomfortable single bed.

Cliff unfortunately has been stricken with diarrhoea and had to relieve himself 18 times on the march.

Fri Feb 16th

We had soup and coffee this am and eventually started at 10.00. We did 18km in glorious weather to finish a 3.00pm.

Cliff was very ill and weak, so between us we carried his kit all day. We arrived at an army camp and were issued with soup.

Hear a rumour that the Ruskies are 80km from Dresden. Today we passed through Altleis, Jessen to Ockrilla.

Sat Feb 17th

After an alright night first we lined up on the road at 6.30. After getting our coffee and rations of ⅓ loaf and slab of meat per man for 3 days, we started at 10.10.

It turned out a glorious day but, I improved slightly yesterday, today my shoulder was agonising.

We crossed the Elbe at Meissen and I must confess the width of it shook me. It is much longer than I expected so far inland. Meissen was in a state of panic, hastily erecting defences and fortifications.

We then followed the Elbe for a short time and in the glorious Spring weather it was lovely. When someone noticed some catkins and said "Signs of Spring" I was almost in tears, so many memories were brought to me. As the day wore on I felt worse. We climbed steep hills and I was boiling hot.

On top of this I have developed diarrhoea. I think it is more a cold in the stomach, in fact all through me as I was shivering at the stops. On top of this I feel very, very weak and worn out. It is in times of suffering and stress like this that I realise how much I have to look forward to. So much. My God, will I have a good time when I get home. My life will certainly be fully occupied in future.

Today we did 17km passing though Meissen, Zehren, Piskowitz to arrive at Lommatzsch at 3.15. After drawing soup we eventually got billets at 7.30.

Cliff rode on the cart today. Too weak to walk.

Sun Feb 18th

A day of rest today, thank goodness. I had to get up 4 times during the night and didn't get an hour of sleep all night, my mind being in a continued whirl. The whole day I spent lying in the straw in between visits to the latrine. I am worried I may have caught Cliff's dysentery.

Thurs March 8th

And now begins the tale of woe.

Since my last entry I have been through, what I now realise, to be the most critical period of my life. I think I have been quite near death.

The interim period 18th Feb to 8th March will have to be completed from memory for I lost all my day to day notes in a frantic search for bumph.

Cliff went to hospital on 19th Feb at Lommatzsch with dysentery and I carried his disease on the road. We were promised that on arrival at Eisenberg we should be at our destination and expected to arrive there on the 25th Feb. This was why we continued to carry on, in spite of the difficulty of having to drop out of line every so often to obey a call. With great dismay I noticed it was blood and slime coming from me. Dysentery.

The next two days were terrible. I tried and wanted to stay with Alex and Johnny but after staying at Dobeln and Leisnig I eventually yielded to their advice to go sick. I was terribly weak and had eaten practically nothing for two days.

At Leisnig the calamity occurred. I let everything go (of necessity) in my trousers. It was all blood. I joined the sick column there and then and had my kit bag carried on the cart. In this way I got to a *Lazarette* at Bad Lausick and there we were greeted by two good English mugs of tea and had a good millet and porridge sweet soup. On top of that we had a good warm billet in the dining room.

We had a medical and I was diagnosed as having influenza and Dysentery. 23 of the boys stayed here and one, Harry Peel, died the following night with D. The following day I walked without kit again but felt increasingly weak and exhausted. All the MOs could do was give me pills and charcoal.

That night we spent at Borna. The next day we did a very short distance but I felt absolutely done in at the end of it. Thommy was with the sick here and in the stable helped me a lot. I was like a helpless child. The next morning I pleaded with the MO to let me go to hospital but to no avail. I really felt I couldn't go any further. That was at Wurchwitz.

Anyway, my kit was carried that day, nevertheless I still had to hold onto a cart and be dragged along 'til I eventually scrounged my way on to the cart and rode. That night we spent at Zeitz. The next day we were due to arrive at Eisenberg. I was very ill. Unable to sleep at night with going to the latrine often in almost inaccessible places. My pants and shirt were by now very messy and I really thought at times that I was going to die. I was so weak.

The last day I had to walk carrying my kit. A strap had broken to make matters worse. I was dawdling along at the rear of the sick, when I had a row with a Hun who kicked me viciously in the shins. The MO Major was unsympathetic but I am indebted to this day to the padre who helped me carry my kit and tried to keep cheerful. The Major was very callous and pushed me along roughly with his stick. Finally after about 20 nightmare km a cart came along and I was put on almost out.

We arrived at Eisenberg, in fact went straight through to a barn. No sign of the mythic camp with Red X parcels. This was the 25th. The next day we stayed in the barn, I spent most of my time on the latrine and the following day the very sick were moved by carts (61 of us) to a hospital at Stadtroda. The rest of the boys went on (God knows where to).

We did the 25km to the hospital and were there comforted by the awful spectre of no room. Nevertheless, stricken cases were taken off, we got a brew of cocoa and after much argument we were allowed in.

As for the march itself, I will say it was the most taxing and difficult experience of my life, mainly due to my physical disabilities. The Huns did make an effort to give us rations but, altho we had our bread, soups and coffee, they were still grossly inadequate and they had too little organisation in finding billets for us quickly.

We were kept hanging around in the cold, hours at a time, lying around on wet ground whilst other things were arranged. I was disgusted at the attitude of our block leaders and column leader and waves of passionate anger went through me when I saw Mac Currie etc in a cart of their own whilst the sick had to trudge along in misery.

A conclusion I have reached also is this; MAN is little removed from an animal at the bottom when it comes to real survival. It is the old animal story of the survival of the fittest. I was disgusted and amazed at the display of pettiness, dishonesty, theft, meanness, selfishness and complete animal callousness that was so often displayed. Rations stolen, trivial arguments and general lack of *esprit de corps*.

It was mostly, I'm glad to say, amongst the lesser educated members of the crowd but nevertheless it still existed amongst the so-called educated clans. They grovelled, snivelled, grabbed, snatched and scrounged, begged and pleaded if they thought there was anything to be given away. It was horrible to see. I sometimes feel ashamed to be an Englishman.

Dad's route through towns/villages (with post-war names in brackets)

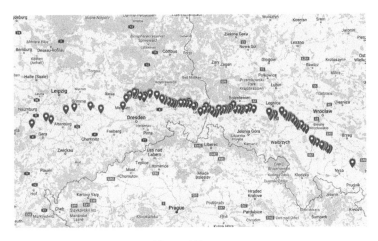

Map of Route

22nd Jan 1945	Lamsdorf (Lambinowice) – Friedewalde	25km
23rd Jan	Friedewalde – Prieborn (Przeworno)	30km
24th Jan	Prieborn – Prauss (Prusy)	23km
	Via: Habendorf (Milocice), Rummels Berg, Gepperdof (Gebczyce), Steinkirche (Bialy Kosciol), Wammelwitz (Wawoinica)	
25th Jan	Prauss – Zobten (Sobotka)	20km
	Via: Jolheita, Grobkniegnitz (Ksieginice Wielkie), Senitz (Sienice), Heidersdorf (Lagiewniki), Langenols (Oleszna)	
26th Jan	Zobten – Domanze (Domanice)	15km
	Via: Marxdorf (Garncarsko), Klien Mohnau (Maniow Maly)	
27th Jan	Domanze – Damsdorf (Damianowo)	22km
	Via: Ingramsdorf (Imbramowice),	

	Pitschen (Pszcyn), Bertholdsdorf (Goscislaw), Gabersdorf (Udanin), Beckern (Piekary), Kuhnern (Konary)	
28th Jan	Damsdorf – St Peterwitz (Piotrowice) Via: Tschinschwitz (Ksiezyce), Merzdorf (Mierczyce), Jauer (Jawor)	21km
29th Jan	St Peterwitz – Goldberg (Zlotoryja) Via: Heldinsdorf, Pramsnitz, Loblitz	20km
30th Jan	Rest day	
31st Jan	Goldberg – Lauterseiffen (Bielanka) Via: Hennersdorf (Chroslice), Pilgrimsdorf (Pielgrzymka), Hockenau (Czaple)	19km
1st Feb	Lauterseiffen – Giefsmannsdorf (Gosciszow) Via: Plagwitz (Plakowice), Lowenberg (Lwowek Slaski), Hartelangvorwerk (Radlowka), Neuand (Niwnice)	21km
2nd Feb	Giefsmannsdorf – Heidersdorf (Wlosien) Via: Siefersdorf (Msciszow), Thiemendorf (Radostow Sredni), Bertelsdorf (Uniegoszcz), Lauban (Luban), Lichtenau (Zareba), Geibsdorf (Siekierczyn)	27km
3rd Feb	Heidersdorf – Gorlitz (Stalag VIIIA Gorlitz Moys) Via: Nikolausdorf (Mikulowa), Schonbrunn (Studiska)	
4th–9th Feb	Rest days	
10th Feb	Gorlitz – Reichenbach Via: Kunnerwitz, Friedersdorf	24km
11th Feb	Reichenbach – Weissenberg	10km
12th Feb	Weissenberg – Bautzen Via: Maltitz, Kotitz, Wurschen, Neuperschwitz	22km
13th Feb	Bautzen – Kamenz Via: Rattwitz, Bloaschutz, Prischwitz,	30km

	Lehndorf, Siebitz, Kuckau, Panschwitz	
14th Feb	Kamenz – Konigsbruck	15km
	Via: Neukirch	
15th Feb	Konigsbruck – Kalkreuth	23km
	Via: Laussnitz, Tauscha, Thiendorf, Schonfeld	
16th Feb	Kalkreuth – Ockrilla	18km
	Via: Altleis, Jessen	
17th Feb	Ockrilla – Lommatzsch	17km
	Via: Meissen, Zehren, Piskowitz	
18th Feb	Lommatzch – Dobeln	19km
19th Feb	Dobeln – Leisnig	20km
20th Feb	Leisnig – Bad Lausick	23km
21st Feb	Bad Lausick – Borna	15km
22nd Feb	Borna – Wurchwitz	30km
23rd Feb	Wurchwitz – Zeitz	9km
24th Feb	Zeitz – Eisenberg	20km
25th Feb	Eisenberg – Stadtroda	25km

The Road to Recovery

Fri March 9th

We arrived here on 27th Feb and I can't describe my heart-felt relief at the thought that at last I ought to get at least a good rest and some proper treatment. I am not frightened of death but I certainly don't want to die like that and I have so much, so very much to look forward to.

As we got on the hospital premises I was really on my last legs. It appeared that the Huns said they couldn't take us but after much argument we were bedded down on straw in a wooden hut complete with stove. It was lovely and warm. We had 22 in the hut to start with which has now been whittled down to 18.

Our first pleasant surprise was the issue of 1 tin of lemon curd pie and a soup of creamed rice. It was delicious and all the dysentery in the world wouldn't have stopped me eating it. We had one slice of bread which I was able to toast.

All my bread for the next 7 days I toasted black and hard, with great damage to my teeth but good effect on my stomach.

The following day we were officially on the ration strength and now have a sweet brew, coffee or tea (Hun) in the am, non-sweet in the pm, 2 slices of bread and honey or jam for breakfast; soup for lunch; 2 slices of bread, marg and meat for tea. Friday is a two soup day when we get a sweet cereal in the evening but no marg or meat. Sunday is no soup but veg of about 6 spuds and 2 veg.

The rations are greatly inadequate for sick men and altho we certainly can't get any worse, I hardly think we can recuperate on these rations. We have put in many moans the last day or two but I doubt whether it will have much effect.

On the second day here we had a shower. I was terrified at my own appearance. I thought the Russians at G. were thin but I was nothing but skin and bone. I was an absolute walking skeleton and still am. I had great difficulty in standing under the shower and the smell of the boys washing away their own excreta was terrible. In fact the whole scene was pitiful. The epitome of human suffering. I have never seen any set of human beings suffering so much.

We were disappointed at there being no Red X but during the last few days we have had a brew of Horlicks each evening at the rate of either 4-5-6 tins between 18 men. These have done us a tremendous amount of good. We were also given some English tea and have had one brew a day.

On top of that we have had about 5 packets of sweets between us, 1/6 tin lemon curd, 1/2 tin of ____, and each morning 1/2 an egg omelette.

One evening I was lucky, for the MO considered me sufficiently ill to have a tin of creamed rice to myself. This was when I was visiting the bedpan up to 20 times a day.

On Mar 3rd two of the boys, McGuiness and Sampson, died of dysentery. This was a great blow to us but on the 7th yet another lad, Pasco, died of the same thing. 3 of us had passed away! Our treatment consisted mainly of pills and quinine. I had 14 pills to take one evening. Never have I taken so many pills in so short a time. Small and large white ones, brown ones, charcoal etc.

It took 'til the 8th to clear up my dysentery and it was almost with a shout of joy that I moved a solid motion. Tho my stomach is in the process of recovery, delicate and tender, my influenza is still not cleared but much better. My main trouble is weakness which is why I have left my diary 'til now. Even this is a great effort to me and makes me puff and sweat. I didn't realise it was possible for anyone to feel so weak and helpless. What I need is good food and plenty of it.

On the 7th the Hun said we were to move by train to a British hospital at Oberhausen. The MO (who is French) said I was one of the 12 still too unfit to move, so am staying. The rest were supposed to be going two days ago but owing to transport difficulties are still here.

Today the Red X commission came round and I believe complaints about the rations are being made. Also the chances of Red X parcels coming through from the depot at Bad Sulza have increased and we are hoping for them early next week.

Last Sunday 4th I wrote a letter home and card to Mary. What relief it gave me to send them off. I only hope they get through. All I've been able to do since being here is sit, lie down and talk, tho this is tiring. We have discussed food, holidays and our future careers a lot and I have definitely decided to take up farming after I get home. I shall have a good time but am prepared to work very hard.

I have planned my next Xmas dinner at home which I shall cook, and various picnics which I shall organise. Menus are a special hobby. My craving for smoking is not too bad but

I would enjoy a good fag. My big craving is food and home, sweet home again. In future I shall live to eat and not eat to live. All my meals and food will be considered and worked out and I shall cook a lot myself. As for holidays, my main schemes are tours in the Lake District and Scotland with Ann and Mary.

As for my present company, now that everyone is a little fitter the *Stalag* secrets are coming out. I again amused the Have-nots, mainly because I can't get out of bed and move around. The Haves here have been discussing their rackets in *Stalag*. It is rather amusing but pathetic. I can see I'm not used to this living from hand to mouth business. Nonetheless we have quite a pleasant spirit in the hut and everyone tries to resist complaining. It is quite good.

The war news is very encouraging especially the W Front news. We are all hoping for an early finish but I fail to see how the entry of Turkey and Finland against Germany will make much difference.

There is a tremendous amount of bombing around here and the food situation is getting grimmer and grimmer.

I am exhausted. I'll have to stop.

Sat Mar 10th

Last night I saw quite a good map of our route. It seems that we walked about 600km which _____ me about 580km.

Today we had a most interesting discussion about principles. What a cynical crowd most of them are and absolutely devoid of principles. One fellow told me all I would have would be a box full of principles whereas he would have a box of food. I still refuse to be so much of a cynic, altho my faith in human nature has been considerably shaken. Thank God I still have my principles.

The padre came in from Muhlhausen *(Stalag IX-C)* today for the funeral but was very supercilious and did little to cheer us except one cig, a Capstan, and very welcome too.

I have a horrible feeling that the boys are still on the march. I sincerely hope not.

Today I was one of six in the room to be given extra food. ⅛ tin of lemon curd and a Horlicks brew.

The sleeping draught last night knocked me cold. I am convinced our rations are below starvation diet. Our 4 slices of bread are like wafers. Everything seems to have been cut.

Mon Mar 12th

I have decided not to write an entry every day or the chances are that I shall fill my book with little hope of a replacement.

Yesterday I had an extra ration; 1 tin creamed rice, ⅓ tin lemon curd and a brew of Horlicks.

An unfortunate thing has occurred. My toothache again starts after a meal. Last night I didn't sleep a wink but had to read from 3 – 6.

Our main topics of conversation are food; special dishes, menus etc. and holidays – we are all planning various tours. I have in mind a cycling tour of Scandinavia and tours of the Lake District, Scotland, Wales and Devon and Cornwall. I would like to do these tours with Mary and Rene. I think they would enjoy it immensely. I also think a lot of my plans and ideas for the future, how shall I amuse myself. As far as I can make out what I definitely will need is a load of money.

The war news is good especially from the W Front where we have apparently crossed the Rhine at Koblenz and established a bridge head. I am also reading some quite good books.

The Hun *dolmetscher* here is a pretty good cove. He speaks excellent English and French, looks 18 but is 31 and when asked where he learnt his English, astounded the boys with a nonchalant 'in China' at Nanking. He has spent very little of his time in Germany, has no time for the Nazi party and has spent a considerable amount of time in concentration camps! On 1st Mar he gave us his cig ration for the month.

We hear some excellent news today, I only hope it's true. We are supposed to be at **Sugham** which is 70km west of Cologne; a 2000 raid on Essen with a death rate of 50000; shelling Essen and most important of all, Hitler is supposed to have made a speech in which he said "All is lost in Germany but we will fight on for the memory of the Reich". If this is true the war should end in a fortnight or 3 weeks' time.

I have decided that my hobbies when I get home will be;

1. Cooking
2. Aero-modelling
3. Gardening
4. Fishing
5. My library

There are certain things I must do;

1. Get a list of war (14-18) (39-45) books from Foyles especially flying
2. Get a catalogue of ____ reprints from the Regiment ____ ____ Book Club

3. Get a copy of James Fighting Ships 39-45
4. Get a complete list of Penguin Specials 39-45
5. Get bound volumes of Illustrated _____ Picture Post in 39-45 and illustrated
6. Buy a good book on nutrition
7. Several good books on cookery
8. A good one on gardening and fruit cultivation. I have also decided to join these libraries; **Whipton** Public library, ___, Foyles and Boots.
9. To join some of Foyles Book Clubs.

It is my intention to make my bedroom a model of luxury, and convert the spare room into a workshop laboratory to cultivate if possible mushrooms etc. and conduct experiments on soil analysis etc. I am also going to get a good book on Carpentry and Handicrafts and try and erect a couple of glass-houses for tomatoes etc. I am going to invest my money in poultry and on advice from Dad, possibly some pigs; make as much money as poss by picking blackberries, shooting and wiring rabbits etc.

I have also decided to put on the Sunday dinner on occasion and to do all the cooking etc of '45 Xmas dining if I am at home. Even to making my rum cake, mincemeat and buying my own spreads and food. I shall try to keep the whole programme a secret. These are just a few of the many plans and ideas flashing through my mind.

We even discuss these ideas and one of the favourite pastimes here is discussing special dishes and menus. We certainly have a food complex but strangely enough, talking about it no longer makes us feel hungry, mainly because our stomachs have shrivelled so much. We can feel satisfied on practically nothing at all.

Our rations at the moment are 4 very thin slices of bread, jam on one slice in the morning, meat and marg in the evening, both very small portions. A litre of soup (sometimes thick, sometimes thin) per day and one cup of mint tea, one cup of coffee. I fully believe we are below starvation diet.

I am fortunately on an extra food diet and got 1/3 tin lemon curd and 1/3 tin rolled oats today. Tomorrow I get 1/3 lemon curd and a brew of Horlicks.

It is rather amusing to note that the Haves when we first arrived, as the fitter man who managed to pinch some extra veg etc. were quite pleasant to we weaker Have-nots. Now that the Have-nots are getting extra food and the Haves little gains have been stopped, they treat us with noticeable antipathy. It is pitiful to see some of them trying to wheedle their way onto the extra food list through the MO. They are usually the scavengers who were well into the rackets in *Stalag*. I am secretly, in fact spitefully, pleased.

Wed Mar 14th

Glorious Spring day today.

Managed to struggle to the dentist and have two teeth filled. I'm afraid the fillings are very, very temporary. He just scraped the hole out and stuck some filling in. No drilling at all.

Wrote a letter home again today. I hope it gets through though I strangely doubt it. Last night we had a little Record programme, highly enjoyable and later Kim entertained us with tales of Tahiti. I'd love to go there.

I find it very hard to sleep at night even after taking a sleeping draft. I want to keep off those things if poss.

We hear that Himmler's headquarters are at Gera about 25km from here.

No news of any importance except that we seem to be widening our bridge heads over the Rhine.

Thurs Mar 15th

Lovely Spring day again.

A Red letter day. The parcels arrived today. A fortnights issue and a number of invalid parcels. We understand that the columns moved on to **Nussaberg**. The parcels are Yank No 10. What a day.

The sickest of us went for screening but after making the stagger the machine was broken so we staggered back. I felt terribly weak. Nobby Clark and Duffy today failed to recognise me. I look so thin and rough. It shook me. I find that when I try to explain how ill I've been and how weak I still am I am inclined to almost burst into tears. It's terrible.

We got our parcels which have to last a fortnight and all I have eaten today is ½ packet of sweets and a few spoons of Klim and 6 cubes of sugar. In the evening we had a ____ soup of 4 tins of pots, 4 tins of Ovaltine, 4 of Le. Curd, 1 of Horlicks, 1 of ____ food. All went into one pot and we had a ____ glop for 18. The *dolmetscher* came in for a brew and a biscuit. He's a wizard bloke.

I feel a little stronger today but am a bit worried about my heart. I also today made friends with a fellow book-worm, who has a library of 1500 books, one Doug Ellsmore. A good lad.

Sat outside today in glorious warm sun.

My parcel contained 4oz choc, 4oz sweets, 100 cigs, 8oz cheese, 7½oz Salmon, 8oz Pork & beans, 12oz Luncheon

Pork, 8oz Pate, 6oz Pineapple Jam, 12oz Klim, 7oz Biscuits, 7 Vit C tablets, 5oz Raisins, 1lb Cleo marg, 8oz Sugar, 2oz Coffee, 2 bars of soap.

Fri Mar 16th

What a night. Everyone was much too pent up to sleep last night so at 2.30 today a brew went on. We had it at 5.00am. Lovely too.

The boys moved out at 7.00am, leaving the 17 sick and a *Sgt Sanitator (orderly)*. Now we should do pretty well.

I tried to get on the moving party to **Holberghanen** a British hospital but the MO would not hear of it. The Huns cut out our usual Friday afternoon soup today and the MO cut out extra drinks. Cuts everywhere. We had a good helping of soup at 11.00.

A glorious day today.

I am very disappointed at Doug Ellsmore going. I felt I have lost a good friend. Still we have each other's address and I have invited him home. I hope he comes. A real genuine lad.

Got our beds today. It seems very strange sleeping on mattresses again, but much more pleasant and clean of course.

At the moment I feel deeply friendless but I console myself with thoughts of home and the future. Oh that glorious future.

I did not enjoy my food very much today as my mouth was so sore I presume with cigs altho I have smoked very few. I now split up the real cigs and out of two manage to roll about 6.

I am now librarian, self-appointed I fear.

Sat Mar 17th

Some rain today but mild.

A good food day. Bread much thicker, a good thick soup and bags of it, a good marg ration. I got 2 kilo loaf for a tin of Yank coffee in the evening and the *dolmetscher* gave us two extra slices of civvy bread. Stan gave us two parcels ___ _____ book and boot loan. The day was marred by the return of the mail I first wrote to Mum and Mary as it was in ____ ____.

Hear that the Ruskies have started a big offensive at **Lation.**

Today we had our longest, nearest and heaviest raid. It was on Weimar and the Zeiss works at Jena just 15km away. The noise of the a/c was terrific and the explosions shook the billet. The dropping of a canister very close to here gave us a bit of a scare. It lasted 3½ hrs.

The MO gave my heart a good test today. It is not quite up to scratch. Got a bottle of beer today but didn't drink much of it.

Sun Mar 18th

Nothing of very great import today. We had continual air-raid warnings.

Had my first hot dinner since *Stalag*. Salmon and mash with *sauerkraut*.

Had my first bath since leaving England. Tepid water tho. Two of us in.

Mon Mar 19th

A glorious Spring day.

The Frogs came in and there was bags of trading but the boys were too ____ and he dominated the rate of exchange which was wicked. I refused to clinch a deal but got some bread and marg, bacon and cake for a singlet. The bacon filled bread in the evening can only be described as delicious. Did I enjoy it. I had bags of soup. We are living really well now.

In the afternoon there was a terrific air raid. The nearest bombing I have ever been near. We saw the formation coming over and I am sure there were many dog flights overhead. Then we heard a swoosh (onomatopoeia) everyone ducked and woomph, woomph, woomph. The building shook violently and then I saw some smoke from the bombs and smelt the cordite.

I forgot to mention that I distinctly saw a stick of bombs coming down. We later found out that the nearest bomb was 50yds away and a number were very close. Altogether about 150 were dropped round about, the main raid was in Jena. The Sergeant *Sanitator* in charge of us was quite scared and has issued an order that we must go down the shelter in future.

Personally, without wishing to boast or show any false bravado, I must admit I didn't feel in the least bit scared, rather was I fascinated; a strange detached feeling of fascination. Nevertheless, I hope they don't come any closer.

A consequence of the raid is that we now have no lights, no air raid warning, no news from the wireless. I think the bombs were very small ones.

We hear that Germany has approached Switzerland with a plan to obtaining peace terms from England. I hope it's true.

Tues Mar 20th

A little colder today here.

I had one tooth re-filled today. I was also weighed and although I have improved tremendously this last week, so definitely put on weight, I still only weigh 8st 4lbs!! A week ago I must have weighed only about 7st 10lbs. My present weight means I have lost 2st since last summer and I am now 3st 3lbs lighter than when I joined the service.

I was thinking today how delightfully peaceful it is here. No screaming Huns, no role calls, we are left extremely alone. Each morning and evening, typical of Spring, a thrush sings in a nearby tree. I love to listen to it. I wonder does it mean something to me or am I just being sentimental? No, I think it brings back dear memories.

Rumours that the Yanks dropped a pamphlet threatening to come back on 23rd and another that the offensive in the W will start on the 24th.

Wed Mar 21st

Mild but coldish owing to the wind.

Last night we had to go down to the shelter for 1½hrs much against my own personal wishes. I was very annoyed at having to suffer for the panic and scare of other people. During today we again had to go down and I was getting thoroughly browned off with it, so it was suggested and agreed upon, that the shelters are optional, thank goodness.

If ever I get a letter from home again there should be bags of news in it. Not that I have much hope actually.

We are now pumping Stan for an issue of the supplement parcels.

The Zeiss works have been completely destroyed. News that they are fighting round Mainz and Frankfurt is being shelled.

I have a feeling we are going to be here a long time and that we shall be very fed up with each other's company before we have finished.

Thurs Mar 22nd

A glorious, hot day today.

Spent most of the day after the MO's parade at 10am out in the sunshine. The electricity came back today but our coal ration has been cut in half. Could hear the rumbling of bombs in the distance. Got a 2kg loaf last night for 20 cigs.

No news today. Read another book today. It is going to be a great, absorbing passion of mine when I get home:- strolling, browsing I think is the correct word, round book shops and accumulating my library.

Had the gramophone on in the evening.

Fri Mar 23rd

As far as the weather was concerned, a glorious hot sunny day.

Otherwise I don't know whether it was a good or a bad day. We were issued with ½ a supplement parcel. Ours contained 1 tin Burger food, 1 tin Ovaltine, 1 tin Cocoa, 2 packets tea, 2 tins Condensed milk, 2oz choc, packet sweets, 2 blocks sugar, 2 tins soup powder, 2 tins porridge, 2 tins egg flakes, 1 tin cheese, 1 tin _____, 1 tin creamed rice, 1 tin fruit, 1 tin Horlicks, 1 tin Lemon Curd. A very good supplement to any parcel, but useless as a fortnight issue parcel which is what Stan intended doing.

Was my duty day but still spent a considerable amount of time outside in the sun. Had a really good feed in the afternoon.

The day was spoilt when in the evening 3 of the boys discovered they had lice. Horror of horrors. Two of them had 4 each and the other had one. We all frantically searched our clothes but I found none on mine. Of course, considering our physical state and also the conditions we have been existing under.

The news from the W Front indicates that the big offensive is in its last stages of preparation. We are looking forward to its commencement.

Sat Mar 24th

This morning at 7.20 poor old Jack Kirby, a Kiwi, passed away. I very much fear that he gave up hope. He was terribly thin and had chest trouble and dysentery. It is the first time I have really seen death close to. Not at all a pleasant sight. I feel very sorry. But his spirit in the last two days was definitely on the ebb.

Had two more teeth filled, one of which was out within 1hr.

We hear that the big offensive of the 2nd Army at **Arnhem** has started and the Yanks have made another crossing of the Rhone. I sincerely hope this news is true. If it is, I give the war 2 more months at the most.

Wrote a letter home and a letter to Mary.

The French Red X lorry arrived from Bad Sulza and we shall probably get another supply of parcels on Monday. If only we can stay here in this haven of rest until the end of the war. We also heard that our column passed through Bad Sulza only 6 days ago and that there had been numerous deaths. These Huns have something to answer for.

A glorious day again.

Sun Mar 25th

A glorious day again.

Nothing of importance to report. Spent the day as usual reading and sunbathing.

Mon Mar 26th

Not quite so sunny.

News that the big British offensive has started and that we have dropped 4 divisions of air borne troops. Montgomery says he will need a fortnight to get all his stuff across the Rhine.

Today we had 4 air raid warnings. 7:30-8:15 *Facallaram*, 10:45-11:25 ____, 1:45-3:15 local alarm, 8:30-10:00 *Fore alarme*.

We went for X-ray screening at 1:30 and had to spend 1½ hrs in the air raid shelter. Awful. My X-ray was negative which is a good thing.

Got another loaf for 2oz tea.

Tues Mar 27th

Cloudy but very mild.

The Yanks are supposed to be 50kms east of Frankfurt.

Yesterday saw some of the staff going to a hospital at **Schbitz**. One said he thought Cyril Ridge was dead. I hugely hope not.

The boys are supposed to have gone on to Kassel and it is rumoured that they are still on the march. Many lads have died. I think we dropped out just in time.

I feel very tired today and in fact feel very tired every evening. Was weighed again today and am now 54.8 kilos. It's a gain of 1.8 kilos since last week.

A *fore alarme* in the evening from 6:30 – 8:30.

I have almost decided not to read any of the good books as I find it impossible to concentrate sufficiently to appreciate their value and really enjoy them. I need a convivial atmosphere with no distraction. Here my mind wanders over the war, food rackets etc. Altho I have bags of grub at the moment I find myself very chary about its use, for I have a terrible fear of being short at some future time. How I long for the day when this dreadful fear of want will be dispelled.

Wed Mar 28th

Mild but cloudy.

No air-raid warning today, but in the distance we could hear a continuous rumbling which we couldn't decide to be either bombing or gunfire, for we hear that **Falda** has gone and the Yanks are in Kassel. There are amazing explosions and we are rather excited.

Had rather bad stomach-ache in the afternoon and evening.

Jack Kirby was buried today.

Thurs Mar 29th

Cold today.

The Huns have cut out our coal issue so we find it pretty cold. Parcel day today. Stomach still bad.

Rumours that the Yanks are at Coburg and Eisenach (80kms from here). I don't believe it myself but hope it's true. Also that 9B has been liberated.

Last night in the local cinema a message was flashed on the screen recalling all SS officers and NCO's to their billets. They then had to patrol the area, *autobahn* and railway.

The *Volksturm* are also patrolling and ____ tank defences are being put up. Also a 5 min long warning means paratroops and *panzers* in the area. They've certainly got a panic on here. Air raid warning. Local alarm 6:00 ____.

Fri Mar 30th

Mild but not too warm.

Good Friday today but rather a misnomer as far as I am concerned for I had my bad stomach-ache and indigestion all day.

We had a large number of air-raid warnings including one local alarm.

Rumours are flying round thick and fast but we have no concrete news.

All I could conjure up today were visions of hot x buns.

Sat Mar 31st

Very cold today.

A lot of warnings including one local when a stick was dropped 100yrds from here. We heard them coming down again and I couldn't get on the floor for the simple reason that it was covered with bodies.

News that the Yanks are at Coburg almost due south of here, E of Kassel and 40kms from Eisenach. Monty is supposed to have advanced 70kms in a day and surrounded Munster.

The news is excellent and everyone is expecting the Yanks here somewhere about Wed or Thurs. I wonder. The talk is all "when the Yanks come" and not "if the Yanks come".

Stomach very bad again.

The French MO has bet to the extent of 3 cases of champagne on the end of the war which he thinks will finish in less than a fortnight.

Sun April 1st

Easter Sunday and no Easter eggs. The only topic of conversation is "where are the Yanks now?"

The Frogs are wildly excited but I'm afraid that after the disillusionment of 344 I cannot work up the enthusiasm the situation seems to merit. Nevertheless, everyone is talking about what they will do when the Yanks get close, 25kms or so. Shall we go down the shelters or into the fields or stay where we are?? Etc etc. I prefer to let them get a bit closer before I really start to worry, altho we hear that they are at Eisenach and even closer.

A group of SS were at the soccer match today when they were suddenly ordered back to their billets to get ready to go to Eisenach. Later they were seen, fully kitted, on their way.

Rumours that the local *Volksturm* have also gone. We are now wondering if Muhlhausen and the boys who went to Hildburghausen have been liberated.

Today I had two good meals porridge in the am and for lunch; creamed spuds, fried meat roll, fried bread, fried onions and it was delicious. It was not without trepidation that I attempted it but my stomach stood it 'til the evening when a slice of bread put paid to a rather quiet day.

The French donated a wonderful brew of coffee!

Mon Apr 2nd

Windy and not too warm.

We awoke to sounds of a fighter patrol overhead and rumblings (gunfire or bombing?) in the West.

I'm sure the MO is more interested in the progress of the Yanks than in the progress of his patients.

A rather amusing thing happened today. We were cursing everyone for being so early with everything and late in the afternoon we heard that the clocks last night were advanced one hour. This makes the days long and the nights shorter.

It is noticeable that certain of our gangs' tempers are getting frayed, probably from close and limited quarters.

Tues Apr 3rd

A nice day after the evening storm.

A big shock today. On weighing I was down to 51.7 kilos i/e a loss of 3.1 kilos on last weighing and of 1.3 kilos on my 1st weighing. This puts my weight at 8st 1lb which is dangerously and absurdly low for a fellow of my size. Also since I was 11st 13lbs at one stage in the RAF.

The MO and medical Sgt in charge of us were a little shocked and afraid of this state of affairs, predicting TB. Roll on these Yanks and let's get some solid and good food, eggs, fruit, milk and meat and good fresh vegetables.

The news today is good. Monty is making tremendous strides in the north and the Yanks have bypassed Eisenach in the South. Our main camp, Muhlhausen, should be liberated by now.

Bags of air activity today with numerous alarms. Increased Hun fighter activity is a positive sign that the front is getting closer. Arrangements have been made for the complete evacuation of the hospital to the main town shelters, should there be any severe fighting in the area.

Played some bridge in the evening but I was not very interested I'm afraid.

Wed Apr 4th

What a day! My appetite is back with a vengeance which puts me in a good mood. So far, and it is now 9pm, we have had 7 air raid warnings, 6 *fore* and 1 local.

During the night there were many warnings and I believe instructions around. There was much traffic on the *autobahn*.

This afternoon we had a wonderful treat. We were just waiting for tea when we heard aircraft over and machine gun fire. Thinking a dog fight was in progress we went outside, only to see seven Thunderbolts flying around at about 2-3 thousand feet. From our vantage point we saw them strafing the *autobahn* about 1 mile away and the No 2 made a beautiful direct hit on a lorry on his first run. The thing burst into flames. It was a glorious sight. They made many beat-ups and circled the town many times with absolutely no opposition. It was just a picnic.

Tonight we hear that the Yanks are about 10kms from Weimer which puts them about 45kms from here.

Yanks for Friday! Certainly Sunday!

Thurs Apr 5th

A nice mild day again.

In the general excitement I forgot to mention that our bread ration is now 200gms per day; one slice in the am and one for tea.

Last night we had an alarm at 10pm. A local. I have never heard so many alarms in my life. The roar was tremendous as the continual offensive passed over in the direction of Leipzig or Dresden. Someone certainly caught a package.

Later, at about 1.30, the previous All Clear having gone at 12:00, there was another local alarm and this time it was much nearer. There was a terrific rumbling and vibration. The All Clear went about 3:00.

Today has been much quieter, one local alarm when a group of squadron of Mustangs beat up the *autobahn* again. Once more no opposition.

At this very moment, 5:00pm, there are more fighters beating something up and we can hear distant rumbling which may be artillery, for the Front is only 36kms away and 18kms from Jena.

What a day today!

I started off with a breakfast of porridge and raisins and during the morning, managed a crafty deal of a tin of coffee for a plucked pigeon and 3 hens eggs. The pigeon was roasted in butter for me so I had a meal, which proved to be easily the best meal turned out yet by any of the boys – namely; roast pigeon, fried egg, 2 slices fried bread, creamed and marged mashed potatoes, mashed swedes. It was glorious, in fact I just couldn't manage the last few spuds and a bit of bread but all the pigeon went.

Incidentally it was stuffed with chopped meat roll, chopped onions and bread rusks. The French cook cooked it beautifully for me. The whole thing cost a tin of coffee – pigeon and eggs; 2 fags – spuds; 2 fags – to cook. In the evening I had tinned strawberries, custard and cream. So ended a perfect day, feeding.

The day was only spoilt by the news that we were going down the shelter in the town with 3 days ration, taking all our stuff with us, there to stay 'til the Yanks take the town. Fortunately, we are not going now 'til we hear the guns which is much better. I personally would prefer to stay here 'til we are liberated. How these Frogs panic!

We were today issued with ½ supplement parcel per man and Stanley has allocated the remaining Yank parcels which we shall take with us if we have to go to the shelter.

Fri Apr 6th

Mild but dull with storms in the afternoon and evening.

Absolutely no near news of our front at all where there seems to be a hold up of some sort. This has put a fit of the blues into the boys who had built up far too much hope of an immediate release. It is noticeable how miserable everyone seems but, altho I must admit I'm disappointed, I'm not morbid.

I spend most of my time reading. Had a good poached egg on toast for supper.

Sat Apr 7th

Cold this am.

What a terrible day of uncertainty and apprehension. A lorry arrived from Bad Sulza with parcels for the hospital, Bad S having evacuated. They said that most of the *Lazerettes* were on the march which doesn't cheer us a bit.

We were issued with ½ a Yank parcel ⅔ English parcel and ¼ French parcel which gives us bags of grub but, oh dear! we shall have to go on the trek again.

The only good part about today is the fact that fighting seems to have flared up on our front and there is increased aerial activity with many air raid warnings. But I am not at all happy about the situation.

Sun Apr 8th

A glorious morning.

Apprehension today worse than ever. 6 more Englishmen, including Gordon Otter, arrived and what a panic. The French MO says that if any more arrive the fittest of us will have to make room for them. I reckon that I will have to move if any do go and I have determined to make a break if this does happen. This waiting and apprehension is terrible. I pray God I do not have to march further. It would be awful.

Many, many air raids this am - a local is on now and fighters have been over strafing.

Rumours say that there is a big tank battle between Erfurt and Weimar.

Air raids continued all day.

Mon Apr 9th

A glorious day today. Sunny and warm.

From dawn to dusk we had continuous bombing and strafing by Liberators, Fortresses, Mitchell Lightenings, Warhawks, Thunderbolts. It is a continual strain on our ability at aircraft recognition.

News seems to indicate they are going north and south of us, driving east. There was a very big raid last night.

Some more British have just arrived; 28 sick and one *Sanitator* from Bad Sulza. They were not allowed into the hospital but have gone to the Commando for the night and the worst of the sick may come up here. I don't know what this will mean to us but I have a good idea!!

Tues Apr 10th

A glorious day after morning fog.

Only one lad came up from the Commando, the rest going on to **Sleitz.**

Today we had a special treat. A RAF WOP AC came in to have his burns dressed. He was shot down three nights ago S of Leipzig and was badly burned about the face. Imagine it! In England 3 days ago!! It seems almost incredible. He was full of excellent news. Everyone at home buying flags and buntings and generally preparing for the armistice celebrations.

The newspapers have headlines "Only another fortnight?" My God, it must be wonderful. The Yanks he said have overwhelming superiority with very little opposition. He certainly expects the war to be over within 3 weeks. I hope he's right.

He said that many PoWs have been liberated, arriving home from Russia, France etc by aircraft. 4000 last week from the Kassel area, which probably means that what was left of our column has been liberated. He has had a pretty rough time since he came down and was almost shot by the SS. Coming from Jena with a *Posten*, the *Posten* noticed an SS man guarding a bridge, so he made a detour of a long way round the bridge to steer clear of him.

The RAF lad is very scared he will be shot before getting to a camp. We knew to dispel his fears. He had a good feed here and took some food away with him when he went to an Air Force station.

He certainly built up our hopes for an early release and victory.

There was a *Feind Alarme (Tank Alarm)* in Erfurt this afternoon which means they are on the move again. Wizard.

Also had a couple of drags of a Players today. What a difference to this American trash.

The boys on the march nowadays have quite a good time. These lads were getting ¼ parcel twice per week and a considerable amount of looting is permitted. They catch and kill pigs and poultry etc which is dished out to them together with ¼ loaf per day. Conditions are quite easy. What a change from our time.

Wed Apr 11ᵗʰ

A lovely morning again.

Raid last night. There seems to be a continuous fire alarm here now. Aircraft were over from dawn. A most momentous day, or I should say evening.

Three more lads came in from the Commando party. Their train was strafed so they jumped off. One made his way back here, the other two were picked up by the SS, almost shot and then brought here.

In the afternoon the *Dolmetscher* came in excitedly and said the *Feind alarme* had gone in Jena 18kms from here. The MOs also heard that and are tremendously excited. Later a French Canadian captain belonging to the 4th American Panza Div was brought in wounded in the shoulder. He was captured in Jena.

The German doctor was in Jena on the W bank of the river and was the last car to get across before the bridge on the *autobahn* was blown up. We saw the smoke as it was up. That was at 7.30pm. He said he was told he couldn't cross but he made a dash for it and was 15yrds over when it went up. He said the Yank tanks were on the west bank of the river.

From 7pm onwards we heard artillery fire in the distance which gradually got closer 'til by 11pm it was very loud and the flashes from the guns were very distinct.

Everyone is terribly excited, woofing what grub they have and smoking as much as they can. We kept dashing out to hear the guns, the tanks and transport moving back from the front and to see the flames. Each one imagines they are getting nearer, which may be.

We have been warned that the *autobahn* bridge about 200yrds from here may be blown any time now. We are preparing to go down the prepared air raid shelter in the town anytime tomorrow.

An ominous note is that when the MO's tried to question the F. Canadian, the SS officer said "Don't ask him questions, he has already been interrogated". This was after he had asked the MO if the patients were fit to march!!! A rather peculiar question to ask.

Also 23 more chaps arrived about 11pm and are in a terrible state. They have been on the march since leaving Lamsdorf having marched to Meiningen and back.

One lad died on the road this morning and they, too weak to wash him or do anything but put his great coat on him, wrapped a couple of blankets round him and paying 80 marks for the hire of a cart, took him to a field and buried him.

A Sgt Mjr offered a prayer whilst the guard fired a couple of shots. But it is really too tragic and pathetic to put on paper. They are in a dreadful state. They also say that there are 73 more coming on behind them.

We are all certainly expecting to be liberated by tomorrow night, if the worst does not happen and we have to go on the march. Pray God we get liberated.

An amusing incident was when a *Posten* (the bread man) came in to ask Phil his advice on what to do. Phil advised him to stay and be taken prisoner.

Thurs Apr 12th

After a night of no sleep, I was up early and the gunfire cleared away. Everyone seemed a little doubtful again.

At 11.30 five Thunderbolts beat up two factories very close to the hospital. It was a marvellous sight and they got two factories which went up in flames very nicely. Some of the boys naturally waved white sheets and then made up PoW in the parade ground with sheets.

In the afternoon things seemed to liven up and at 4.45 the fun started. I was just eating beans and spuds (the same meal I was eating at Lamsdorf when we were told to move) when we were told the *Feind alarme* had gone in Stadtroda and the tanks were approaching.

We quickly got ready what we wished to take down the Commando shelter but were told that the Commandant had left the town and a civvy had taken over town. So we stayed in the hospital, thank goodness.

Reg and I were in the hut but the rest panicky down the shelters when two fighters zoomed over and dropped a bomb each very close to and then strafed the town. We thought discretion the better part of valour and went down the basement but the smell was so bad I soon came out again.

At 8:00 we heard a terrific rumbling on the road which we assumed to be tanks and then I heard them firing their guns and saw ___.

At 8:30 we considered ourselves fine men and shook hands all round, my first hand shake being with Dave Gawby. I excitedly told the news to the boys down the shelter.

The *unteroffizier* on the gate handed over his gun and keys to Stan and the rest of the *Postens* put down their rifles and wanted to be taken prisoners. I then saw a little ceremony I shall never forget. The *Oberzahlmeistan* handed over his keys to Ted with the words *"Gott scidank". (Thank God)*. I shall never forget it.

I then went to one of the gates and opening it just walked outside the wire. I imagined the air smelt purer. I'm sure it did. I was so impressed by freedom that I almost burst into tears.

The sight of two Jerries sitting disconsolately on some wood, waiting for the Yanks to take them PoW filled me with pangs of pity. Their country beaten, a beaten nation, they have little to look forward to.

The boys then went mad, many of them getting drunk on the bottles of Cognac of course. I had a sip of Cognac but had no real enthusiasm for it. I have more respect for my stomach. Nevertheless we had some.

Frenchmen sang the Marseilles and various other songs, had brews, ate and generally made merry. I later slept like a log.

What a great day. The greatest day of my life without a doubt. We have been waiting for this for two and a half long weary years and now it seems hard to realise it's time. I can hardly believe it.

Fresh Food, Fags and Freedom – at last!

Fri Apr 13th

Friday the thirteenth, but far from unlucky.

I woke up early and had the most wonderful breakfast since being in Germany. Porridge and raisins, fried egg, chips, bacon and bread, toast and marmalade, coffee. It was great.

Just as I finished, a Yank jeep shows up to the hospital at which we all rushed down and cheered like mad. A glorious sight. Chewing gum and smoking, they looked the typical Yank, say "how many Yanks and British yer got here?" It was great.

Later I went up to a jeep guarding the hospital and had a chat with them. They gave me gum, sweets etc., and then I had a marvellous snack. Eating the whitest and loveliest bread I have ever seen. We had two slices of this with an egg and ham omelette about an inch thick smothered in butter and red raspberry jam. It positively melted in my mouth. I've never enjoyed anything so much in my life. I was most amused at their equipment; small frying pans etc., _____ methodical.

We heard the news that Roosevelt is dead. Now we are spending the rest of the day eating, drinking and smoking. It's lovely to be free again. When the tanks went through the town it was apparently amazing. A few shots were fired, they then threw chocolate, food and sweets to the civvies and kids, telling them to come out of their holes. They were free. They then said "Auf Wiedersehen, we're off to **Gerapaoso**".

In the afternoon Reg and I went for a walk. It was marvellous walking out in the county, with green fields, quiet roads, blossom on the trees etc. I felt most strange, as though I was walking on air. We were then picked up by a jeep

A walk in the countryside

and after a ride round, went round with the billeting officer appropriating billets for the boys coming in.

Since they had to hand over their cameras, revolvers and binoculars, we had our pick. I got two lovely cameras, one a wizard affair, a pair of binoculars and smashing little pistol.

The people had to clear out in 20 minutes and the officer brooked no excuses. It was a little pathetic at times but I haven't much sympathy for the Huns.

We also got 2 eggs each. Later we went up to the town hall where I got another pair of binoculars and a Hitler youth dagger with emblem. The Yanks were extremely good to us, very interested and gave me a breakfast, dinner and supper K-rations, a box of cocoa, bags of sugar and a copy of March 'Readers Digest'. I have done nothing but eat today.

It's great to wander around unmolested.

Sat Apr 14th

Today, a glorious day, spent wandering around again, talking to Yanks etc and in the evening Jim **Catrell** and I went a little ride on an auto____. It was grand and we were both a little overawed. We have been warned to be careful as we are only a ____ and there are still snipers in the area.

We moved into the civvy hospital and have good beds and billets.

Sun Apr 15th

A glorious day.

Today we got hold of a motor car, an Opal. Jim and I went a good ride in it and got ourselves some eggs. We just walked into the homes and demanded them. I find it hard to describe the feeling of riding around in a car again. I would love to go home that way.

We saw some photos a Yank had got of hanging Poles in a concentration camp. Gen Paton saw the camp and told the boys to take no more prisoners.

In the afternoon we went another ride and had tea with some Yanks. It was marvellous, white bread etc.

Mon Apr 16th

A glorious sunny day.

I've arranged to swap a camera for a _____ and my pistol for a dress sword.

Reg and I drove into Jena today, or tried to but the roads were too blocked by debris.

We then had a wonderful ride round. It was rather funny in Jena when the supposed owner of the car came over (a Dutchman) and wanted his car to go home. What's more, he proved he was the owner.

Tues Apr 17th

Again a lovely day.

There are still a number of SS and Hitler youth fanatics around the place who are in the woods and at night cause a little trouble.

We are supposed to be going either tomorrow or Thursday.

Since Jim is sick I have a monopoly over the car and a glorious little effort too. Reg and I had a good drive round today and managed to get a hen and a few more eggs.

Wed Apr 18th

Lovely again.

My new peace is very much disturbed by constant toothache. Every time I eat a meal I have violent toothache so that I never know whether to go hungry or eat and have toothache. I shall certainly be glad when I get home to have them properly seen to.

Today I had a most interesting and unusual experience. In the afternoon I took Hans and a civilian, with Reg and Jack Nath, into Jena. The bypass from the *autobahn* almost sealed our fate and the ___ bridge proved a bit of a trial. Nevertheless we made it.

Bombed ruins.

We went to the police headquarters where Hans and the civvy proceeded to act as most active collaborators. They had various evidence against certain Nazis and Party members, who are apparently still free in Stadtroda which is supposedly a nest of Nazi officials. These men are organising a secret society against the allies, called the Wolfgang, led by the Werewolf.

The civvy is very fearful for his life and asked for protection, having already been threatened by anonymous letter.

When we arrived back his wife invited us in to supper when we had roast pork, spuds, tomatoes and celery. It was very lovely.

Thurs Apr 19th

Lovely day.

After a terrible night of _____ and toothache I saw the dentist today, but he only put in the temporary filling.

We are getting very impatient for home, the novelty of freedom having worn off a little and Jim, Reg, Jack and I have decided to try and go home by car as far as Gotha and there pick up a transport plane.

We hear that they are stopping all cars between Jena and Weimar commandeering them, so we are going to try and get a permit from the police in Jena before we go too far.

Went another drive round in the car.

Fri Apr 20th

Glorious day again.

Big toothache, I must get something done. The boys went into Jena saw the major, but have to wait 'til tomorrow for

GII to come when we may have our credentials checked and possibly go home.

Today Jim went up to the Yank hospital and brought an MO down who was a little disgusted at the treatment we've been having. One fellow was moved into a room on his own, but, too late, he died in the evening. I feel very sorry for his people. The MO says he will get the very sick away to a hospital.

A Hun a/c straffed the *autobahn* last night.

Sat Apr 21st

A bit overcast today with some rain.

Went to the Yank dentist who filled one tooth and put a temporary filling in another one. He told me to come back tomorrow and have one extracted but since one of the boys left today, while we were away, and went to Botha I don't think I'll leave the place 'til I know exactly what's happening. Even now I get toothache very badly after a meal.

Had our boiled fowl today. Delicious.

Jim **Catrell** has gone which leaves me owner of the Opel. The first time I've owned a car in my life.

Sun Apr 22nd

A lovely day today.

I have some stomach trouble and slight diarrhoea. Phil wanted me to go on a funeral party today but I wouldn't go because I believe it would be sheer hypocrisy to do so. I don't know the fellow, have never spoken to him and never saw him before in my life 'til he was at death's door.

I do not believe in attaching hypocrisy to religion.

Went a little drive in the evening through Neustadt.

Mon Apr 23rd

Lovely day but I couldn't appreciate it owing to my chronic stomach-ache and diarrhoea.

In between visits to the lavatory I was in bed all day and didn't eat a thing.

Tues Apr 24th

Lovely day again.

The Yanks MO has put me on special medicine and pills. On request I got some tinned fruit but couldn't eat it all. Very bad stomach-ache. In bed all day.

Wrote a letter home.

"Dear Mum, Dad & Rene,

At long last I am a free man and now only raring to get back to you, which I am hoping will be in the very near future. My, we'll have some yarns to swop won't we? It seems very hard to realize that soon my hopes and dreams of the last two years and 8 months are to be realized. I will not attempt to describe on paper my first impressions of regained freedom.

Well, if my last letters got through to you, you will know where I am and why. If they didn't get through then I fear you must have had a most worried and anxious time since Xmas.

Nevertheless, I am in hospital, and have been here for two months, now recovering from an attack of influenza and dysentery which I contracted whilst being marched across Germany. At one time it seemed as tho' it was touch & go but now I am happy to say I am well on the way to complete recovery.

If I do come home within the next week or so, which I sincerely hope I do, don't be unduly shocked at

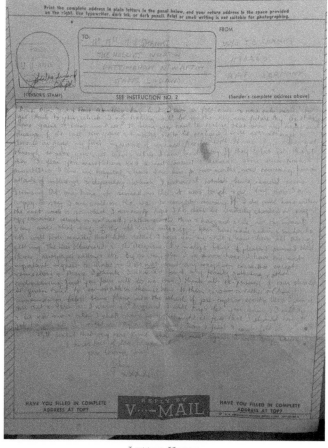

Letter Home

my appearance which is naturally rather on the thin and haggard side at the moment. I am sure that bags of the old fresh milk & eggs, your homemade cakes and sandwiches etc will soon remedy that little detail.

I hope you are still, & have been all along, getting "The War Illustrated" & "The Aeroplane". I visualize hours of pleasant perusal through those, newspaper cuttings etc.

By the way, when I do arrive home I have one most important request to make – I do not want any reception committee except yourselves and Mary. I think I should find any family gathering rather embarrassing. Just you four will do me fine. I think all ex-prisoners of war should be given time to re-establish themselves to their new – or rather old – surroundings before being flung into the whirl of pre-captive society. Also I promise you that as soon as I arrive in England I will try & let you know, & I will try & let you know when I shall arrive home. I thought at first that I should have a job to get all I wanted to say on this sheet, now I find I can't fill it.

Well, until that very near time when we meet again I will say,

Cheers, & here's tons of love to you all,

> *Your loving son,*
> *John*
> *Xxxxxxx"*

Wed Apr 25th

Lovely day. I am missing some glorious weather.

Today the Yank MO gave me a sort of rough diet, doubled the medicine ration and ordered the French MO's to give me glucose injections. Phil explained to him how much weight I have lost etc but he didn't seem unduly worried and said we will be home shortly. He said the Major is back and is going to get the Hun insane out first and then a couple of days later we shall go.

In the evening I was moved into another room by the three nurses who have been assigned to look after me. One of them bathed me. Imagine it! The first time since I was a kid. I wasn't the least bit embarrassed except for the amount of dirt on me. She also washed my hair and then they put me to bed with sheets and blankets, clean pyjamas etc. it is almost embarrassing the way they look after me, always fussing around. I haven't had anything like it since I left old Mum. They completed the feminine touch with a bowl of flowers by my bedside.

My thoughts today have been on the things I could and would like to eat. Herring, plaice and tomato sauce, bread and butter and greens and tomatoes.

I would give anything for any of these.

Thurs Apr 26th

A glorious day again.

Today our hopes ran high at 10:00 as the lorries and ambulances came to take the Hun insane away. They promised faithfully to return for us.

Consequently I got up and packed up my bit of kit, mostly souvenirs and fags and waited around in great pain in my stomach for the rest of the day but no Yanks turned up. We were bitterly disappointed. What's more, I have lost my ____ and my car, for the Yanks who borrowed it returned this am, thought we were going and took it away.

The Jocks, Slim, Doug and George went off in their car early and are making for an airdrome near Erfurt. Reg and I would have gone with them if I hadn't been sick. Curse my luck.

They did not return.

Fri Apr 27th

A bit cloudy today.

After a shaky start my stomach improved during the day with a considerable return of appetite.

Reg has gone out to see if he can locate the car and inform them we want it back tomorrow. If we do, we shall go on Sunday and if not we shall still go on Sunday, only we shall have to hitch-hike. Staying here is like being free with our hands tied behind our backs.

In bed all day.

Sat Apr 28th

Showery today.

I got up in the morning and felt rather weak and dithery about the legs which wore off during the day. Eating like a horse again.

Went for a walk in the evening to locate the car and eventually found the fellow who borrowed it who told me the sad story that another fellow had commandeered it and refused to part. We eventually found the car in new rigout but by this time it was ____ so we decided to leave it 'til tomorrow morning before we pinched it again and set off straight away for Erfurt. Apparently the fellow is a tough, nasty ____ to deal with.

Four more of the boys set off for the airdrome **Nola** near Erfurt this morning but in the afternoon returned with an Aussie, who advised us to stay put for another day or two as we would not get beyond Erfurt. He said there were about 700 ex-____ in a camp at E with bad accommodation, no blankets and little organisation.

They are in charge of an Aussie Sqd/Ldr but a Yank evacuation Col arrived there last night to organise their evacuation by diverting transport kites to E etc.

They went back taking all our forms and particulars etc so we are now getting something down. Apparently we shall be flown to Brussels and from there by RAF ____ after being kitted out etc to England.

At last we have got something definite. So now we are going to hang fire for a day or two.

In the evening Flash and I walked over to see another Sgt about the car and he is going to do all he can for us. We have to see him tomorrow again. I walked home by myself and felt wonderfully happy for the first time for a long time. I wandered slowly through peaceful, quiet countryside, on a glorious Spring evening after a fresh rain. The air smelt beautifully fresh and clean and the birds were whistling. The trees in glorious green. As I looked over the growing crops, I thought of Dad as he would wander round on a Sat evening. It was lovely and I thoroughly enjoyed it.

According to the BBC an offer of unconditional surrender has been made by Himmler to Grt Britain and America which has been turned down as it was not also offered to Russia. I do hope I'm home before the end.

Hitler also is supposed to be very ill and not expected to live more than another 24 hrs.

Sun Apr 29th

A glorious morning but turning rather cold and stormy later.

I am getting very impatient with waiting here. Every minute seems like an hour, every hour a day and every day a month. It's worse than waiting for liberation.

Heard the BBC for the first time in 2 yrs 8 months at 3pm this afternoon when we rigged up a small wireless and heard the news. It was grand listening again.

Unfortunately the radio has gone again.

Mon Apr 30th

Cold and cloudy again.

Today the whole hospital was evacuated apart from us, the British. The MOs, dentist, Froggies, Ruskies, Serbs etc have all gone to Gera.

We are supposed to be going tomorrow but the Erfurt lads called again and said that, owing to bad weather and low cloud at Brussels, there has been no flying and consequently no evacuation. But we are definitely on the list there and are the tenth lot to go which should be on Wed if conditions are favourable, so we shall probably stay here tomorrow.

I wish we could get to Erfurt tho, to be on the spot when our time does come.

My toothache is still very bad and what with that and the nervous tension of waiting, I am getting very little sleep.

News that Mussolini has been shot.

Tues May 1st

And I did not forget the *"white rabbits"*! A glorious day so there should have been some flying. Maybe we shall go tomorrow.

Was in bed most of the day trying to make up for sleep I have lost through neuralgia which still persists.

In the evening took a walk into town to collect some eggs and then went to the Company headquarters to see the show. It was a film entitled 'A *Guest in the House'* a very poor film of love intrigue etc. I'm afraid I wasn't impressed. Nevertheless an evening out and something to take my mind off wanting to go home.

George turned up an excellent dinner today. We had bread and marg and syrup for breakfast. Meat, spuds, peas and gravy for dinner with rice pudding as a sweet. Bread, marg, meat for tea. Yank rations were a tin of beans and pork, supper was a tin of pork.

A good day.

Wed May 2nd

Sleet in the morning, which may account for the neuralgia I've been having lately. It cleared up about 10am and there is a good chance it was good enough for flying. That's all I'm worried about.

Breakfast today was 2 fried eggs on fried bread (supplemented by ½ tin beans, 2 slices toast and another fried egg); dinner – tomato soup, meat, creamed spuds, gravy, prunes and custard. It was as good as a civvy street meal. For tea, rissoles, bread, marg and bloodwurst. No Yank rations today.

It was very cold and damp all day and I hear that there is extremely bad weather in England with 5 inches of snow. Maybe we're better off here. Anyway it is certainly very cold here for this time of the year.

Heard today that the whole of the German army in Italy – 18 divs – and 6 Italian Fascist divs have surrendered on block. The terms were supposed to have been signed on Sunday. Is this the start of the big pack-up? I wanted to be home for that.

No news yet of moving. I think the weather must be too bad for flying.

Thurs May 3rd

A nicer morning altho still a little cold.

At noon we saw 9 Yank transport a/c flying towards Jena. Our hopes are high that they will land there and we may go home tomorrow.

Managed to get some milk and sugar from a shop today. We are now living much better than we would do in any service mess in Blighty. For breakfast we had fried meat, scrambled egg on fried bread, bread, butter and syrup and English tea; for dinner, fried spuds, onion sauce and steak, followed by bilberries and cream, followed by a cup of tea with a ____ bread issue for lunch. I am now eating wonderfully well, have a good healthy appetite and have replaced the fat in my face which I lost during my illness last week. And what's more I have the feeling that some of my lost vitality is returning.

For tea we were given 2 raw eggs and the usual bread and butter etc.

Fri May 4th

A glorious morning turned cloudy later in the day.

After breakfast of 2 fried eggs the lorry from Erfurt arrived with the Aussie Sqd/Ldr. It didn't take me very long to pack my kit most of which was food.

After lunch of pork chop, spuds, peas and Yorkshire pudding we all embarked and after a mad 1hr dash in the lorry arrived at the big Army camp at Erfurt which is No1 evacuation centre. Our group is no.39, so we shall probably have a few days to wait.

We managed to fix ourselves up in rooms and now our life apparently consists of waiting for meals, bed, waiting for meals. We have three meals a day, the same grub as the Yanks get. Unfortunately we are told there is not enough of it.

I met some of the boys from Lamsdorf and, to my intense regret learn that I have missed seeing Cliff by a whisker. He was here but left last week and is now home. I would love to have seen him.

Also I am told the RAF personnel go to Cosford before going on 28 days leave. I hope this is true. I'll soon be home. Also that there is very little chance of demobilisation.

Sat May 5th

A very dull morning with absolutely no chance of any flying but it cleared up in the evening.

We've had very good meals today. Breakfast; porridge and milk, meat, flap-jacks and syrup and an orange. Dinner; meat stew, rice, 2 slices white bread and peanut butter. We should have had cheese but they ran out ____ _____. Tea; meat, peas, spuds and beetroot, 2 slices bread and apricot jam. Coffee and tea for each meal. Very good indeed.

The orange was the first I have had since leaving home. It was wizard. The only fly in the ointment is we have to queue up for meals which is rather unpleasant in the rain.

Reg, Dig, Flash and myself are lucky enough to have get ourselves installed in a little room of our own. Quite comfortable too. We might as well make ourselves as comfortable as possible even tho we hope to go as soon as possible.

I am still getting chronic toothache.

Sun May 6th

Windy and wet again but clearing in the afternoon.

The day was of the usual routine, meals, reading, bed.

13 transport a/c went over heading west but I believe they had Froggies on board.

Heard that 1260 more PoWs got home and that many more PoW were liberated, including Viscount Lascelles, John C **Wisents** son, the Queens nephew and another big shot.

Also according to the news the war is expected to end any moment now and that Churchill and the King are to make speeches. It has always been my big ambition to be home when the war ends. I would give a lot to be there for the finish.

It is amazing what little comment or stir was created by the death of Hitler. No-one seemed the slightest bit interested.

Meals today. Breakfast; porridge and milk, bacon, fried bread and syrup and sausage. Dinner; rissoles and tomato ketchup (delicious) spuds, beans, peas, bread and butter, coffee. Supper; stew, spuds, beetroot, apricot, bread and jam, coffee.

The meals are very good in quality but a little lacking in quantity.

Today also we had 20 cigs, small bar of chocolate and chewing gum.

Reg, Dig and I were today shoved up from 39 group to 24 group making up their number. I wonder if this will make any difference to our length of stay here. It could make a difference of a few days.

There are various rumours of our moving. One that we shall fly home tomorrow, another that we shall go home by train part of the way and then fly on etc, etc. No one really knows in my opinion and I think the weather is being most unkind to us.

Today I had a conversation, all too short, with some Yank fighter pilots (Thunderbolts). It was extremely noticeable what a different type of fellow they were, compared with the type of fellow we have so far met. They were quiet, well-spoken and had nothing of bombast about them. According to them the Tempest is the fastest fighter in the world – a wonderful a/c.

Let's hope I can fly them against the Japs for my ambitions are once again against the Yellow men. I really want to go out there and shall be very disappointed if I can't for any reason. From the news we have just heard Mr Churchill is expected to make a statement tomorrow announcing the end of the war.

Mon May 7th

A glorious day with lots and lots of a/c passing over.

This morning 4 groups and the Yanks were flown away so that leaves 12 more groups to go before us.

Maybe tomorrow.

TODAY AT 2:00 PM THE WAR ENDED. THE GERMAN GENERALS SIGNED TERMS OF UNCONDITIONAL SURRENDER TO BRITISH, AMERICAN, RUSSIAN AND FRENCH GENERALS.

At long, long last. I heard the news at 3.10pm whilst listening to the radio in the camp here. The announcer, in strong Yank drawl said "Just over an hour ago, the German foreign minister broadcast from *Flensberg* radio to the German people telling them that Grand Admiral Donitz had announced that the High Command ordered the unconditional surrender of all German troops".

Boy! Would I like to be either at home or in London. What are we missing? It has been an ambition of mine ever since I was taken prisoner. And we came so near to it. So near and yet so far!! I am very annoyed and disappointed.

In camp here there were no celebrations and no excitement at all, everyone naturally only anxious to get home. That is the only thing to cause excitement here.

I must admit, now that the war is over, except in Czechoslovakia where they refuse to pack in, that the Huns have given us a very good run for our money. They have put up a staunch fight against overwhelming odds, especially since Italy packed in, altho I think they were more of a liability than an asset.

The way they have held out for so long against the land, naval and air might of Britain, Russia and America has been, in my opinion, nothing short of miraculous. Fast diminishing food and raw materials, tremendous losses in men and material, terrific air bombardment blockades etc, etc. Truly an amazing effort of endurance.

But we must never forget that there are some Germans who applauded the laying waste of Rotterdam, laughed at the burning of London, cheered the laying waste of Warsaw. They are still the same rackets who have massacred, tortured, pillaged and raped the Jews and political prisoners. They must be made to pay for their crimes of the past – and I think they will too!!

Today for meals we had breakfast; scrambled egg, porridge and milk, bread and butter, coffee. Dinner; rissoles, spuds, tomatoes, cherries, coffee. Supper; fried chicken, spuds, peas, prunes, bread and butter, coffee.

This evening I learnt that only 19 of the boys left by air, the remaining 81 came back very disappointed and browned off. The a/c were taking home Yanks and allied wounded personnel and Yanks going on leave. In spite of the fact that the Aussie Sqd/Ldr said we came before everyone going on leave.

If they carry on with that game we'll never get home now that the war has ended, for there will be thousands going on leave. I don't know how the end of the war will affect us but I'm hoping the RAF will take over this evacuation business and then we shall probably get somewhere.

Anyway I'm not expecting to get home tomorrow as it has been declared by Mr Churchill to be VICTORY day and a National Holiday. All essential services are to carry on but my! will there be some rejoicing and merry making in London - or any town for that matter.

Mr Churchill is to make a speech at 3pm tomorrow and the King at 7.00pm.

Saw a film in Technicolor in the evening 'Greenwich Village' with Carmen Miranda and Don Ameche. I'm afraid, through the combination of circumstances, I didn't enjoy it a bit.

Firstly I had bad toothache and neuralgia (as usual) secondly, we had to sit on the hard floor which was most uncomfortable, thirdly, the film was rather poor, and forth, my mind was continually on the fact that the war is over and we are still here.

Tues May 8th 1945

VICTORY DAY

A glorious sunny day with bright sunshine shining down from a cloudless blue sky. Very warm.

Today is Victory Day. VE day and according to the 1:00 news, flags and bunting are gaily flying in the streets of city, town and village. Crowds cheer and throng the streets and the world over telegrams are being sent from one nation to another, one being to another, leader to leader; in fact, everyone seems to be congratulating everyone else.

The official cease fire is to be sounded at 11.00pm tonight. I presume the sirens, factory sirens, ships and trains will all add this quota to the noise of bedlam as Big Ben sounds the momentous hour. I am sure it will be an occasion never to be forgotten altho the authorities will attempt to make it plain to everyone that we are still at war in Japan. This I believe will go on for another 12 to 18 months and will be a grim, bitter difficult task. I have no illusion about the magnitude of the task ahead of us against Japan.

On top of that I am one of those pessimists, full of trepidation with regard to the consequences of the European war. I believed that Britain and America, whilst not in complete agreement themselves over the dispensation of the spoils, are dramatically opposed to the ideals and ambitions of Soviet Russia.

I very much fear the consequences of the attempt of each to outdo the other in the matter of territorial and economic acquisitions. I will go as far as to prophesy also that Russia will be at war with Japan within the next month.

I will also be rash enough to prophesy another World War, started by a rupture between G Britain and Russia within the next 5 years. I refuse to believe the argument that either of the two countries is materially or economically unable to pursue another war, in that time.

War and power politics are synonymous and power politics is becoming more in evidence every day. If we are to dispense with war, we must first dispense with power politics.

Well, as I write, this victory day is almost over and I now have the correct times of the various events as given by Mr Churchill. It was at 2.41am yesterday that the surrender terms was signed at General Eisenhower headquarters in Rheims. It is at ONE MINUTE AFTER 12.00 PM TONIGHT the official CEASE FIRE is to be given.

The Hun navy and ships today had orders to either dock in allied ports or stay in the ports they were already in and U-boats had orders to surface, fly a black flag and make for the nearest allied port.

There was heavy fighting in Czech and the position at Prague seems obscure but Marshall Stolen announced the capture of Dresden.

I listened at 3pm to Mr Churchill's historic speech when he gave thanks to God for our victory but urged the people on 'til final victory over Japan. Then there were commentaries from the various provisional cities where it was obvious that there was great rejoicing.

In glorious weather in London crowds thronged Trafalgar Square, Constitution Hill, Whitehall and outside Buckingham Palace. Flags, bunting and streamers were flying and red, white and blue frocks, shirts, hats, ties were very much in evidence. The commentator said it was one of the most wonderful scenes he had ever seen.

Various nationalities had their own minor processions.

In Liverpool the ships horns could be heard making a terrific din as they blew ...- (V for Victory). In Edinburgh a pipe band (that of Edinburgh University) could be heard floating through the streets in drizzly weather. In Belfast some RAF lads were mobbed and carried shoulder high through the streets. In Cardiff one could hear the voices of the Cardiff City Choir as they led 40,000 Welsh people in song.

Everywhere (on the radio, of course) even the old tower of Coventry Cathedral standing over the bombed ruins and in the little Dorset village of Puddingstone, one could hear the chiming of church bells.

It was a most historic and moving broadcast, but I wonder in how many homes was there, not rejoicing, but tears of anguish and sorrow, where loved ones will never return. Also it was obvious that reminders of the war against Japan were in evidence and tended to damp down the celebrations as Mr Truman, USA President said, until the last Japanese division has surrendered unconditionally.

In the USA celebrations were very conservative and mostly on the scale of thanksgiving for victory and for the men who had lost their lives to enable that victory to be secured. They were very quiet and sober in most of the big cities with work proceeding as normal.

Reg, Dig, Flash and I went for a little stroll in the evening. I had my photo taken sitting in a destroyed German tank.

I did not hear the King's speech at 9.00pm which was again one of thanksgiving and went to a film from which I came out very early. I wasn't enjoying it a bit.

There are supposed to be 25 a/c coming tomorrow to take us back. That means that I should go but some more Yanks came in today having been liberated yesterday so I don't know how that will affect us as they have priority.

Dad in a deserted tank.

We heard on the wireless that 4500 PoWs were flown home by RAF _____ today. I wish the RAF would take over here. Anyway we have been told we shall go tomorrow. The boys that were back yesterday went away today.

Meals today were breakfast; semolina and milk, bacon, pancakes, tomato puree, biscuits, butter, coffee. Dinner; stew, beans, spuds, peaches, biscuits and butter. Supper; stew, spuds, carrots, cherries, biscuits and butter, tea. Not too bad but rather moreish.

Wed May 9th

Another glorious day.

During the day we saw many squadrons flying west. Thunderbolts, Lightenings etc, all going home. Today thousands more Frogs and English and Yanks came in. The Frogs arrived in the morning and were off home in the afternoon. They go by train.

There are now so many English and Yanks here that they cannot feed us properly. Consequently for dinner today we had to go to another room _____ and are now fed on German food again.

I think it's disgusting that the Yank PoWs should get good food, different to the trash we are getting. If they can't feed us properly the obvious remedy is to get us home. The promised 25 a/c did not materialise of course.

Some of the boys in today were liberated from the march only yesterday.

More on the radio that Hun a/c raided Prague this am in contravention of the cease fire order. There was much panic as the sirens were out of order etc.

Meals today were breakfast; fried egg, porridge and milk, one slice of bread and butter, coffee. Dinner; a small ladle of meat stew, carrots and horrible *ersatz* soup, too small biscuits, dishwater that had a packet of tea standing near it. Supper; water over which a hen had flown (chicken soup?) beans, two biscuits, the usual tea. Terrible meals. We are very browned off with the whole affair.

The Aussie officer went to Rheims today, as we believe to demand a/c to get us out.

Thurs May 10th

Another lovely day.

A month ago today we were liberated and here we stop. I feel like a lion in a cage. Many transport a/c seen sculling around this morning but of course nothing turned up at **Nola**.

We heard that 10,000 PoWs were flown home today. If all this is going on, why in Pete's name, can't they get us out. In my opinion it is complete lack of organisation.

I went to a cinema show but came out very soon after the start as it was much too hot, making me sweat like a bull and we had to stand right at the back too, where it was very difficult to see. But I suspect the real reason is psychological, for I cannot enjoy the show at all whilst I am wondering all the time when we are to go home.

Fri May 11th

A glorious day, very hot and just like mid-summer.

We started early with the old binoculars for this being

Friday, which seems to be our lucky day, we expect something may happen.

Our superstition was not unfounded, for groups 11-21 moved off – in company with 300 or so Yanks of course – in the morning. Our hopes ran high and yes sure enough, just after lunch we were told to pack and get out on to the parade ground to go to the drome on spec, in case more a/c came in.

Needless to say it didn't take me long to pack for I had been expecting something of the sort all morning. Altho as a gesture of contempt for the Erfurt organisation, I had resolved not to pack until actually told to go.

After a few hours of dashing to the window with the binoculars constantly accompanied by the irrepressible Reg, I could stand the strain no longer and put away my 'kit' with a very small K, for all I have is a few cigs, some of which are souvenirs, a camera, binoculars, Hitler Youth honour dagger, and officers dress sword, with of course, towel and toilet gear.

Inwardly excited, we _____ (horrible neologism) in the square and proceeded to the airdrome with the usual mashing of gears and shattering roar from the exhaust.

After a nightmare drive we arrived to find some groups still waiting to go but more a/c expected. Then we sat on the grass and dejectedly awaited the arrival of a/c. I say dejectedly because as the minutes fled past, in spite of our constant watch on the horizon, we realised that our hopes of going today were gradually, nay, all too quickly, diminishing.

Altho two groups did go while we waited, at 7.30, after we had eaten our 15 rations, it was decided that no more a/c could arrive and either we go back to camp or stay the night on the drome. We stayed, finding reasonable beds in dismal huts and, after I had boiled myself some spuds, which I quite enjoyed in the camp fire atmosphere, I went to bed.

Sat May 12th

Today has been the day of days. Another cloudless sky heralded good flying weather.

I brewed up some coffee (I really enjoyed doing this amongst the trees on a fine, fresh, sweet smelling morning, intermixed with the glorious smell of wood-fire) and all ate our breakfast of 15 rations.

Whilst sitting on the grass waiting for things to happen, a Yank Air Corps officer came over to us and asked us where our officer was. He had not yet arrived. He told us he was expecting 40 a/c (imagine it) to take us to Brussels.

No sooner the word… when 17 a/c were seen by our ever watchful eyes approaching the drome, low and in formation. Are they coming in here? Yes, a beautiful peel off and within 10 minutes they were all safely parked just waiting to take us yet another stop towards our long awaited destination - Blighty and Home.

But again more waiting, during which time many photos were taken, until, at 10.15, Lt/Col Ball and many more truck-loads of lads came in from the camp. Immediately we boarded our a/c and at 10.30 exactly, ours, the 4th off the line, left the deck.

A glorious trip of 2hrs exactly, during which time our heads were constantly at the window taking in all that was to be seen, saw us over Brussels airport. We crossed the Rhone, so leaving a Germany we had grown to hate, at 1.45pm.

There were a tremendous number of bomb and shell craters a little later and much evidence of a terrific battle.

This was the Siegfried Line area. But even after ___ 2hrs we still weren't there for we had to circle the drome for 50 minutes before we could get in. The traffic was terrific; round and round we went and a few of the lads were sick.

Once on the ground we were greeted by the spectacle of a Lancs on the ground and a number PoWs just about to take off on the last stage to Blighty. They had arrived here this morning. We still thought we might get off today. Trucks took us to St Anne's barracks in Brussels.

Here we got out, formed up in our respective groups of nationalities, services etc to be marched away to get first of all an FFI, then a kit bag, clean socks, shirt, vest, pants (mine were made for Hong Kong and I told a major they were hardly designed for an ex-PoW) boots, cap, tunic and trousers if we wanted it. I didn't take these last three as they were khaki and I shall be getting these in England.

Then a glorious, much needed and very welcome cold shower (I forgot to mention we had also a clean towel and ___).

Before the clothing business we had to fill in some forms and get an ident *(identity)* paper. After putting on new clean clothes, I took sadistic delight in flinging away my old clothes which I am told will be burnt. They were German. Then we were taken to our billets which are comfortable and clean.

Following this, it being 5.45 and I being ravenously hungry, I went to the canteen and there got tea by the cupful, buns, cakes, biscuits and in the highly interesting surroundings of newspapers, mags, periodicals etc had quite a good tuck-in, free of charge.

Previous to this, the Canadian Red X (the camp is run by Canadians) had given us ___ gear, handkerchief, chocolate and 50 cigs, towel etc again free of charge. By this time my toothache was in full swing but I nevertheless went to the mess and finished off with a meal. I was disgusted by the amount of stuff being wasted.

Now there were four alternatives of action open and the one decided upon was a walk around Brussels. This being the one thing we could do which we shall not be able to do in the future. Certainly not under these conditions.

After a glass of beer and buying 60 cigs (Players) and two ___ bars of chocs for 25 francs (we had been paid the equivalent of £5 (including a 10/- note for Blighty), we (Dig, Reg and myself) set off into the city.

Street Scene in Brussels.

The first thing we noticed were the enormous number of pubs, cafes and cabarets which seem to outnumber the shops 4 or 5 to one. We sat at a table on the pavement outside one of them to eat apples I had bought and drink lemonade. How embarrassing a similar situation would be at home but here it seems the natural thing to do.

Then I bought sweets (everything we could wish for seems available but the prices are exorbitant) and a little later we came, hey presto, to an ice cream parlour. Two ices satisfied our, by now, protesting stomachs so we strolled on. Everywhere was lit up and it was a glorious sight.

At 11.30 we set off back and after staying in the canteen, two cups of tea again, 'til 1am. I had bacon sandwiches and am now preparing for a little needed sleep. I don't really feel like it tho.

Reg and I both thought the attitude of the civvies was a little hostile but either it was our imagination or they were so surprised to see three English ex-PoWs behaving themselves as we were, for I was disgusted and ashamed to see, as usual, some of the louts displaying themselves in drunken bawdiness in cafes, pubs and on the streets, why do some of these senseless, loud, unintelligent louts have to let us down so in front of foreigners?

But now, after the end of a perfect day I will try and get some sleep. Tomorrow for old Blighty. Who knows?

Sun May 13th

A glorious day again.

The hopes we were having all day around the camp, in the canteen etc., drinking tea and reading the mags, but our hopes were unfounded. Atho more came in and more went out, we stayed here.

In the evening we went to an open air cinema show but after the news reel of horror pictures I went back to the canteen.

They told us over the Tannoy not to worry as we should be going first thing in the morning.

Mon May 14th

A lovely day again.

Today was the BIG day. After an early breakfast the message came over the Tannoy telling us all to parade on the square for departure. Our hearts leapt. We all went out and gradually the square emptied as the lorries took the boys away.

We drove to the drome there to await the arrival of a/c. After what seemed an eternity we eventually boarded an a/c and left the continent at 2.00pm. We flew over flooded Belgium where it was possible to see the roofs of houses poking bright and red from the deep water. Whenever will they get the place cleared?

We eventually crossed the coast near Dunkirk and soon espied the coast of Blighty. We crossed over Dover, the white cliffs standing in all their rugged glory. I must admit I felt very little emotion, probably because we were too detached from the earth itself.

We finally landed at Dunsfold, south of Guildford, after 2hrs 10mins. Feet on English soil at last. What a feeling! We were ushered into a larger hanger where tea, sandwiches and cakes were waiting for us. RAF flags of the nations fairly bedecked the hanger.

After tea I went to look in the cockpit of a 5 bladed Spitfire 14. I was amazed. There was hardly any resemblance at all to the glorious Spit I knew. Everything was altered and I hope improved.

At 11pm we moved by lorry to Basingstoke where we took the train for Cosford. By this time I felt for some unaccountable reason, violently sick and was violently sick.

Anyway we arrived at Cosford at 6am Tuesday morning.

Tues May 15th

We arrived at Cosford at 6am in cold damp weather.

We were allocated a flight and taken to breakfast. Then we went through all the regimental kitting, identify cards, pay accounts, telegrams, MO filling in forms about _____ etc. until we finished in the afternoon. I was given, funnily enough, a malnutrition card to enable me to buy "more milk and eggs" from the shops!!

After tea I rang them up at home and out Rene came to fetch me. Naturally she was full of emotion and couldn't speak for at least 5mins. I felt very queer and found it hard to start a conversation. Of course the same thing happened at home when Mum burst into tears and Dad was on the point of doing so. It is impossible to describe how really good it was to see them all again.

The house and garden are wonderfully improved, almost unrecognisable. I am delighted. I went in, had something to eat chattering away the whole time. Here I learnt of Alex an old Stan's visit. How grateful I am. The quality of true friendships.

I went back to Cosford at about 10.30.

Wed May 16th

After getting my pass etc I went to the dentist. I had to have two teeth extracted and then went home for my month's leave. I didn't meet anyone today as my mouth was swollen and rather painful.

I am overwhelmed by the books, magazines, paper cuttings, letters etc, etc. that have been accumulated for me.

I am extremely pleased to learn that my Do217 was confirmed for me by the squadron.

Thurs May 17th

Going into town today I am once more amazed at the rationing system. Nothing seems obtainable without these beastly points and everything is frightfully expensive. The value of money is little compared with pre-war. No wonder they are scared of inflation. A chap was telling me he was offered £500 for a second hand 1939 Vauxhall 12.

In the evening I saw Mary. She is lovelier than ever and just as full of life. Rene, she, Mum and I went to the flics in the evening.

Fri May 18th

Once again I went to the dentist at Cosford and had one more tooth extracted. I then went to ___ and had another look around.

In the evening Rene and I took a walk up to Wrottersley where we saw Uncle John and Aunt Kate, Peter and ___ who are visiting them. They were all very interested in my experiences.

I am a little embarrassed at my eating capacity. I am eating everyone out of house and home. Thank goodness for double rations.

Sat May 19th

Today Mary came for tea and supper and lo and behold who should turn up in the evening but Stan Jones. I am very pleased to see he is a Flt/Lt. He has done reasonably well. We naturally had a good chat but I am looking forward to a couple of hours or so on our own.

Dad with his trusty MG.

Sun May 20th

Thunderstorms today.

Everyone, if not coming round here or asking me to go round to their homes, is ringing up. I'm getting a little cheesed but must put up with it for a bit.

In the afternoon took Rene to Jones's then went to Symmond Syde for tea and Parkside for supper. Everyone is very interested and sympathetic and the lads are just great. Full of misbelief but looking extremely fit and they have all grown tremendously.

Stan showed me all the grand photos of bombing trips. He is lucky to have them.

Mon May 21st

I don't know when I shall get everything done. I have so many people to see, so many to write to, so much to do and little time to do it in.

This afternoon Stan, Mary, Rene and I went to a Gymkhana at Albrighton. Very _____ and mediocre performance.

In the evening we went to a film 'The Constant Nymph' which was quite good.

Tues May 22nd

Dull and thundery again.

More teeth filled. There is still a tremendous amount to be done to them.

I later went to see Stan and got my petrol (leave) coupons. They gave me 12 gals for the 300 miles which is quite good.

I saw Mrs Fowler and Marjory and thanked them for their kindness.

In the evening we paid a visit to Aunt Edie after Maurice, Petie, Urtie and Mary had been over. Maurice was his usual affected self, professing disappointment at not being able to join the services. I hate hypocrisy.

Urtie doesn't look too well after her holiday but maybe that is due to the fact that she is expecting another kiddie.

Aunt Edie was of course itching to tell me all about Humphrey – of course when she did it was accompanied by the inevitable flood of tears. I feel very sorry for her but think she should make an effort to get over her sorrow and just cherish a memory. Hard, I know, but a brave woman can do it.

Today I received a reply from the Strand regretting no accommodation.

Wed May 23rd

A thundery day again.

More teeth filled. I had to act as 'official photographer' to the dental sector and took two shots. The dental officers are extremely nice chaps.

Cosford is a most mysterious camp. I can't quite make it out, ____ wandering around with brevets up, others with white bands round their caps etc, etc.

Apparently the reception centre is a bit of a mix-up. Some have received two leave extensions, others none; some clothing coupons, others, including myself, none; some double rations, others none. And when they come back, no-one seems to know what's going to happen, when, where or why.

Stan, Rene and I saw an excellent play *'Claudia'* in the evening by the Rep Company at the theatre. It was a modern play as evidenced by the broad-mindedness in respect of the sex question.

Today the political situation reached its climax with the resignation of Mr Churchill. He had no alternative after the allegations made against him by the Labours Socialist parties. I should hate to be in this dirty political racket.

Thur May 24th

A lovely warm day.

Today I had my first day to myself since coming home so I wrote a long letter to Betty. I love to just laze around, it's grand, but I am convinced I shall never settle down in England unless I can get a flying job. If I cannot get a flying job I just don't know what I shall do.

Fri May 25th

A thundery day again.

Had two more teeth filled. The dentist down there is amazingly good.

Stan came in the evening so we went shooting. There are a terrific number of hares around. We startled a lot but with no success. I enjoyed the chat and the walk round. Naturally we talked a lot of 'shop'. He has a chance of getting into BOA for 3yrs as a navigator. I wish I had the chance.

Himmler, after being captured, has committed suicide by taking potassium cyanide. Why do they give them so many chances to commit suicide.

I see the Labour Party are advocating equal gratuities for all service men regardless of rank and sex. Good scheme!

I also noticed in an *'Aeroplane'*, that Larry Smith was awarded the DFC in '42. Good show.

Sat May 26th

Thundery rain.

A letter writing day. Wrote letter of thanks to Mrs Dumbell, Mrs Schofield and a long letter to old Stan L.

In the evening mum, Mary and I went first to Donnington and then Lower Wood. I had a most interesting conversation with Uncle Jack who has an extremely wide knowledge of politics and social affairs. Uncle James was very interested in my experiences but I thought he looked very thin.

Sun May 27th

Thundery again.

Collected 5 mushrooms - my first for 3 years. I wish Dad had put some salt down, but of course it's too late now.

I see in the paper that JEA Hartill (Flt/Lt fighter pilot) was killed on Wed.

Went with Mary on a pleasant little drive round the various farms.

I had, today, my first proper hot bath for 3 years. It was grand.

The fires in Tokyo have been fanned by a 70mph gale doing enormous damage.

Mon May 28th

A glorious day after morning fog.

Had mushrooms for breakfast my first for 3 years. Caught the 9.40am train for Blackpool and arrived about 2.30pm. Quite nice private Hotel the Clifton___ only a long way from the centre. North of the North Pier. Went to a good musical show *'The Lisbon Story'*. Excellent.

Tues May 29th

Rain in am; nice later.

Went into St Annes in am. Quite pleasant and select. Tried to see Cliff in afternoon but he was out. The woman next door said she knew Cliff was staying at home because she could "hear him laughing".

Went to the pleasure beach and had a good laugh. In the evening I danced Rene off her legs at the Winter Garden. Enjoyed it very much.

Wed May 30th

Nice day.

Saw Cliff this am. My stay there was all too short. His company is as good as a show. I felt I could have stayed chatting all day. So much to say, so little time to say it in. Invited him down.

Central Pier, Madam Tussauds in afternoon. *'On with the Show'* in evening. Grand show.

Took a few snaps and sent a card home and one to Mary.

Thurs May 31st

Nice day again.

Saw old Stew this am outside the PO. He looked in fine

trim very fat as well. He showed us the famous Pablo's ice cream merchants. The queue was about half a mile long. We had a little chat and then Rene and I went round the shops a little further.

In the afternoon, we went on the Grand National Science railway, it was great. I had a terrific laugh over Rene's fright. She didn't know whether to laugh or cry, she was so scared and hung on for grim life. I then went on the Big Dipper and got a great kick out of these things. I'd love to take Betty on them.

Saw 'Western Approaches' in the evening.

Fri June 1st

Did our shopping in morning and a little sunbathing in the afternoon. In the evening went dancing at the 'Town'. Not such a good floor as W Gardens. Met more lads from Germany. I'm getting a bit fed up with meeting them. I had hoped to get away from prison camps for a week at least.

Sat June 2nd

Wandered around during the day and in the evening went to another good stage show on the Central Pier.

Sun June 3rd

Very wet today.

In the afternoon went on North Pier and spent quite a pleasant time. Chatted to two very pleasant people. In the evening saw a good Technicolor 'The Fighting Lady' a film of an aircraft carrier in the Pacific.

Had dinner this evening.

Mon June 4th

Our last day.

We caught the 2.35 home and, after changing at Crewe from where we had to stand, arrived in Wolves at 6:45. So ended a most pleasant holiday and if Rene enjoyed it, then I consider I achieved my purpose which was that it was her holiday in principle.

Hear that Derek Beresford has at last arrived home from the Russian held camp.

Tues June 5th

More teeth filled.

Saw many of the boys at Cosford including Johnny Rankin and Garry Hemmings.

Opinions seem to differ about the chances of flying in the Far East. I shall be bitterly disappointed if I can't go. It is my big ambition at the moment. The farming life seems, strongly, completely alien to my life. I have no inclination towards it whatsoever and am certain I would never be happy as one. My heart is in flying and I think it is a cruel fate that my eyes should not be perfect. It is my biggest and only worry.

Had my hair attended to today in an effort to prevent it coming out so rapidly.

Very wet today.

More mushrooms in the evening.

Wed June 6th

A nice day.

I spent the morning in bed and the afternoon outside in the sunshine, if any.

This evening I went to see Mary. She was going down to Pattingham to a dance in aid of the Welcome Home Fund. I was caught like a rat in a trap. Harold Taylor, whom I didn't recognise (incidentally my greatest difficulty these days) asked me if I would be embarrassed if he officially 'welcomed me home'. I lied. I said I wouldn't mind! He then made a little speech on the platform and I of course had to reciprocate. It was very short and snappy, thanking them for their kindness. Strangely enough I didn't blush. I was very nervous tho.

Thurs June 7th

The usual morning and afternoon.

In the evening Rene and I (Mary unable to come) went to a dance at Brewood. Young Farmers affair. I met many strange faces, young people I had never met before. Brookes, Smiths etc. I enjoyed it very much and was very much impressed by the younger clique of Young Farmers. They are a very nice crowd and have a certain stamp of education, manners and breeding about them lacking in the crowd of our own day. Their company is to say the least, most pleasant.

Fri June 8th

Fine but windy.

The political situation is at the moment anything but amicable. Russia is pursuing a policy of obstructionism and non-cooperation which in my opinion can only have one result, that which I have fore-shadowed for years. Their portion of Germany is exactly half Germany and means the withdrawal of the Yanks and British to another 150 miles, B___ to Eisenach. I hope we don't accede.

The San Francisco fiasco is proceeding with its usual stalemate. Russia again being the stumbling block over the veto process of the Big Five.

The Levant crisis has been temporarily (I fear) subdued but I was glad to see a firm attitude by the British Government.

Recently I have had mail from Thommy T., Betty (including wonderful photos), Mrs Schofield and the Red Cross. Also £150 from the RAF as the main balance of my account. This gives me a bank balance of approx. £760.

Mon July 9th

It would be an impossible task to try and remember the events chronologically of the last month. I will attempt to record some of the incidents of importance. The months has been spent most pleasantly with our round of visiting and a little work.

I have at last succeeded in seeing all the relations, every one of whom I suspect has been briefed by Mum to harangue me on the attributes and pleasures of a farming life. This has been (I mean my future career) constantly in my mind, in fact, altho I am not subject to much worrying, thank God, I have worried rather a lot over this most vital question. It must affect my whole future happiness in life. I realise full well the gravity of the decisions I shall be compelled to make within this week. I am prepared to say that this will be the most momentous week in my life.

My heart, of course, is and always will be, in flying but unfortunately I strongly doubt if I should have any chance whatsoever of getting into civil aviation since I have had no experience on multi-engined aircraft. I doubt whether I should enjoy the permanent discipline and regulations of a regular peacetime service career. On the other hand I have achieved an interest (considerable but far from all-embracing) in farming and think that I could make a success of such a career. My decisions have been precipitated by the decision of Uncle John to leave Wrottesley for if I did go in for farming that is the farm I would like.

To sum up, I feel I have three duties to perform;

1. My Duty to Myself
2. To my Parents
3. To the Royal Air Force

My duty to myself is a) to assume that whatever I do regarding present and future career, that I choose that giving me most happiness and chance of success; b) to ensure that I am physically and mentally fit enough to maintain a decent place in society; c) to obey the calls of conscience. Here my mind is split for I should feel guilty if I shirked danger and duty whilst there is still a war on and guilty also if I caused my parents any more worry and anxiety after what they have been through already.

My duty to my Parents is a) to relieve them of all unnecessary worry and anxiety by pursuing a less dangerous career and to give them more help and comfort as they grow older.

My duty to the RAF which is synonymous with my duty to King and Country is a) to obey orders; b) to do whatever and go wherever the needs of the Service dictate.

Those briefly are my ideas of my duty. In addition I feel I would like to do my bit towards the release of the PoWs still in Jap hands. That, I fear, is personal for I know just how we felt when waiting for the 2nd Front to start.

I would also like to do a little more travelling.

Against this I feel that my future career will be jeopardised if I stay in uniform any longer, for if I went to the Far East I should be away for at least 18 months, possibly more and then I should be a little old to start farming. I am hoping that the authorities will say "you have got to do this" or "you cannot do that" etc, when I go through the Disposal Board at Cosford on Friday or Saturday.

If I am unfit for further flying, I shall have no hesitation in asking for my discharge but if I am fit, I shall ask for a conversion on to multi-engined aircraft with a view to the Far East ops or Transport Command, and an eye on civil aviation prospects.

The work I have been doing is in the hay harvest and pea picking. I hope by this to reduce some of my fat (my weight at present is 12st 2lbs!!) and to attain some sort of physical fitness. To supplement this, tennis has been my sport of late and I think I have improved. I think and hope I have made a good friend in Peter Smith. I like him very much.

Outside my own sphere, the world I fear is still in its precarious state of unstable equilibrium. Events have perhaps been overshadowed in England by the general election which took place last Thursday. I did not vote for my views are strongly liberal and we have no liberal candidate. I think the Conservatives will get in for the socialists have rather spoilt their chances by disputes and controversies mainly the Lashi dispute who, it seems, imagines himself to be a Labour Party potentate.

Last week I had 50 supplementary clothing coupons from the Customs & Excise after a protracted correspondence. With them I have bought shirts and a sports jacket. It is Mum's ardent wish to see me in civvies again.

Russia is still pursuing her policy of cantankerous obstructionism and intimidation of the smaller powers. Is this in accordance with the terms of the Atlantic Charter? Is the foundation of the League of World Union *(United Nations)* at San Francisco to be another idiotic farce? I fear so. As the days and weeks pass and each event succeeds another with unfailing monotony, I am afraid a war with Russia is inevitable.

July 17th

The last day of my leave was the revelation of something that has been worrying me for some time.

I went across to see Mary on her birthday and found I was the unwanted guest at a small party. Chris Morgan of course was there. I thought Mary had been rather cool since I came home but could only have suspicions. That was my proof. Anyway it's all finished now.

I went back to Cosford and on Friday had a preliminary medical interview on Tuesday - the full one. I passed A 1 which, being the highest grade, felt full flying duties ___ me. I had a WAAF for the man part!!!

Then I went before the disposal board and was told I could not fly, not because I had been a PoW but because they had already 80,000 redundant aircrew. Chaps who were flying right up to V day are redundant. Consequently, rather than have a ground job, I asked for my discharge after resettlement at Scarborough.

On Sunday I had a release medical and Monday I got civvies from Hednesford. The civvies are a suit, shirt and two collars, tie, 2 pairs socks, shoes, mac. And hat. Only the shoes and mac are any good.

Now I am on indefinite leave 'til resettlement and do I feel browned off. I wish I had stayed in, even in a ground job. If it hadn't been for Mum I would have done. No one knows how I miss the bright, boisterous, sparkling, happy-go-lucky companionship I found amongst comrades in the Services. I yearn for their company and always will do. I fear I will never settle down to farming.

Flying and friendship are the only things that give me that complete happiness which is the essential to success. God alone knows what I will do now. I am only hoping we shall have another war with Russia in the near future. How selfish. I may even, when the RAF is reduced, try to join again on the Fleet Air Arm on a Regular Service basis.

I saw Stan, Alex, Bas (who all came up here) Ron Farmer, Lofty Martin, Roy Gilbert, Bert Farmer, Jim Mercier, George Brassey, Dave and a crowd of others. I thoroughly enjoyed a long chat with Bas.

Aug 25th

To try to remember all the events of the past month would be an almost super human task. I will deal with Mary first.

To my great disappointment, and I must say surprise, I noticed she was rather strange in her attitude towards me. I realised just before I went back to Cosford that she had another affection – Chris Morgan – the little twerp (mild language!) To my intense consternation they were engaged about July 26th!! I was staggered. I thought of writing a letter to her but decided, fortunately, against it. On Aug 6th she broke off the engagement. She found out she was not as much in love with him as she thought. Last Sunday Rene and I went over for supper. I am still very much in love with her.

Betty Smith, the nurse arrived back from Italy full of her usual vim and vigour, more attractive I think on account of her slimming. She had many varied and interesting tales to tell of her experiences. We went one Sunday afternoon, our old walk around Patshull Park. It was grand. We had a really good chat. I think Betty is the only one I have met since I got home who really understands me. I feel I can tell her anything and get a sympathetic hearing. It's so nice to meet anyone like that when I feel I am so misunderstood at home.

She volunteered for service in Burma and was on a month's embarkation leave. When she told her mother, she eventually submitted to her pleas and said she would not go. Oh! that parents would not be so possessive and influence their children. I think it most unfair. Why should anyone try to rule anyone else's life. I can't understand it.

Since her return, Betty has met Tom Swinnerton, home from India and a romance has been fixed for her. She is not so keen but may succumb. Of all the things people should not arrange, careers and marriages are the two most vital. They are purely matters for the individual in fact, any affairs of the heart should be for the individual to decide.

I got some information on Norman Steele, who I hear has completely changed since joining the army, is now a Lt in Norway. Tom, the Aussie, is over, his ship is in Davenport undergoing repairs after attacks by the Kamikaze boys in the Pacific. He is as full of umph as ever and we've been swimming at the Kingfisher a few times. We did a few gymnastics and I thought a lot of Cyril Rudge.

A fortnight ago I went with Stephen to Newquay for 10 days. The place is dead as far as life is concerned but is pretty and has good swimming and surfing. I really enjoyed the surf riding after I had mastered it at the expense of much bruising and scraping.

I don't think S really enjoyed the holiday as it was so dead but I try to adapt myself to the surroundings and quite enjoyed it. I met some extremely nice people there, especially a 10 year old lad, Brian Sennitt of Wyshodene, Wildernesse, N Sevenoaks, Kent. He was the most amazingly intelligent and charming little chap I have ever met. I was amazed at his language knowledge and his engaging manner.

What a ten days they were. When we went away, the war looked a cinch for another 18 months. When we came back it was all over. First Russia came into the war (as I had expected of the cunning and avaricious devils) then we dropped the Atom bombs which shook the world and then it was all over.

The evolution of the Atom bomb I think means the dawn of a new, almost terrifying, era. Practically every other invention is now obsolete and I only hope they have not got hold of something they can't quite control. The world was first pleased and then aghast at the power of the new invention. They are a little sceptical and doubtful of the consequences.

Victory night S & I spent in the train coming home. Plymouth, with all its lights on the ships, ___ lights, searchlights Aldis lamps, fireworks and bonfires all reflecting on the water, was a sight I shall never forget.

On VJ & I night we went into Wolverhampton where there was a wild and gay crowd.

Now I have settled down to some hard work on the harvest and am enjoying it. I think I may eventually settle down to farming when my break from the Air Force becomes more absolute.

To return to our world, what is England faced with now that the war is really over. Six years of soul searching, ghastly terrifying war (fearsome!!) have left poor old England, the self-styled bastion of freedom, impoverished, economically weak, in fact almost desperate, physically tired.

Our Labour Government, having such an amazing majority, has rather disillusioned its impressionable, and impulsive supporters. They have not much to offer. Less food, less clothes, less petrol, less beer, less tobacco. What are our fruits of victory? A mere pittance. Who has won? True it is that no one wins a modern war. We have before us a long time of hard work, disappointments, sweat and toil, of self-sacrifice when everyone must devote their energies to re-financing an almost destitute nation.

The drastic, unthinking, despicably sudden termination of Lend-Lease by the Americans has been a great blow to all Englishmen. I believe it was America's war just as much as ours from the word go. I wonder if they think that. They who have never heard the drone of enemy a/c, the shriek of bombs, the wail of sirens, have undergone none of the ravages of war. Their lot has been a comparatively rosy one. For many it has been a fortune making episode in an age of money grabbing commercialism. It would have done them good to have suffered as many other countries have suffered and I have NO qualms or compunction about saying this.

Sept 2nd

Today the war ended. Exactly 6 years ago to the day, we went to war with Germany and Japan when we listened to that fateful 11.00am broadcast of Mr Chamberlain. Today at 2.30am BST, the war officially ended by the surrender of the Japanese. McArthur, Truman and Co. all made sentimental speeches, even if they were historic, but I notice that no one is under any illusion that this may be the end of wars. Rather the disillusionments of the pact have inaugurated a new era; an era of scepticism and doubt and distrust. What a terrible foundation for the future of world peace.

I have been seeing quite a lot of Mary recently. I am very much in love with her and continually thinking about her. I have told her all this and more but I don't think she is really in love with me. I have the terrible impression that she doesn't really want me, maybe because I am so different to the fellow she knew long years ago. I know I am different and can't help it. She cannot be other than what she really is, no matter how we would like it otherwise.

I feel I have lost my youth; that I am prematurely old. I find I can talk to older people more easily than I can young. I can talk about war and political social relations etc, whereas I find lighter breezy bright conversation with young people, especially women, a terrible trial.

As far as females are concerned, I attribute this to my confinement in Germany where I missed so many vital years in my mental makeup. The years I missed were absolutely essential and I fear I shall never replace them socially. On top of that I feel I have lost my youth.

These perhaps are the reasons why Mary is not impressed

by me. She knows what I once was like and what I am like now, she doesn't seem at all enthusiastic about me, rather cool and disinterested. As for myself, I feel (I hope wrongly) that young people find me a frightful bore.

Sept 7th

Two things have happened today which have once again unsettled me.

Firstly my posting to Scarborough has arrived and secondly Norman Steele paid me a visit. I am to go to S on Tuesday. Norman has just arrived back from Norway. He is attached to the First Airborne Div (the Red Devils). He looks well but naturally a little older and very smart in his uniform. He is a Lt. He was telling me he is not very happy at home. His sister and another having died, his brother and sister being a bit mental and his father having remarried. This wife expecting a kid. I feel very sorry for him.

He has got engaged to a Norwegian millionaire's daughter and has been having a grand time with her. But he is yet another one of the gang of unhappy warriors suffering from terrible disillusionment of post war England. I doubt it will have a permanent effect on my future happiness. He is staying in the army as he says he has no time for civvy street England. I am inclined to agree with him.

Set 21st

On Sept 11th I left home for Scarborough. A most disturbing feeling possessed me when I started on the train journey. I felt really happy for the first time for two months. I am worried because that can only mean one thing. Firstly that I should continue to be unhappy if I stayed at home and secondly that I still have that urge to travel around and go places. It also means that I am a victim of repressions endured in the sober atmosphere of farm life.

As far as my future career goes I am nervously considering a permanent commission in the RAF as an alternative to civilian flying. Today I wrote in answer to an advert in Flight which requested a pilot for internal airways and I strongly doubt whether I shall hear any more about it but am hoping.

Here we are at a Resettlement Centre more properly called an Unsettlement Centre for no one wishes to leave. The punishment for non-attendance at classes is to be sent home on indefinite leave. We have a re-orientation lecture at 9.00 and a class at 10.30-12.00. I haven't been to any classes yet.

The lecturers are all first class men and I find the re-orientation lectures extremely interesting. We also have periodic visits to various places. I was on one the other day to Duffield airdrome to see a preview of the exhibition in honour of Battle of Britain day. We also have film exhibitions of films we have missed whilst away.

The billets and food are very good, our billet having two lounges, two dining rooms and an entrance hall. The bedrooms have hot and cold water. The most hectic part is the night life. I've been drinking a terrible lot.

I was lucky to fall into Cliff's gang straight away which includes Al, Mac, Cliff, Mack, Harry, Bob H, Bob, Mike, Nobby, Shorty, Frank, Bas, Arthur, Cyril and others. They're a great crowd especially Bob and Mac. Mac incidentally is a farmer's son from Falkirk but he's going in for auctioneering.

But there have been some most amusing incidents 1) Lamp-posts and PC 33; 2) Traffic & PC 39; 3) Hats in the sea; 4) Kiddie in the road; 5) Any complaints on the Wessex; 6) Altering the early calls; 6) Late lunches and late trains; 7) The shirt signatures; 8) Knickers from Marks & Spencers; 9) The show at the Arcadia (beer bottles on stage, cigars, whoo-hoo to chorus girls, pennies on stage, Cyril helps the conjuror, Frank's note); 10) Loitering and the police.

I have met a Scotch VAD nurse working at the Wrenney. Betty Smith by more of a strange coincidence. But I don't want to get involved as I like Mary much more. But she's a nice kid all the same.

I have played one game tennis with Bob H who has now gone.

World affairs show what I consider an unnerving antagonism between US and Russia especially over the Balkan governments; the sentencing to death of Lord Haw-Haw and now they are on the Belsen trials of Kramer and co.

Oct 2nd

Al, Mac, Cliff, Frank, Bob H, Laurie, Arthur, Shorty, Mike, Cyril have all left here now. Harry is going tonight. I am very disappointed. When I saw Cliff away last night, I felt that a 3yr service friendship was breaking. Nevertheless I intend keeping up with civilian friendships.

I have been worried recently about the prospects of a career. I applied for the flying job but have had no reply so far. I think it is hopeless as there is too much competition. Now I am considering what I should really do. Stay in the service or not for I am convinced there will be a war with Russia in a few years' time. The Council of Foreign Ministers has been a complete and disastrous failure. They cannot even agree on the wording of the protocol of their activities!! Having failed to make the cake they cannot even agree on the ingredients used.

Furthermore, Russia, without consulting the other powers, has signed a trade pact with Hungary which almost completely monopolises Hungarian trade.

I sincerely hope we shall make use of Hun technicians and designers as I really think they have us licked hollow, especially in the sphere of aircraft and jet design. Some of their jet fighters and bombers are indeed revolutionary and superb. Altho we claim to be the first to reach 500 over mph with the DM jet Meteor, I fear many reports contradict this as they seem to have many aircraft almost 600mph, 597 & 598 mph for two in particular.

American public opinion seems to be against a loan to Britain. They seem to fail to realise how much this would affect them economically. Recently we have been bombarded by reports of Jap atrocities to PoWs and yet we still give them a lenient (in my opinion) defeat. The Canadian Army PoW collaborators have got off very lightly with sentences of hard labour. Their stories I think were compete fabrication and I think they should be have been shot.

Dave has arrived here in all his glory. He and Roy are buying a yacht 14½ tons for about £150 and very nice it is too for I have been over it. Dave certainly knows a lot of the big shots around here but I think they endure him as an oddity.

Alex is getting married on the 12th Nov and I am going to Gloucester on the weekend for a bachelor party and then to the wedding. He is lucky in buying a house near Manchester very cheaply according to present day standards.

I cannot understand the attitude of Mary. She has not replied to any of my four letter as far as I know. I have written her a letter demanding to know why, and if she doesn't write I shall never forgive her. Each day I have searched the mail box three or four times over, but to no avail.

One evening last week Cliff and I had a most interesting conversation with a Lt/Col on FM Montgomery's staff. He thinks the trouble will come not from the present Hitler Youth but from the 25yr olds demobbed from the Army. They are the chaps who saw the Youth in its hey-day. The others have seen it under trying and disciplined conditions.

Went to Rowntrees last week. Quite interesting.

Oct 5th

I am in rather a mess. I have a feeling that Betty Smith, whom I've met again, is in love with me; even wants to come home with me, and I don't want to get too involved. She's going on leave next week and I think I am a little relieved altho she's a great kid.

Have read that the C of FMs *(Council of Foreign Ministers)* was a disastrous failure. Molotov and Bevin had some fiery clashes; once when Bering said Molotov's attitude reminded him of the Nazis and when Molotov rose, walked towards the door, turned round and demanded an immediate apology or he would leave the conference. Bevin without saying a word got up and walked out. The other time was when Molotov said the reason the conference was not a success was because Eden and Hull weren't present. I think that the real reason for wanting to keep so many people in the forces is for fear of Russia ____ to ____ ____

Very decent crowd and quite generous with lots of chocolate. A remarkable point has been raised why are the new crowd here so dull compared with the old. Is it because they have been home too long and have now got the wretched veneer of Civvy Street and conventionalism in them or is it because the old crowd were mostly 5yr PoWs.

I have applied for a job with a business firm in W. Africa. Am going to apply for another as a plantation assistant on the Gold Coast.

Oct 15th

Not a great deal has happened in the last 10 days. Dave has been getting into his usual scrapes but acquitting himself quite well in verbal witticisms. The crowd at the Royal intrigue me more every day. I have my ideas about them but it is all very interesting.

I have made enquiries about staying on in the RAF but since they have no concise instructions concerning the re-engagement of air crew I am leaving it for the time being.

I have also met a smashing little Wren. Mary Poole. She is a delightful companion quite natural and unassuming and it is very refreshing to be in her company.

Politically I think the whole world is getting ready for a really big bust-up.

Oct 31st

What on earth is happening to the world today? It seems unbelievable that after the mistakes of the last war the leaders of World affairs could be so incredibly stupid as to precipitate conditions incomparably worse than they were in 1939. The sombre picture becomes more chaotic every day. Our spasmodic glimpses of a hopeful future are becoming rare as gold in a pauper's house.

As the proverbial drowning man clings to a straw, so we are grasping the torch of peace whose light is fading fast.

In England we are afraid of America's economic imperialism. Mr Truman said, in his 12 commandments, which are hardly an improvement on the original 10, that he has no territorial imperialism. Then why is he trying to get control of more Pacific islands and why does he resent intrusion in Japan? Is it for defence? Defence against what and whom? I thought we were working for world trust, faith and peace. Why does he allow his capitalist economists grasp markets in their own vicious vortex?

Why doesn't Russia let us know what is happening behind the iron curtain at the River Elbe? Why this ghastly repetition of callous brutality in forcing millions of people to trek across Europe in mid-winter, without food, without clothing, without transport, without shelter, with nothing but an indomitable spirit and an instinctive urge for self-preservation?

Why allow this fertile breeding place for rampart disease to persist, with all its pernicious consequences? Why have War Crimes trials if we are going to allow worse bestialities than the original perpetrators allowed? Arrant hypocrisy, in the name of Justice.

Why keep ½ million men under arms in Yugoslavia whilst their population is starving for want of agricultural labour?

Why clog up the waterways of Europe for reasons of security when the only security needed is security to reinstate the war-ravaged countries?

Instead of pursuing a policy of continuity of purpose, we are all drifting apart 'til we shall set up impassable barriers in our various spheres of influence. There should be no sphere of influence, nowhere where one side has more interest than another.

Let us blast to hell this inconsequential chatter of blocs and parties, markets and money, reparations and sanctions, justice and revenge. There is no justice unless we face facts as they are and bravely carry out our principles of morals and ethics.

The whole world is fast approaching a crash far worse than any we have yet had. I feel that something ghastly is fast approaching.

Dad aged about 20.

Dad aged 80 with Mum.

Postscript

Dad did take over from his father and was very successful, purchasing the farm from the Wrottesley Estate in the 1950's. He retired at the age of 82, but still kept a diary where most entries were about the weather.

He met and married our mother, Sheila, in 1952, at the age of 30. Sheila was 10 years his junior. They went on to have 4 children and celebrated their 63rd wedding anniversary just a few months before he died.

Bridge became a life-long hobby, which he shared with Sheila, and his love of reading was evident (although it's unclear how many of the books on his 'list' he managed to read.) He also became a very keen and knowledgeable gardener, with a special interest in trees.

His passion for aircraft, especially his beloved 'Spit', never wavered. He occasionally said that being with his squadron, and especially flying, were some of the happiest times in his life.

Dad rarely had a day's illness after returning home (although his tooth trouble persisted and he had to have all his teeth removed shortly after the last diary entry) but was always vulnerable to stomach upsets after his bout of dysentery. He gave up smoking when he was in his 70s and, with Sheila, continued to travel and enjoy adventures all over the world well into his late 80s.

Dad was an honest, fair, honourable man and a loving husband and father. He was incredibly hard-working, culturally aware and tolerant and held a fascination for the lives of those from different nations, religions and ethnicities. He was extremely generous with his time and knowledge, always putting himself out for others and he had a wonderful sense of humour.

Dad never did cook a meal…

Acknowledgements

I'd like to thank Michael Tattersall for generously sharing his research into his father and MO Major McLardy's route regarding all the village names on the Long March. Without this invaluable help, I would doubtless still be searching in vain, as much of the route was in Germany at the time, but changed to be part of Poland post-war and the village names were changed accordingly.

It is possible that Major McLardy was the doctor on the March with Dad.

I'd also like to thank Sebastian Mikulec from the Lamsdorf Museum for his help and finally my niece, Leonie Shanks for her valued support, comments and editorial contributions.

JK